Gender, Development and Disasters

In memory of John Bradshaw

Gender, Development and Disasters

Sarah Bradshaw

Principal Lecturer in Development Studies, Middlesex University, UK

Edward Elgar

Cheltenham, UK • Northampton, MA, USA

Published by
Edward Elgar Publishing Limited
The Lypiatts
15 Lansdown Road
Cheltenham
Glos GL50 2JA
UK

Edward Elgar Publishing, Inc.
William Pratt House
9 Dewey Court
Northampton
Massachusetts 01060
USA

A catalogue record for this book
is available from the British Library

Library of Congress Control Number: 2012951742

This book is available electronically in the ElgarOnline.com Social and Political Science Subject Collection, E-ISBN 978 1 78254 823 2

ISBN 978 1 84980 446 2 (cased)

Typeset by Columns Design XML Ltd, Reading
Printed by MPG PRINTGROUP, UK

Contents

Acknowledgements

This book began life in October 1998 with Hurricane Mitch and has developed via discussions in Nicaragua, Hawaii and India and through thinking and writing in the mountains of Switzerland and the Lake District. It is based on work undertaken over a number of years and, as such, thanks are owed to many people. Thanks are due to all those in Nicaragua who undertook the research in the communities and, more importantly, all the men and women who gave up their time to talk to us. Thanks also to the women leaders in Nicaragua, Honduras and El Salvador interviewed after Mitch, especially Martha Isabel Cranshaw and Maria Hamlin-Zuniga, and to Deirdre O'Reilly for all her support. The research studies were part financed by Oxfam GB and the UNDP and supported by CIIR/ICD (now Progressio). My thanks go to Patricio Cranshaw, the country representative of Progressio in Nicaragua, for all his help and hospitality. In the CCER, I thank Ricardo Zambrana and Rebeca Zuniga, and Jorge Arostegui of CIETinternational for being such great work colleagues. In Puntos de Encuentro, I thank Teresita Hernández and Vilma Castillo Aramburu for sharing their knowledge and, especially, Irela Solórzano for always welcoming me back; also, Verónica Campanile, Ana Criquillon, Amy Bank and Ana Quirós – all are inspiring people to work with. In Middlesex University, my thanks go to all the staff who covered for me while I was away in Nicaragua, and to Eleonore Kofman for her continued support. I would like to thank all those at the various Gender and Disaster conferences but, in particular, Elaine Enarson for being so welcoming and supportive of my work, and Maureen Fordham for her commitment to the GDN. I am grateful to the team at Edward Elgar for their professionalism and patience. My thanks to Hazel Johnstone, Charlie Weinberg, Allan Cochrane and Sarah Neal for their good-humoured support, and to Sylvia Chant who has supported me since my PhD and took the initiative of sending the idea for this book to Edward Elgar – many thanks. To Cathy McIlwaine who is always there to discuss ideas, for a good moan and for a good night out. My family in Huddersfield, which because of them I still call 'home'. Most of all to Brian Linneker, who read all the manuscript not once but twice, for his knowledge and insight, who was there in Nicaragua and is an ever-constant supportive presence: many, many thanks.

Introduction

This book aims to provide a critical gendered reading of disasters in the developing world context. The focus of the book is not only on the 'Third World', but it also seeks to draw on academic debates within development literature to problematise current disaster thinking. While concepts such as poverty have received a great deal of attention within development writings, they are often taken at face value within disaster literature. Similarly, notions such as 'participation' and participatory processes now have as many critics as supporters among development professionals, yet they continue to be seen as an intrinsically good thing among many disaster practitioners. Despite the efforts of a small, but growing, group of women and men, this lack of critical engagement within the disaster literature with key concepts is echoed in the debates around gender and disasters.

Gender has now become part of the official disasters discourse and on the ground reconstruction is often targeted at women. Women are also increasingly being seen as a key to ensuring adaptation to the disaster risks presented by climate change. Many of these new gendered initiatives are drawing on development thinking to justify and design interventions. However, while there are lessons to be learnt from development theory and practice, development does not necessarily provide a good blueprint for how to 'engender' disasters. As the book seeks to highlight, the call to engender disaster risk reduction is a valid one but women's inclusion in relief, reconstruction and mitigation activities can at times be as problematic as their exclusion. To be successful, it is important that initiatives do not just assume women to be more vulnerable to disasters than men, but that they seek to understand how women and men experience disasters differently.

This book, then, will not explain why volcanoes erupt or how tsunamis form, but instead it will explore the differential impact of these events on people and places, and in particular different gendered experiences of these events. While disasters are often pictured as cyclical with the hazard presented as the central 'event', it is the processes that such hazards provoke that will be the focus of the book, not the hazard itself.

The traditional depiction of disasters as cyclical (see Figure I.1) suggests there are discrete stages of planning and response to disasters, with different specialists working in each – structural mitigation being seen as something for engineers, preparedness for emergency planners, response as the domain of the emergency services, and reconstruction that of the United Nations and humanitarian relief organisations. It also suggests that activities are not only undertaken by different parties but are also sequential, suggesting, for example, that only when reconstruction of destroyed roads and houses is 'over' does preparation for the next event occur. This sequence of events will provide a structure to the book, which, after introductory chapters on disaster, development and gender, will focus on relief, reconstruction and mitigation. However, this is not to suggest that these should be seen as discrete or sequential, merely as providing a logical and well-established means of addressing the many issues raised by disasters.

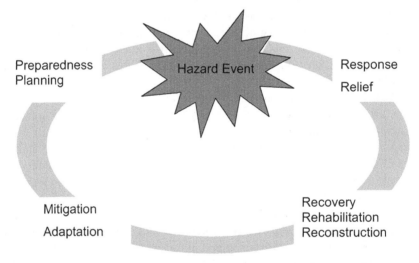

Figure I.1   The disaster cycle

Hazardous events occur on a regular basis so the logic of presenting disasters as a cycle is clear. However, a cycle suggests that a disaster is an inevitable outcome of a hazardous event. This is questionable. Contemporary understandings of disasters highlight that preparation should and could prevent the next disaster by reducing the vulnerability of the population to the natural hazard. Rather than cyclical, the stages represent a progression of activities that build on each other. Reconstruction merges into development, or reinforces development processes and, in turn, development projects should seek to mitigate the impact of future hazard events.

The need to 'disaster proof' development is increasingly being recognised by actors such as the World Bank amid the twin fears of the impact of climate change in increasing the number and intensity of events, and the fear that such events pose a threat to achieving planned advances in poverty reduction and the Millennium Development Goals (MDGs). There has also been increased recognition of the gendered impact of events such as the Indian Ocean tsunamis in 2004, which saw more women than men die due to culturally prescribed gender norms that helped dictate their relative risk. This has led to calls to mainstream disasters into development, and also gender into disaster risk reduction.

As noted above, it is important to demonstrate how and why women should be involved in disaster work and the consequences of their exclusion from disaster risk reduction, but it is also important to critically analyse this inclusion. To this end, the book will draw on existing studies to explore the impact of disasters not only on individual women but also women's groups and movements. In particular, it will utilise empirical research undertaken by the author in Central America to highlight the point that women's inclusion in post-disaster reconstruction can be as problematic as their exclusion. Studies undertaken after recent large-scale events such as hurricane Katrina, the Haitian earthquake of 2010 and the Indian Ocean tsunamis demonstrate that women are not a homogeneous group and they highlight the importance of understanding differences between women in how they experience disasters. The book then seeks to provide a critical reflection on the gendered impact of disasters and disaster response in the developing world and to problematise the way women are being incorporated into disaster-related work and the consequences of this for wider processes of development.

Chapter 1 will provide an introduction to 'disasters' and explore ideas around what is a disaster. It will contest the idea of 'natural disasters', noting that natural hazards only make 'disasters' when they impact on vulnerable populations that cannot withstand, respond to, and recover from the event. Thus the subjective rather than scientific nature of disasters will be highlighted, and the importance of vulnerability and risk for understanding experiences of disasters will be explored. In turn, risk and vulnerability will be deconstructed to reveal the complexity of these notions. The conceptualisation of disasters will be further explored through consideration of how those working in development often construct disasters as unusual, extraordinary events that 'set back' development rather than as a common feature of the developing world.

The consequences of this for both disaster response and for processes of development will be a key theme throughout the chapters that follow.

Processes of development will be the focus of Chapter 2, which will present an introduction to development actors, development theorising and more recent development initiatives in practice, including key policy initiatives such as the Structural Adjustment and Poverty Reduction Strategy initiatives, in order to provide theoretical and policy context to the discussion of disasters. Particular attention will be paid to the notion of 'poverty', how it has been conceptualised and what this means for gender and for 'disaster proofing' development. The third chapter will continue the focus on gender and will provide an introduction to key concepts and feminist theories as well as explore the different ways gender has been integrated into development. A key issue will be the notion of 'mainstreaming', and attempts to 'engender' development by actors such as the World Bank will be critiqued. The chapter will conclude by asking how evolving understandings of gender and development have influenced understandings of disasters. The ideas raised in this chapter provide the basis for the analysis in the remaining chapters, as they explore the provision of relief and reconstruction post disaster as well as the ability to mitigate large-scale events in the future.

Chapter 4 will look at the period during and immediately after an event, focusing on how people help themselves and as well as the 'humanitarian' response of national and international actors. It will draw on existing studies to highlight that how an event is experienced may be shaped by culturally prescribed gender specific roles. It will critically explore the notion that these gender roles will, in turn, be shaped by the event, as cultural boundaries are, through necessity, crossed in the event and its aftermath. The coping strategies that households and individuals adopt will be critically examined and the discussion will highlight the corrosive as well as therapeutic nature of household and community response. The arrival of relief organisations, and the changing status of those affected – from 'survivor' to 'victim' – that this can bring about, will then be considered, as will the role of the media in shaping how the event is understood and responded to. This focus on the practical aspects of the relief period will be complemented in Chapter 5 by a conceptual discussion of the evolving, and contested, understandings of 'humanitarianism' and its implications for those working in the field. Much of the writing around humanitarianism has focused on conflict situations. This chapter will highlight the growing links between conflict and disasters, given the nature of contemporary crises, but also, given the response to recent crises, the increasing role for the military post disaster. It will also highlight the links increasingly being seen between relief and development, and the resultant involvement of actors such as the World Bank in post-disaster work. A gendered reading of the processes will be presented, something that has largely been absent from the debate. The discussion will not only question the extent to which a distinction should and can be drawn between relief efforts, reconstruction and wider processes of development, but also the consequences of a closer relationship between them.

The evolution in thinking around the reconstruction period will frame Chapter 6: from the notion of building back what was lost to the idea of transforming lives to be more resilient to future events, as popularly captured in the idea of 'build back better'. Once again, a discussion of the practical elements of reconstruction will be combined with a discussion of the relevant conceptual debates. In particular, echoing calls for 'participatory development', there has been a move toward ensuring the participation of individual and civil society organisations within reconstruction. Problematised within the development discourse, the chapter will use the post-disaster context to explore the potential issues raised by ensuring women's 'participation' in reconstruction. The chapter will suggest there is a need to challenge the seemingly received wisdom within the disaster literature that participation is automatically a good thing. The empirical data presented questions that there is a 'window of opportunity' for change post disaster. This is an assumption that has been used to justify the promotion of the participation of women in reconstruction by donors. While case study evidence points to a change in gender roles occurring after an event, with women assuming non-traditional roles, there is little evidence to support the view that there are long-term changes in gender relations for the better. Rather than focus on seeking to prove that change does occur, it will highlight how different women may have different experiences of the same event. The chapter will provide the background for a more detailed discussion of some key issues for women and for gender roles and relations raised by reconstruction.

Chapter 7 focuses on some of the 'secondary disasters' that may occur as a consequence of how post-disaster reconstruction is handled. This chapter will provide two 'case studies' of secondary disasters – violence against women and the psychosocial impact of disasters. In each case the theme will be introduced through a summary of the key thinking and contested areas, as well a presentation of relevant empirical studies. It will relate back to issues raised in the first chapter around what is a disaster, suggesting that, while this may be understood as the tangible loss of livelihood, it may be felt more as an intangible loss of well being through experiencing violence or poor mental health. This may be the 'real' disaster, at least for many women.

Chapter 8 will seek to move from discussion of individual men and women to considering the role of civil society organisations in responding to events and how this response may impact on them. While disasters may lead to greater cooperation between groups and organisations, they may also lead to old conflicts re-surfacing and new conflicts emerging. The discussion will draw once again on primary research undertaken by the author as it considers the tensions that may be set up within women's movements as well as between women activists and male dominated spaces and processes. The conceptual framework for the chapter will be the notion of civil society and specifically the phenomenon of Non-Governmental Organisations (NGOs), drawing on debates within the development literature to explore and contest their role in the post-disaster context. While noting the key role for women's groups and for gender NGOs in reconstruction, it will contrast the high visibility of women's leadership in the reconstruction period with women's limited engagement in longer term 'mitigation' initiatives, highlighting the changing official discourse – from the social focus of reconstruction to the more technical focus of mitigation – as having a role to play in explaining this.

The last substantive chapter continues to examine the changing discourse around disasters, focusing on the international policy discourse. It will consider how Disaster Risk Reduction fits within other related discourses, including Climate Change Adaptation. Two key policy initiatives will frame the discussion: the Hyogo Framework for Action (HFA) and the Millennium Development Goals (MDG). It will critically examine the HFA in terms of its purported 'gender perspective' and discuss this in relation to the gendered critique of the MDGs in order to highlight the debates around the inclusion of a gender focus in such initiatives, and the key contested areas of this inclusion. How such global initiatives are to be operationalised will be considered and, in particular, the lack of acceptance of global responsibility for disasters will be highlighted. It suggests that at present, at the macro level, international agencies and governments have not accepted responsibility for disaster risk reduction. However, at the micro level, it is women that have been obliged to assume the responsibility for disaster response. Recent critiques of engendering development have focused on the inclusion of women in development as efficient providers of services, or the engendering of development on efficiency rather than equality grounds. They suggest there has been a feminisation of responsibility for ensuring that development goals are met. The chapter suggests a parallel process may be evident within processes to engender disasters and, as such, warns that care needs to be taken before welcoming such processes uncritically.

Rather than present a handbook on how to include women and gender in disaster response and risk reduction, the book seeks to reflect on processes to date within both disasters and development. It highlights that while there are valuable lessons to be learnt from processes of engendering development to date, a valuable lesson might be how best not to engender disasters.

1.   What is a disaster?

INTRODUCTION

The focus of this book is on disasters. Whilst seemingly a straightforward concept, and an objective fact, what constitutes a disaster is based on subjective understandings and experiences of an event, which differ between people and across time and space. This chapter explores how disasters have been understood and defined. It highlights that, while represented as a scientific phenomenon, unlike the natural hazards that may provoke them, disasters are actually socially constructed. A hazard need not become, or be seen to be, a disaster. Vulnerability has emerged as a key concept to help explain how and why natural events have severe negative socio-economic outcomes or become 'disasters' for some groups of people and not others; that is, why some groups are more at risk than others. However, even identifying those 'at risk' is not straightforward, since risk is also a highly subjective notion and, while experts may define individuals or countries as 'at risk', this risk may not be perceived in the same way by them. In particular, the Third World has been constructed as at risk of, and vulnerable to, disasters due to its lack of development. In turn, when disasters occur they are seen as setting back the development achieved to date in these countries. This suggests disasters are something unusual and outside the normal processes of development. This chapter seeks to problematise this conceptualisation of disasters as extraordinary, and suggests that disasters need to be understood as part of the development process and thus mainstreamed within development.

WHAT IS A DISASTER?

> Unfortunately people often view disasters as if they were the same things as the phenomenon that caused them. (Cardona 2004: 41)

The question, 'What is a disaster?' may seem to be one with an obvious answer, but in fact it is something that has troubled academics working in the field for many years. In 1998, an edited collection under the same name was published (Quarantelli 1998). Twenty one chapters and

300 pages long, the book demonstrates that the answer is not as obvious as might be assumed. When asked what a disaster is, most people will name an event such as a cyclone, hurricane or typhoon (the same event with a different name in different parts of the world), an earthquake, or a tornado, volcanic eruptions, tidal waves and tsunamis, or related events such as flooding and mud or land slides. Increasingly, events related to extremes in temperatures may be included, such as heat waves, droughts and wildfires, or freezing conditions, blizzards and avalanches. That is, they will define a disaster in relation to a 'natural' event. This is why the phrase 'natural disaster' is often used, not only by the general public but also by journalists, political leaders and, until recently, agencies such as the United Nations (UN). This common-sense view has also informed the dominant discourse among disaster professionals: traditionally, disaster experts have focused their attention on nature or the natural event. In the 'naturalist' disaster discourse, nature is constructed as a 'hazard' and the focus is on the violent forces of nature (Wisner et al. 2003). Contrary to the more usual notion of a nurturing 'mother' nature, nature is constructed as a monster (Hoffman 2002) punishing society and/or the human population and 'the cause, the condition and the propelling force that damages, destroys and kills' (Hewitt 1983: 5). Disasters then are the 'negative of normal nature' (Anderson 2011: 5). On the one hand, they are conceptualised as unavoidable extreme physical events (Varley 1994) and have been conceived of as messages from God (or the gods) and mediated through mythological and theological frameworks. On the other hand, disasters are seen as needing structural responses to control their damaging effects (Smith and Petley 2009), making science and technology the main tools with which to address disasters (see Phillips et al. 2010). What such 'technocratic solutions' aimed to achieve was to modify the impact of a hazard, that is, to prevent a natural hazard becoming a disaster.

Many natural events popularly constructed as 'disasters' occur across the globe every day. Estimates vary but, for example, it is suggested that several million earthquakes occur in the world each year and the US National Earthquake Information Centre 'locates' about 50 earthquakes each day, or about 20 000 a year. Many events go unnoticed because they occur in uninhabited areas, remote places, or are of a very small magnitude. Only when natural events pass a certain threshold of intensity, or become extreme events, are they said to be a hazard. The United Nation's International Strategy for Disaster Reduction (UNISDR) defines a hazard as 'a dangerous phenomenon, substance, human activity or condition that may cause loss of life, injury or other health impacts, property damage, loss of livelihoods and services, social and economic disruption, or environmental damage' (UNISDR 2009a). In comparison a disaster is a 'sudden, calamitous event that causes serious disruption of the functioning of a community or a society involving widespread human, material, economic or environmental losses and impacts, which exceeds the ability of the affected community or society to cope using its own resources' (UNISDR 2009a). Put simply, a hazard has the potential to bring about loss, while a disaster is defined by that loss occurring.

A large earthquake out at sea presents a potential hazard as it may produce a tsunami but, as Smith (1992) notes, it is only when people and their possessions get in the way of natural processes that hazards really exist. If the earthquake produces a tsunami that threatens the coastline of a populated area, it is a hazard, but if all the residents are evacuated to safety would we call it a disaster? The natural hazard in itself is not a disaster; it merely has the potential to produce a disaster (Drabek 1997). Put another way, disasters do not cause effects, the effects are what we call a disaster (Dombrowsky 1998). That is, the same tsunami that impacted on a populated coastline that did not evacuate, leading to the death of a large number of people, would be labelled a 'disaster'. However, even here the label disaster may not apply.

For a disaster to be entered into the database of the UNISDR, at least one of the following criteria must be met:

- a report of 10 or more people killed;
- a report of 100 people affected;
- a declaration of a state of emergency by the relevant government;
- a request by the national government for international assistance.

Two sets of criteria for identifying a 'disaster' are apparent from the above – the level of loss and the fact the loss cannot be coped with. So the definition has both a quantifiable, objective component in the level of loss, but also a more qualitative, subjective element encompassed in the idea of coping.

However, quantifying loss is also a subjective exercise. Quantification has been refined through the 'Bradford Disaster Scale', ranging from 32 deaths, defined as a 1.5 magnitude disaster, through to 'destruction of the planet' as magnitude 10, with various points in between (Horlick-Jones and Peters 1991). The quantifiable aspect has also been considered by Sheehan and Hewitt (1969: 20, cited in Smith 1996), who suggested that disasters should be defined as events that cause at least 100 human deaths, or at least 100 human injuries, or at least US $1 million economic damages. Applying the reasoning behind the Bradford scale to this definition raises the question, Which would be the greater 'disaster': 100

dead; 1000 injured; or $2 million in economic damages? Dynes (1998: 112) notes that a definition based on numbers is problematic, since thresholds are of little value for comparative studies in different social systems, and economic thresholds quickly become eroded by inflation.

Disasters are often classified by their onset, with the majority of events that are seen as 'disasters' being rapid onset events such as earthquakes, which give little if any warning they will occur, or events such as hurricanes which offer only a short window in which to prepare. Other events have a slow onset: droughts are a good example of a potential disaster that takes time to unfold. Climate change, environmental degradation and desertification are also slow onset events that can lead to disasters in terms of the damage and disruption to lives they may cause. Events also differ by where they impact: they can be intense localised events bringing great loss to a few, or have a widespread impact with low levels of loss felt by many. As noted above, loss of life may be low but economic damage high. Even where loss of life is concerned, there is a question around how human lives and losses are valued. Are some lives valued more than others? Is the death of an 80-year-old man understood or felt by a society in the same way as that of a 30-year-old mother or a 13-year-old boy? Sen's (1990b) suggestion that across the globe there are more than 100 million 'missing' women would seem to suggest women's and girls' lives are less valued than those of men and boys. A related question might be: Are some deaths seen to be 'worse' than others? For example, an estimated 1.3 million people die every year through road traffic accidents, making it the ninth leading cause of death in the world today and the biggest killer of people aged between 15 and 29 (United Nations data). Despite this, death on the roads seldom generates the media or public response 'disasters' do, and, despite the scale of the problem, only in 2011 was the first global 'Decade of Action for Road Safety' launched.

How a loss is valued or felt may decide how the magnitude of the loss is understood, and this in turn determines whether the loss is seen to be a 'disaster' or not. The actual magnitude of the loss may not be the most important factor in determining how it is understood and, in fact, during events such as earthquakes and tsunamis it is difficult to know in the immediate aftermath what the actual loss is. This means the response is often not based on the actual level of damage but on the perceived level of loss, and how this loss is perceived. As such it might be better to understand disasters as telling us about how society views and defines physical harm and social disruption (Kreps 1998: 35). This may differ between societies, between the First and Third World for example, and between people within a society, by characteristics such as gender or ethnicity. It suggests that disasters should be understood in relation to the response in itself, rather than the physical damage (Dynes 1998). Cannon's (1994: 29) definition reflects this in suggesting that a disaster is 'an event associated with the impact of a natural hazard, which leads to increased mortality, illness and/or injury, and destroys or disrupts liveli-hoods, affecting the people or an area such that they (and/or outsiders) perceive it as being exceptional and requiring external assistance for recovery'. This moves away from 'how many' to 'increased', and rather than trying to quantify loss talks of 'perception' of loss as being seen to be 'exceptional'. As Kroll-Smith and Gunter (1998) suggest, there can be no adequate attempt to explore what 'disaster' is that is not centrally concerned with what it has been said to be. The discourse of disaster will vary over time and space. It is also gendered. Consider the example below where a young man was asked what he and his family thought about methane plumes under the town:

> My dad says this is a disaster. He goes on and on about his business losing money and the government not doing much to help. ... Mom? She thinks it's a disaster but not like dad does. She thinks we could all end up dead or something. ... I don't know. It seems to me like a flood or earthquake like in San Francisco is a disaster. ... I did say yesterday or sometime that if my fiancée moved because of the gases, it would be a big disaster. I don't have a car right now. (Kroll-Smith and Gunter 1998: 165)

The subjective notion of a 'disaster' is well illustrated by the quote, and the gender and generational differences, in terms of how the same event, as well as the word 'disaster', may be understood, are also demonstrated. As the discussion highlights, disasters can be real or imagined events (Oliver-Smith 2002), and Kroll-Smith and Gunter (1998: 170) draw the conclusion that 'it is a mistake to attempt to define what disaster is independently of how it is thought about, talked about, and experienced'. Disaster is a 'conceptual negative' that has no inherent meaning other than being outside what is understood to be 'normal', but through personal experience abstract notions of extraordinary events become extraordinarily substantial (Anderson 2011). Gilbert (1995) suggests that the common element when thinking about disasters is uncertainty, and highlights that disaster means a difficulty in understanding reality through ordinary mental frameworks. This 'outside of the ordinary', or the 'un-ness' of the situation (Rosenthal 1998: 147) is what may be seen to be the common feature in defining disaster.

Disaster academics have long pointed out, however, that the natural hazards that may potentially produce a disaster are not unusual or even surprise events. The Atlantic hurricane season, for example, runs from

June to November every year. Earthquakes are continually tracked and modern technology allows early warning of the tsunamis they may produce. All natural hazards are therefore 'known unknowns'. Such hazards are far from extraordinary in many countries and regions of what is defined as the 'Third World'. For many low-income people they are part of their 'ordinary' existence and the frequency with which they occur means natural hazards become part of daily life, constructing a 'culture of disaster' for those living with them (Bankoff 2003a). In contrast, development professionals continue to construct natural hazards and the disasters they provoke as extraordinary events out side of 'normal' processes of development.

Given that natural hazards may occur on a regular basis, may be predicted in advance and that, if not predictable, the best measures for a population to take to avoid their impact are known, the question is, Why do natural hazards become disasters? On a simple level, as Varley (1994) points out, disasters can be seen as 'communication breakdown'. Disasters are the outcomes of warning and response systems that did not work, or are not in place, or are not known about or not responded to. However, this still leads to the question: Why? It is this question that has troubled disaster specialists more recently and discussion has focused on a number of key concepts such as vulnerability and risk, which will be explored below.

VULNERABILITY

> Vulnerability, however, is not just concerned with the present or the future but is equally and intimately a product of the past. (Bankoff 2003b: 10)

While popular discourse may continue to suggest a shipwreck was caused by a storm, in reality the wreck was caused by the inability of the ship and its crew to withstand the storm or its vulnerability to the hazard (Gilbert 1995: 15). That is, a disaster occurs when a hazard impacts on a society, group or individuals unable to cope with the event or the level of damages it provokes. It is not an inevitable outcome of a hazard but, rather, the result of the intersection between hazards and vulnerabilities (Flint and Luloff 2005). This has been captured in a popular 'equation':

$$R = H \times V$$

where R is risk of disaster, H is hazard and V is vulnerability

Recognition that the risk of disaster is a product of both the natural hazard and the relative vulnerability to that hazard has grown since White (1945: 7) noted that while floods are acts of God, flood losses are largely 'acts of man'. While agreeing that disasters are the product of the intersection of a hazard on a vulnerable population, there is still disagreement among disaster specialists over the extent to which a disaster can be seen to be caused by the severity of the hazard or the vulnerability of the population (Prowse and Scott 2008). Since the 1990s, there has been increased recognition of the 'mutuality' of hazard and vulnerability, or the interactions between nature and society (Oliver-Smith 1998). This is not new and builds on earlier 'structuralist' thinking. What is important is that climate change has highlighted that, while people are vulnerable to hazards, hazards are increasingly the result of human activity. Vulnerability may then be thought of as a measure of societal impact on the environment as much as the impact of the environment on society. As Stonich (1999: 24) suggests, there is a need to 'balance the cultural/social construction of nature with a meaningful consideration (and analysis) of the natural construction of the cultural and social'.

While the risk of disaster is a product of hazard and vulnerability, vulnerability is in turn a product of the social, economic, political and cultural characteristics of individuals, communities and nations. It has been suggested that when people say the word 'vulnerability' there is an unspoken word that precedes it, since vulnerability has different dimensions: physical; organisational; legal; technical; socio-economic; political; psychological; and cultural. A whole nation may be seen to be vulnerable to a specific hazard due to:

- its geographical location (in the path of hurricanes for example);
- its lack of institutions charged with responding to such hazards, by evacuating the population for example;
- the lack of laws to enforce evacuation;
- the lack of technical ability to get out warnings;
- the lack of money to provide transport to move people;
- the lack of policing to ensure people feel it is safe to leave their property;
- a mistrust of the government; or
- due to a cultural belief that each individual should look after themselves.

Despite this range of different dimensions to vulnerability, the examples above suggest that some countries and regions, such as the developing world, may be more vulnerable than others. Similarly some people may suffer a greater range and greater magnitude of vulnerability than others.

At the individual level, Cannon (1994) suggests that vulnerability is a complex characteristic produced by a combination of factors derived especially (but not entirely) from class, gender and ethnicity. Despite the complexity of notions such as class and caste – and colonialism might be the equivalent country or macro level concept – income is often used as a proxy. A low-income country is usually assumed to be more vulnerable than a Western nation. Similarly, a low-income person is usually assumed to be more vulnerable to an event than a middle or high-income earner, given that lack of income means that they will not have a private car to use to evacuate, may not receive warnings due to a lack of TV or radio, or may not know to act due to a lack of education. Similarly, the suggestion is that women and ethnic 'minorities' or ethnic groups will also be more vulnerable. Other characteristics such as age may also be important, and both the very old and the very young may be more vulnerable to hazards.

Although the UN states that 'women always tend to suffer most from the impact of disasters' (UN/ADPC 2010: 8), the evidence for this is far from clear. For example, despite assertions that more women suffer injury or die during disasters, post event the 'tyranny of the urgent' often means that basic information like the sex of the injured or even the deceased is not recorded, especially when bodies are burnt where they lie to stop the spread of disease. Figures are usually reported as total numbers, such as the 227 000 deaths in the Indian Ocean tsunami in 2004, or the 739 'excess' deaths due to the Chicago heat wave in 1995. What is not generally reported, since figures come from small-scale or academic research, is that in some locations three or four times as many women as men died from the tsunami. During the heat wave, elderly men were twice as likely to die, even though elderly women were considered more likely to be vulnerable (Sanz 2009: 14). As this latter finding illustrates, in terms of death and injury, it is actually difficult to predict who will be most vulnerable and while the assumption of women's greater vulnerability is not wrong, it cannot and should not be assumed to be always or necessarily the case.

Response to an event is subjective and will be framed by individual understandings of appropriate behaviour, which in turn are shaped by cultural norms, including gender norms. Within Latino cultures, for example, the cult of *machismo* may make men rather than women more likely to suffer loss of life during an event, whatever their relative poverty, due to their socially constructed roles and associated riskier behaviour patterns in the face of danger – a suggestion backed by data post hurricane Mitch in Central America (Gomáriz 1999). On the other hand, women's social status may make them so risk adverse that this becomes a risk in itself. This may be linked to ingrained cultural practices. In Bangladesh, observance of *purdah*, for example, may mean that women remain in their homes, despite cyclone warnings, waiting for a male authority figure to arrive and grant them permission to leave or assist them in doing so (Ariyabandu 2009). Such behaviour may affect middle-income women who are 'housewives' as much, if not more than, low-income women workers, since the former may be less accustomed to going out of the home alone and face greater social stigma for doing so.

The second problem with the UN's assertions that 'women always tend to suffer most' is that women are not a homogeneous group and not all women will experience the same event in the same way. Income may be key but, as the example above suggests, it is not always the defining factor. The stage reached in a life course, understood as the intersection between age and key events in many women's lives, such as marriage and childbirth, widowhood and caring for elderly parents, may be equally important. In general, gender needs to be understood as it 'intersects' with other characteristics such as age, sexuality, marital status and income. Enarson (2000) has noted over 20 different intersections of characteristics of women that may mean some women are living in highly vulnerable conditions. These include: low-income women; women whose income is insecure; and women in poverty; women with chronic health problems, from asthma to HIV; caregivers with primary responsibility for disabled or seriously ill spouses, children, and seniors; single mothers and women who are *de facto* heads of households; refugee women and undocumented women migrants; rural women isolated geographically; lesbians vulnerable to disclosure (outing) if accessing relief systems, especially in small communities; women experiencing violence and/or sexual assault; women needing pre-or post-natal care.

However, while it is important to take into account the different characteristics of a woman when determining vulnerability, care needs to be taken that checklists are not used in a cumulative fashion to predict who will be 'most' vulnerable. For example, post Katrina, research also highlighted that the assumption that women over 65 years of age would be more vulnerable to the negative impact of the hurricane was not borne out; but, what was important was the twinning of race and gender (Willinger and Knight 2012). Characteristics of vulnerability are qualitative, not quantifiable. For example, is it possible or useful to say if a middle-income, black, lesbian woman with a stable partner is more vulnerable than a poor, white, single mother? It is also important to remember that the risk of disaster is a product of both hazard and vulnerability and, in many ways, checklists of vulnerability are nonsensical without a hazard to relate them to. It is not possible to say with certainty who will be the most affected given that the impact of any event will be time, place and person specific, or depend on a mix of location, event and vulnerability. Moreover, while gender, age, income, race and migrant status may be key characteristics when thinking about vulnerability, they are not in themselves what defines that vulnerability – they are outcomes of other processes of discrimination and marginalisation. Being a woman is not in itself what leads to vulnerability. Vulnerability lies with the lack of access to the resources that allow people to cope with hazardous events and this access may be gendered, in that women in general tend to have less access to or control over assets. Vulnerability is not just about characteristics women have but also about having these ignored (Phillips and Fordham 2010). As such it is better not to think, 'Who is (more) vulnerable?' but 'Why are some people vulnerable, and what are the processes that made them so?'

Most obviously, people equate vulnerability with poverty. This is so at the macro level, with the Third World being perceived as more vulnerable than the West due to the low-income status of many countries, as well as at the micro level. Within 'the poor', some groups are considered poorer, and one such group is women (see Chapter 2). The Global Facility for Disaster Reduction and Recovery, a partnership between the UNISDR and the World Bank, suggests there is 'ample evidence' that poverty is the most important trigger that turns hazards into disasters. The UK's Department for International Development (DFID 2004), notes how poorer people tend to be more susceptible to hazards and how disasters can induce poverty, making the poor destitute. However, poverty and vulnerability are not one and the same thing. The development literature has demonstrated this (see Prowse 2003), and Moser's (1998) Capital Assets Framework, which looks at how 'the poor' respond to economic shocks, is useful in this context.

In the development literature, 'vulnerability' was brought to the fore to highlight the fact that not all poor people remain poor all the time, and as an attempt to shift away from static conceptualisations of poverty (see McIlwaine 2002). It recognises that people may make themselves income poor now to reduce their vulnerability to shocks in the future, through, for example, investing in education – denying themselves an income now in the hopes of attaining a higher and more stable income in the future. Conversely, the idea is that the poor have assets they can use to protect themselves during times of (economic) crisis such as income, human capital (health and education), potentially productive assets (things to sell such as jewellery or to use to make money such as a room to rent), family, and social capital.

In this context, social capital is best thought of as an asset that people obtain through their participation in social networks and institutions that they can use or call upon in times of need. Stocks of social capital are built over time as a by-product of other activities and social processes. However, it is important not to fall into the trap of accepting simplistic notions of social capital as necessarily and always a good thing, especially for the poor. Social capital and the social relations on which it is based can, in reality, be embedded in unequal existing social structures and relationships, such as unequal gender relations, and reinforce rather than transform them. While all may 'gain' from the relationships, not all gain to the same extent and as social capital is a resource available through social networks, the resources gained by one individual will be at the expense of losses for another individual. An extreme example of 'perverse social capital' is where membership of a group, such as a gang, produces positive benefits for the group members but negative results for other groups of people, often the majority (Rubio 1997; Moser and McIlwaine 2001).

As in the context of economic shocks, in the disaster context, social capital has been seen as a useful asset if stocks of social capital can be converted into monetary capital or other resources, such as access to transport. However, as work post Katrina notes, social networks do not always function as they should (Barnshaw and Trainor 2007) and the ability to transfer social capital into tangible resources to help withstand crisis seems to be limited (see Chapter 4), thus leaving even those individuals and groups with strong networks vulnerable.

If a person or group of people are asset poor, this may make them more vulnerable to shocks. DFID (2004) suggests that female-headed households are amongst the most asset poor and thus suggest they have been found to be among the most affected by natural disasters. It is not income *per se* that is the issue – women heads may have greater control over the income they earn than women who live with and depend on a man for money – but they may have poorer housing, less education and fewer familial and social relations due to the social stigma attached to being a single mother, and this is what makes them vulnerable.

The issue of assets also underpins another key development concept – that of livelihoods and more specifically the notion of 'sustainable livelihoods'. Livelihoods are the ways in which people access and mobilise resources that enable them to pursue goals necessary for their survival and longer-term well being, and thereby reduce their vulnerability. One of the earliest and most often cited definitions of a livelihood is that it comprises 'the capabilities, assets (including both material and social) and activities required for a means of living'. A livelihood is sustainable when it can 'cope with and recover from stress and shocks (drought, flood, war, and so on), and maintain or enhance its capabilities and assets, while not undermining the natural resource base' (Chambers and Conway 1992: 9). With its focus on coping with shocks, the usefulness of a livelihoods approach to disasters should be clear. Livelihood assets can include: natural resources (such as land, forests and water sources which people can access and use to build their livelihoods); technologies; skills; knowledge and capacity; health; access to education; sources of credit; or networks of social support. The extent to which individuals and groups can access and use these assets is influenced by the prevailing social, institutional and political environment. The more choice and flexibility that people have over what assets they can use, and how they can use these assets, the greater their ability to withstand, or adapt to, shocks; that is, the less vulnerable they are. It may be predicted that women, who will tend to have less access to a smaller range of assets, and less ability to use the assets available to them, will have less capacity to respond to shocks, be they economic or environmental.

It is interesting that, in the development literature, the focus is very much on the ability to use assets, and to adapt and respond to shocks. By contrast, in the disaster literature the focus tends to be on what people lack or cannot do, not what they can do. This has been the basis of some of the critiques of the concept of vulnerability and new concepts have emerged as a result of this. A relatively new concept is 'resilience' and the 'disaster-resilient' community. A focus on resilience means putting greater emphasis on what communities can do for themselves and how to strengthen their capacities, rather than concentrating on their vulnerability to disaster or their needs in an emergency (see Twigg 2007). Community resilience can be understood as:

- capacity to absorb stress or destructive forces through resistance or adaptation;
- capacity to manage, or maintain certain basic functions and structures, during disastrous events;
- capacity to recover or 'bounce back' after an event.

While a welcome development, a note of caution is needed since the idea of 'community resilience' does tend to construct 'community' as a benevolent, collective and equitable space and this may not be the case. Communities are not flat structures but have hierarchies of power and influence and thus may be highly unequal spaces. Care also needs to be taken in assuming we know what and where a community is (see Coates 2010 for discussion). While the term 'community' is often used by academics and practitioners, it is often not well defined. Community is often taken to mean a physical or geographical locality – a village or a town, for example. Alternatively, 'community' may be used to mean a specific group linked by common characteristics, such as sexuality. These common characteristics can be geographical – those living in houses located on flood plains are the at-risk 'community'. However, the notion of community is not simple even when location is the determining factor and it cannot be assumed that all those who live in a village, for example, see themselves, or are seen by others, as part of that community. A community is socially constructed, and as such can be an exclusionary as much as an inclusionary body. Often membership comes from 'partici-pation' in communal activities not merely occupying the space. Com-munities are, then, as much political as geographical spaces. They are spaces of power and inequality and how hazards are felt within them will differ between members of the community depending on the space they occupy – physically and politically.

For the more 'radical' disaster thinkers (see Radix), disasters are all about 'politics', suggesting they are as much political and historical processes as they are natural processes. The focus then should not be on vulnerability *per se*, but on what causes vulnerability. This is perhaps best illustrated by Blaikie et al.'s (1994) 'Pressure And Release' model (see Figure 1.1), which presents vulnerability as an outcome of 'dynamic pressures' at play which in turn arise from 'root causes' of inequality within society.

Gender and disaster researchers have also focused on inequalities for the better understanding of vulnerabilities, and have noted that disasters may help us better understand social processes. As Enarson and Morrow (1998: 2) note, disasters reveal inequalities of power at all levels, national, regional and global, as well as power inequalities within intimate relations. The suggestion is that issues of power and inequality of power, including gender inequalities and power imbalances, should be central to how we understand vulnerability and, thus, our understandings of disasters.

While vulnerability has received a great deal of attention from disaster academics over recent years, it has also been critiqued (Cannon 1994; Blaikie et al. 1994; Bankoff 2001, 2003a, 2003b, 2004; Oliver-Smith 2002). Hewitt (1998: 82) suggests that vulnerability encourages a sense that society or people are passive and, as noted above, this may be due to the way it is used in the disaster literature. Its usage may tell us

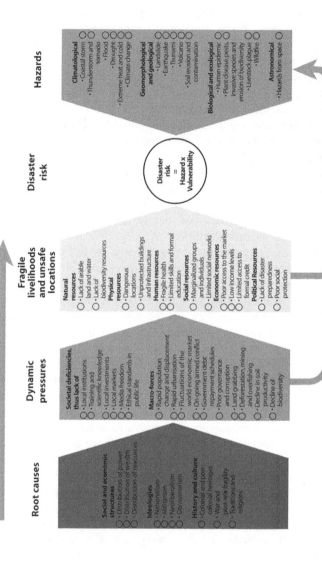

Source: Wisner, Gaillard and Kelan (2012); see also Blaikie et al. (1994)

Figure 1.1 'Pressure and Release' model

something about disaster experts, many of whom see people as needing
to be 'instructed, led and managed' (Phillips and Fordham 2010: 9).
Critics have suggested that vulnerability is a paradigm that has been used
to divide the world into two (Hewitt 1995; Bankoff 2004) – the
developed and the developing world – with the developing world
assumed to be more vulnerable while the developed world offers instruc-
tion on how to reduce that vulnerability.

Bankoff (2001) notes how, while initially the developing world was
constructed as 'paradise found' by its colonisers, this quickly changed as
conquerors and colonisers succumbed to tropical diseases. The developing world then became constructed as a dark, dangerous 'other'. Over
time, while the traditional dangers have been overcome through Western
medicines and interventions, the nature of the danger has been transformed. Countries have transitioned from being conceptualised as
disease-ridden, to poverty stricken, and then to disaster prone. The
vulnerability approach reinforces this notion of the Third World as
'other'. The 'developed' world also faces natural hazards but what makes
it distinct from the developing world is its ability to deal with these
events, or the inability of the developing world to do so. Developing
world countries are constructed as spaces of vulnerability or as defence-
less spaces. Yet defences are available and, as such, they are seen to be
spaces that require outside assistance to protect the vulnerable peoples.
Disasters then provide further justification for Western interventions in
the developing world under the remit of providing Western, 'solutions' to
the 'problem'. This is a theme that has been much discussed in
contemporary debates about development (see Chapter 2). However, the
extent to which natural hazards are seen to be a problem or conceptualised as a key risk by those who live through them in the developing
world is open to question. It is this notion of risk that will now be
explored.

RISK

Risk can never exist in the present, only in the future … (Cardona 2004: 47)

Risk, like vulnerability and hazard, is a key concept within work on
disasters. At the global level, the risk of disaster occurring is said to be
increasing. Notions that the world is becoming more prone to disasters is
linked to the climate change debate. While climate change is much
discussed in the academic literature and popular press, and is a phrase we
may use ourselves, it is important to remember it is a contested notion

and its existence is questioned. Within the discourse, shifts in weather extremes are presented as one of the most prominent anticipated impacts and of concern to many (Bouwer 2011). Yet care also needs to be taken not only around suggesting that the risk of disaster is increasing, but also what an increase in 'disasters' might mean.

If the number of extreme events were increasing, this would suggest the world is becoming more hazardous and, if these hazards result in disasters, it also suggests that the world has not been able to cope. The two are, as explored above, different issues. For example, to suggest the world is more hazardous would mean the number and intensity of events is increasing. The Intergovernmental Panel on Climate Change (IPCC) reported in 2007 that the frequency of heavy rainfall and heat waves has increased, that the area affected by drought has increased in many regions, and that tropical cyclone activity has increased in the North Atlantic Ocean (Solomon et al. 2007, cited in Bouwer 2011). This data suggests the world is becoming more hazardous. However, a hazard does not necessarily a disaster make, and we cannot suggest just because there are more hazards there will be more disasters, as disasters are a product of the hazard's interaction with people and things. The argument may then be that it is not the events themselves that are increasing, but the impact of events is increasing. This may arise from population increase. Population growth is usually associated with the developing world and has been constructed as a (global) problem within the neo-Malthusian discourse, and this, of course, is a gendered discourse (see Hartmann 1987). Rapid population growth may mean unsafe areas become populated, and strong population growth in coastal areas puts populations at greater exposure to floods, cyclones and tidal waves in particular. Population growth may also mean areas become more or over populated, meaning the impact of an event may be greater, not because the event is larger, but because it impacts on more people. While the number of people impacted may be increasing, in a world with ever more material goods to lose, the material loss from events may also be on the rise. Bouwer (2011) reviewed 22 studies of natural events and found there was a general trend for an increase in economic losses over time. However, after normalisation for changes in population and wealth, only eight studies identified increases in losses. This suggests that at present there is little evidence to support the idea that any increases in hazards are having a significant impact on increasing material losses at least.

Bearing in mind that disasters are social constructs, the idea that they are increasing may not reflect an increase in events, nor an increase in loss, but changing ideas around what constitutes a disaster – for example, loss of forests and mangroves may now be viewed as an (environmental) 'disaster'. The idea that disasters are increasing may also be due, on a scientific level, to improved information, meaning the number and intensity of events is now better recorded, as are losses. On a popular level, it may be due simply to the fact that we, as the general public, now know more about more disasters, due to the media beaming images of events into our living rooms, making us feel that the world is becoming more unsafe. Similarly, tourism and travel also contribute to bringing disasters closer to us, and the Indian Ocean tsunami is a good example of a disaster 'felt' across the globe because of the media reports providing 'as it happens' coverage, coupled with the number of tourists involved. Rosenthal (1999) captures these ideas in the notions of 'transnationalisation', 'mediasation', and 'politisation' as characterising contemporary disasters.

Whatever the origin, the above analysis suggests that our understanding of how safe the world is may be changing, and there may be a heightened feeling of risk from 'natural' events. The notion of risk has become central to disaster response, captured by the notion of Disaster Risk Reduction (DRR). This broad and relatively new concept has a number of definitions but it is generally understood to mean the broad development and application of policies, strategies and practices to minimise disaster risks throughout society. DRR thinking sees disasters as complex problems demanding a collective response from different disciplinary and institutional groups.

Not only are disasters complex, but so is risk itself. One reason why it may be suggested that the world is becoming more risky is not because of changes in the risks we face, but because of changes in how we perceive events as 'risk'. Things that were once seen as day to day annoyances can come to be seen as a threat, while events once perceived as risky can be normalised. Kroll-Smith and Gunter (1998: 169) use the example of a woman who has lived for many years in a mining town prone to fires. She noted that, until recently, her understanding of mine fires was that they were something 'that you lived with when you live in a mining town'. Two events changed her mind. One was designed to protect her and her family – a gas monitor was installed in her house that would set off an alarm if dangerous amounts of gas were present. Suggesting the need to take measures against a risk highlights the existence of that risk. The second was a study, which was designed to look at the issue. This altered her understanding of risk since, as she noted, 'What are you here for if there is nothing to worry about?' The example highlights the way that what is seen to be a risk will be influenced by external actors and events, and is subjective, not objective.

It also highlights the fact that there is a need to recognise that 'public logic is not the same as scientific rationality' (Stephens 2002: 103).

For scientists there is a clear definition of risk – probability of damage inflicted by one or several hazards to a vulnerable unit. The objectivist definition rests on risk as being about probable and measurable outcomes. It is no longer a neutral term denoting the probabilities of both positive and negative outcomes but in the scientific discourse risk has become only negative (Douglas 1992), something that should be avoided through technical and/or non-technical measures.

It has been suggested that risk can be understood as a set of differing ways of ordering reality, as part of the move from the theological discourse of divine danger to rendering the world into a calculable form (Anderson 2011), and as such it is not possible to speak of an incalculable risk (Dean 1999: 177). While it is presented as something known, in fact Liverman (1990) suggests there is substantial confusion, and that for many years risk was used to refer to what is now defined as hazard, while currently vulnerability is being used as if it were the same thing as risk. Disaster scholars, such as Cardona, have for many years sought to refine the means to calculate and evaluate risk and vulnerability and, while recognising the utility of quantitative methods, conclude that 'the quantitative approaches for assessing vulnerability need to be complemented with qualitative approaches to capture the full complexity and the various tangible and intangible aspects of vulnerability in its different dimensions' (Cardona et al. 2012: 67). One such dimension that has received attention has been gender, and advances have been made in designing tools to evaluate and enumerate women's relative, and specific, risk and vulnerability (see Enarson 2000).

What the general literature on risk highlights is the subjectivity of 'risk perception' (see Sjoberg 2000) and while what informs the perception of risk is contested in the literature, there is a shared view that it is 'in the mind', and closely related to personal or collective psychology (Cardona 2004: 47). Past experience can influence risk perception, particularly among those who suffered a high impact event, while repeated events and recent events will also heighten the perception of risk (Bonin el al. 2010; Burn 1999; Lindell and Perry 2004). However, personal experience may be 'misleading' (Burn 1999: 3452). If people were able to cope with the event, a similar event may not be seen to be a 'risk' in the future and/or people may not believe it will happen to them again (Botzen et al. 2009; Burn 1999; Martin et al. 2009). On the other hand, those who have never experienced an event may find it difficult to imagine. If an event cannot be imagined, it cannot be prepared for. Those without experience will have little to draw on and may rely on images from the media, which may lead to errors in judgement (Parker et al. 2009). Technology can also lead to 'errors' in judgement since structural measures or defences may give people a sense of security and, through feeling 'safe', they may actually take riskier actions, for example, setting up home at a risky location or not evacuating (White 1945).

Once again populations are not homogeneous and ideas of risk will vary. For example, migrants in the UK who have suffered floods in Bangladesh may not perceive the threat of flood in the UK to be great since they will not see it as being on the same scale, plus they may perceive there is the technology to deal with it (Lindell and Perry 2004; Robertson 2004). Studies suggest adolescents and youth may have lower perceptions of risk and what are risky activities in general, and may thus be more likely to take risky actions in hazardous situations. Risk is also gendered and this relates to how men and women are socialised into their male and female roles and what these mean (see Chapter 3). For example, men may see a threat as less than women and may display riskier behaviour in the face of an evident threat. As different characteristics intersect and build, then, for example, a young male may walk through fast flowing water, putting himself at risk of drowning, whereas a young female may not. Lack of recognition of a threat as carrying a personal risk may lead to risky behaviour and produce vulnerability to a particular event. This denial or non-acceptance of personal risk may, however, have a rational explanation.

Nathan's (2008) study of a precarious community built in La Paz on top of extremely steep mountains and within ravines illustrates how subjective the understanding of risk is. He notes that when asked what risks and hazards they faced, the inhabitants generally focused on interpersonal insecurity, the struggle to earn and secure a living, and their fear of health problems. Even when asked specifically about landslides or the potential collapse of their homes, they often denied the risk or reported that they felt secure. Research suggests people may become hostile to the idea that they are at risk of experiencing negative life events, such as contracting disease, or being impacted by a disaster, due to 'optimism bias'. People generally judge themselves to be impervious to events, or less at risk than the general population (Weinstein 1980). However, denial or repression of risk may also be a rational choice for those who feel they have no other choice than to live with that risk. What Nathan's research highlights is that people tend to prioritise some risks over others, in particular it has been suggested that people tend to give less importance to low probability events, such as earthquakes, even if they may bring high losses. People also 'learn to live' with the risks they face, especially when there are few other options open to them. That is, there is an element of adaptive realism around how risks are perceived – those that are manageable are perceived as 'risks' while those that are not easy to change, are lived with, become familiar, and are minimised or repressed. However, risk may also be 'repressed' or denied by external actors, and this can be explained through reference to the responsibility to respond that would arise if the risk were not repressed.

Risk is not a 'fact' but depends on perception and representation and thus if a risk is not constructed as a threat by society then it is not seen as a risk. Experts and governments, then, have a key role to play in ensuring risks are recognised by society. However, they may actually play the opposite role. Risk may be repressed by governments for the simple fact there is no politically acceptable way of transmitting risk messages. For example, what scientists see as the acceptable risk associated with nuclear power may cause alarm among the general public. However, a government cannot construct an issue as raising risks for the general public and then avoid taking action. Therefore, it is decided that it is best not to inform them of this (minimal) risk (Paine 2002). If recognition of a risk means accepting responsibility to respond, there may be large economic and political costs involved. Conversely, if risks are constructed as 'natural' by experts, and become accepted as such by the individuals exposed to them, then governments can deny their responsibility to respond to what are 'Acts of God'. This 'naturalness' of events undercuts demands for the problem to be made part of the political agenda.

In societies where there are high and multiple risks, such as poverty, violence and conflict, and a history of a lack of response from governments, there may be higher tolerance of risk. So high toleration of (high) risk is something that may characterise Third World countries. The community studied by Nathan (2008) in La Paz do not see their situation as 'risky' as they have no individual choice and no notion that the government could be responsible for them and their situation, even when that situation results in loss of life. In precarious communities, a relatively high level of loss may be tolerated without the community or society seeing it as a problem, or a 'disaster'. In this context, the impact of a natural event is understood as being only a more acute or extreme form of chronic daily suffering (Cannon 1994: 16).

DRAWING THE LINKS: DISASTERS AND DEVELOPMENT

Asking why disasters happen is essentially a political question but understanding how they occur is a fundamentally historical one. (Bankoff 2003b: 11)

Disasters are a subjective concept and what may be seen as a 'disaster' by one individual, community or society may be seen by another to be merely another instance of daily suffering, albeit in an extreme form. Given the understandings of disaster, risk and vulnerability explored above, it is clear how the developing world may be seen as 'vulnerable' to natural hazards and deemed 'at risk' of disaster. However, it is equally clear why those who live in poverty within the developing world may not see the risk presented by a natural hazard as being a priority, or indeed a disaster to be a 'disaster'.

What is interesting about disaster writing in the developing world context is that while disasters are such a common occurrence for so many Third World countries, the topic is generally not discussed within mainstream development literature, and disasters are noticeable by their absence from development textbooks and courses. When discussed in relation to development, immediately after an event, it is not unusual to hear commentators talking about how the disaster has 'set back' development. Even UN disaster training materials suggest that 'disasters set back development programming, destroying years of development initiatives' (UNDP 1994: 10). Despite the regularity with which they occur, disasters are conceptualised as extraordinary events that break the 'normal' or established process of development. This conceptualisation is in part related to the traditional focus of disaster professionals on the natural hazard and the popular construction of disasters as acts of God. Yet, understanding disasters as a product of a hazard interacting with a vulnerable population highlights the way disasters are not outside human agency and, as such, not outside the development process, but instead are shaped by that process. As such, disasters may be better understood, not as interrupting development, but as the outcome of historical processes of development that create vulnerability (Bankoff 2001). They are an outcome of the 'development' to date that has not improved the ability of the population to respond to the natural hazard and thus avoid the associated potential 'disaster' (Wisner et al. 2003).

This conceptualisation of disasters highlights how disasters should be understood not as outside development processes, but as linked to them, or even as products of them. It suggests that to understand disasters there is a need to understand how 'development' has, or has not occurred. As with disaster, risk and vulnerability, the notion of development is subjective and as a lived reality it is experienced differently by different people. In particular, women may understand and experience disasters and development differently from men. The next two chapters will provide a brief review of the notions of development and gender and how they relate, or do not, to disasters.

2.   What is development?

INTRODUCTION

Development, like disaster, is a contested notion with a long history of discussion and debate around its meaning. Many textbooks explain what development 'is' and many pages have been filled in exploring how best it can be achieved (see for example Allen and Thomas 2000; Chant and McIlwaine 2009; Crush 1995; Timmons-Roberts and Hite 2000; Desai and Potter 2008; Potter et al. 2008; Willis 2005). In general, it captures ideas of progress and advancement: inherent in the idea is the notion of change. This change is generally assumed to be all encompassing, to occur at both the social and individual levels, and to be a continuous and cumulative process. However it is not always positive or 'good' change (see Thomas 2000). While much discussion has focused on how to achieve development, economic growth has been presented as key. Events in the 1990s, however, called into question whether economic growth alone is sufficient to bring about development and saw a new focus in the development discourse on factors that influence growth, including gender. In recent years, the notions of poverty and inequality have also become more central to the debates around development and while growth remains key, social protection for the poor is now also recognised as important. The evolving development discourse overlaps with that of the disaster discourse, including a common language focused on poverty and vulnerability, on risk and protection. However, the way in which these concepts are understood does not necessarily coincide, and disasters have certainly not been a central concern of development. Mainstream development texts do not discuss disasters, and disaster writing has not informed the way in which ideas such as vulnerability or risk are discussed within the development discourse.

This chapter will present some of the key ideas related to the notion of 'development' and suggest how they relate to the ideas around disasters presented in the previous chapter. It will consider the key actors in development, the key development theories, and some key moments in the history of Third World 'development' to date. It will explore a number of development concepts related to ideas of well being, which are important for the study of disasters also. It does not pretend to be an exhaustive consideration of what 'development' is but it does aim to provide a context within which to understand how strands of thinking around development and disasters have inter-related and still do.

EARLY IDEAS AROUND DEVELOPMENT

The contemporary notion of 'development' as a professional planned process is generally thought to have emerged at the end of the Second World War. Prior to this time, many of the countries that are now classified as 'low income' or categorised as 'Less Developed', 'Developing' or 'Third World' countries were colonies. As such, the idea that they and their people could 'develop' to be like the colonising nations was not given any currency. Processes of de-colonisation occurred from internal processes, with the colonised peoples demanding the end to colonial powers, and external events, such as the Second World War, demonstrating the declining power of the former colonisers. The end of the Second World War marked a new era across the globe in terms of changing power balances, with the rise of the US and the (former) USSR as power blocs, the demise of Western Europe, and the formation of newly independent countries. Ideological differences, especially those highlighted by the notion of the 'Cold War', marked this era. However, there were also common agreements, not least the idea that never again should open conflict be seen on the level of the Second World War. It was this understanding that underpinned the formation of a number of global institutions formed toward the end of the War.

The United Nations (UN) was formed as a global peacekeeper in 1945. The idea for such an organisation originally emerged after the First World War and the formation of the League of Nations. However, while the League of Nations was unable to survive, the United Nations has grown and now has a diverse range of programmes and funds covering a range of issues from children, to drugs and crime, and a series of specialised agencies, such as the World Health Organization (WHO) and the Food and Agriculture Organization (FAO). There is no programme, fund or specialised agency that is directly responsible for natural hazards and disasters but a number of programmes are important in post-disaster situations, such as the Human Settlements Programme (UN-HABITAT), and the World Food Programme (WFP). The UN's direct work on disasters is through the International Strategy for Disaster Reduction (UNISDR), which aims to 'mobilise, guide and facilitate action at national and regional levels to integrate disaster risk reduction and climate change policies and practices, through close collaboration with national platforms for disaster risk reduction, regional platforms and networks, and by providing guidance materials, tools and methodologies.' The lack of a dedicated 'disasters' agency perhaps seems surprising, given the UN's founding aims of peacekeeping, peace building, conflict prevention and humanitarian assistance. However, this needs to be understood within the context of how 'disasters' have been conceptualised (as discussed in the previous chapter) as 'natural' hazards rather than social, political and historical events. In short, disasters were seen until recently as unfortunate 'Acts of God', but not the responsibility of international agencies such as the UN. More recent changes in conceptualisations of disasters and 'humanitarianism' (see Chapter 5) mean that the UN is now the key coordinating body in post-disaster relief and reconstruction and has taken the lead in advancing a global agenda on disaster mitigation (see Chapter 9).

After the Second World War, reconstruction was not, however, the remit of the UN but rather that of two institutions set up at a meeting of the main industrialised nations close to the end of the Second World War in Bretton Woods. Collectively known as the International Financial Institutions (IFIs), the World Bank and the International Monetary Fund (IMF) have had an important role to play in shaping the developed and developing world for over 50 years, and some critics suggest their power has only increased over time (see the Bretton Woods Project website). It is interesting to note that, although they were set up to help bring about post-conflict reconstruction and they focused on bringing development out of crisis, neither have played a key role in post-disaster reconstruction and only recently have disasters entered the World Bank development discourse.

The initial thinking behind both the World Bank and the IMF was similar to that behind the UN – the need to ensure global harmony. The two institutions reflect recognition of the role economic disharmony played in the Second World War. It also reflects recognition of the need to re-establish trade in the wake of the War as a tool to reconstruct the devastated economies of Europe and Japan. This was also important since, while the US had emerged wealthy, this wealth could not be maintained without trade. The International Bank for Reconstruction and Development (now known simply as the World Bank) was set up to improve the capacity of countries to trade by lending money to war-ravaged and impoverished countries for reconstruction and development projects. The second institution, the International Monetary Fund, was to play a supervisory role and aimed to create a stable climate for international trade by harmonising members' monetary policies. The final institution born at the meeting but not formalised until 1995 was the World Trade Organisation (WTO), which aims to ensure that trade flows as smoothly, predictably and freely as possible.

While, more recently, these three Bretton Woods Institutions (BWIs) have been the target of global campaigns against the powers they are seen to represent, it is important to remember that their ideology in general reflects the dominant paradigm of the day and this has evolved over time. Their initial remit reflected the key thinking of the time and was influenced by the British economist John Maynard Keynes.

At the time, Keynes presented seemingly radical ideas around economic policy, seeing a role for the State, not just in protecting the nation or providing goods that otherwise would not be provided (such as traffic lights) but in managing the economy, and in ensuring employment and welfare for the population. While not anti-market, Keynes believed the depression of the 1930s raised questions about the traditional (classical) view that a boom/bust cycle was 'natural' and that, after a bust, the market would re-establish the economy at its former level. He suggested that this process was not always quick and did not always re-establish the pre-crisis levels of economic development. In the post-war context, he suggested a role for the state in 'kick starting' the process of recovery, most specifically through large-scale infrastructure projects such as rebuilding and improving dams, bridges and ports. Such projects would provide employment for many, which would provided wages; wages would provide the money to buy goods, and the demand for goods would in turn influence the supply of goods, because manufacturers would be encouraged to produce more. For this they would, in turn, employ more people, who would in turn have wages to spend, and so the 'virtuous' circle would continue. From this description the relevance of Keynes' ideas for post-disaster reconstruction should be clear. However, then, as now, an initial impetus was needed post crisis through an injection of money to pay for projects. Since post-War governments had few available funds, projects would be financed through borrowing. Borrowing was not seen to be a bad thing in this optimistic era, as money would be invested to generate growth and loans would be paid back as growth occurred. This thinking not only influenced post-War reconstruction but also influenced early development thinking, and continues to influence post-disaster reconstruction projects.

Development as a planned process began in the 1950s and many of the former colonies sought to find a new, 'third way', to advance their newly independent countries. The 'non-aligned movement', created in 1961, sought a path for Third World countries that was neither tied to the First or Western World, with its focus on capitalism, nor the Second World, the

Soviet bloc with its focus on communism. However, processes of de-colonisation did not alter the need of the industrialised nations for raw materials, many of which had in the past been extracted from the colonies. With progress in manufacturing in the West, mass production called for mass markets to sell goods to, and the newly independent countries also offered opportunities for the West in terms of sales of manufactured products. Thus the Western nations sought to continue links with the former colonies. However, while economics was important, there was also an ideological impetus to forging links with the new nations – to ensure they remained within the capitalist bloc. The classic development text of the time, Rostow's (1960), *Stages of Economic Growth* highlights the importance of this ideological battle with its sub title: *A Non-Communist Manifesto*. Rostow's work falls into what has been termed the 'Modernisation' school of development theorising, a school of thought whose influence can still be seen within contemporary development and disaster discourse.

DEVELOPMENT THEORISING

Much has been written about Modernisation theory both at the time (see Friedmann 1966; Hirschman 1958; Hoselitz 1952; Myrdal 1957; Parsons 1960; Rostow 1960; and Timmons-Roberts and Hite 2000 for selected readings) and in textbooks (see Potter et al. 2008; Rapley 2007). The intellectual roots of the theory lie in the work of nineteenth century sociologists, Max Weber and Emile Durkheim, and also draw on the ideas of Adam Smith and David Ricardo. It essentially sought to learn from reflecting on why some countries had developed in the past, especially those of Western Europe during the industrial revolution, and use this as a 'blue print' for how countries could develop now. While Modernisation did not concern itself with 'disasters', what is interesting for the current discussion is the language used by the Modernisation theorists and their underlying ideas around what characterised the 'Third World'. Modernisation theory divided the world into two types of society. The traditional, characterised as rural and undeveloped, was constructed as backward and uncivilised, superstitious and fatalistic, with people living in 'extended' families producing for subsistence and essentially without drive to achieve change in their status in life. Such was how Western Europe had been prior to the industrial revolution. In contrast, the contemporary urbanised and industrialised 'modern' nation was a complex society of nuclear households interconnected in production and consumption by markets, where individuals are driven by the 'protestant work ethic' and make decisions as 'rational economic man'. While industrialisation is important in bringing change, what differentiates the two types of society is not technology and machinery, but the characteristics of the people. As the work of Talcott Parsons (1960) highlights, changes in attitudes and values are seen to be critical to economic progress and development. Lack of development is then due to internal 'obstacles' – the people themselves, their beliefs and ideologies. Thus, Modernisation theory posits far-reaching changes in social relations and social structures, modelling these changes on the development of the West. Western interventions focused on education, technology and capital are then presented as the 'solution' to the development 'problem'. As later chapters will highlight, these ideas are still apparent within current development and disaster discourse.

Modernisation was very attractive to the leaders of newly independent countries, presenting as it did an optimistic view of their future and the role of the West in helping them with this. However, not all were convinced, and, particularly in Latin America, new leaders and thinkers in the former colonies saw a flaw in the Modernisation rationale. They pointed to the importance of history for understanding both how the industrialised nations had developed and why the rest of the world had not. Again, much is written in development texts about what is known as 'Dependency theory' (see Potter et al. 2008; Rapley 2007), and the writers of the time provide a rich and detailed view of the relations between the First and the Third World (see Baran 1957; Cardoso and Faletto 1979; Dos Santos 1970; Frank 1967; and Timmons-Roberts and Hite 2000 for selected readings). While differences exist between the key thinkers within the Dependency school about the extent to which 'development' could occur within the current global system, there are ideas in common. In contrast to Modernisation, Dependency theory has its roots in the ideas of radical nineteenth century thinkers, Karl Marx and Freidrich Engels, and its proponents applied a neo-Marxist approach to understanding why Less Developed Countries were less developed. Dependency theorists suggest that Third World countries are not 'undeveloped' but rather have been actively 'underdeveloped' and the process by which this occurred was colonisation. While the former colonies might have been at the same point as Europe prior to the industrial revolution, Europe 'developed' through colonisation and the colonies were 'underdeveloped', that is, their situation became worse. The two processes are the different faces of the same coin; one occurred because of the other. This means there can be no Western blueprint to follow, and that the barrier to development is not internal to the Third World but external. The benefits for the Third World of Western 'development' interventions are questioned and are seen instead as the means by which the West can prolong the current unequal power relations between the First and Third worlds, which act to their advantage. This thinking has resonance with the thinking of the more radical disaster scholars such as Bankoff (2001, 2004), who see the conceptualisation of disasters as a means to divide the world into two halves and as a justification for Western interventions in the developing world to 'help' lessen their vulnerability (see Chapter 1) – a vulnerability the First World is seen to have helped to produce through the Modernisation development paradigm.

Dependency theory offered an explanation why the Third World is under developed but little by way of what to do about this. Its ideas had something of a resurgence in the 2000s, especially in Latin America, with the election of leaders such as Lula in Brazil, Chavez in Venezuela, and Ortega in Nicaragua. Ideas of dependency can also be seen in a more radical formulation within the post-development discourse (see Escobar 1995; Illich 1973; and Rahnema and Bawtree 1997 for selected readings). Here the very notion of 'development' is disputed and presented as a construct promoted by the West as a means to maintain its power through offering the notion of advancement, which is in fact a myth. It is important to note that, while development within the post-development discourse is constructed as a myth, as Escobar suggests 'as a discourse development is a very real historical formation, albeit around an artificial construct' (Escobar 1995: 53). That is, development practice exists, but the notion of 'development' does not, or at least not as something achievable and desirable for the Third World. The modernisation process does not produce 'development' but, actually, it systematically produces risk, thus modern society is a 'risk society' (Beck 1998). That, despite 'development', disasters continue to occur and, some suggest, with greater frequency, intensity and impact adds support to such notions.

While Dependency theory and post-development thinking contest notions of development put forward by the West, Modernisation theory offered the West the means to continue growing its industrial base through trade and it seemingly offered the most obvious and attractive way forward for Third World leaders. Development as Westernisation remains the dominant conceptualisation and its legacy can also be seen in how 'natural disasters' are conceptualised as something to be overcome through the application of science and progress and lessons learned from the West.

THE ORIGINS OF THE CONTEMPORARY DEVELOPMENT LANDSCAPE

Whatever the ideology of the governments of the First and Third Worlds and the relative influence of Modernisation and Dependency theories on their designs for development, the 1950s–1970s were characterised by two key features: industrialisation and borrowing (see Rapley 2007). The Third World, in particular, benefited from the 'petro-dollars' earned by the newly rich oil producing nations. These nations invested their money in private Western banks in order to accrue a return on their savings. These banks in turn lent the deposited money to individuals and business, earning money through the difference in the interest given to savers and charged to borrowers. In the post-War period, the banks expanded their clients to include offering loans to Third World governments across the globe. When the US and UK governments chose to increase interest rates in a response to 'stagflation' in their economies and the fear of First World recession, the interest rate rises were passed on to borrowers by the banks, including indebted Third World borrowing nations.

Over and above the apparent misuse of the money borrowed by the governments of many nations of the Third World, the sheer amount they had borrowed meant they struggled to continue to service loans, particularly as interest rate rises meant that people in the First World were reducing their consumption and thus the demand for exports from the Third World also declined. In 1982 Mexico was the first country that threatened to default and many others soon followed, leading to what has been termed the Third World 'debt crisis' (Corbridge 1993). Borrowing in itself is not a problem, as long as savers and bankers are confident that borrowers can and will pay back loans, or have assets to the value of the loan that can be seized if they cannot pay them back. The fear was that, as these were large borrowers with debts to familiar high street banks, a threat to default would lead to a loss of confidence in the banks and the global financial system would unravel. To avoid this, the debts were rescheduled in consultation with the World Bank and the IMF. This 'bail out' came with conditions, and the countries were required to change their economic polices as recommended by the IFIs and in line with a global shift in thinking with the rise of neo-liberalism. It is interesting to note how 'crisis' can allow radical changes to occur within governments and governance, and how the threat of economic crisis is used to justify quite extreme austerity measures. Similarly, endogenous shocks to countries, such as natural hazards, may bring radical change to policies and processes in the aftermath of the crisis they provoke. Disaster scholars may be able to learn from studying other economic shocks and crises.

The debt crisis of the 1980s produced one such radical change as neo-liberal ideas emerged in its aftermath, reflecting changes in governments in the US and UK with Ronald Reagan and Margaret Thatcher coming to power. These 'new' ideas were then exported to the Third World via loan conditionalities. The 1980s and 1990s have been seen as the 'lost decades' for development as the World Bank and the IMF insisted on Structural Adjustment Programmes (SAPs) being put in place across the Third World. SAPs should be understood as the manifestation of neo-liberal thinking in the developing world, an extreme application of neo-liberalism rather than something distinct from neo-liberal thinking. SAPs were designed to stabilise economies, and then restructure them to promote economic growth, growth needed in order to generate foreign currency and pay back debts.

A reaction to, and rejection of Keynesian economics, neo-liberalism is more than an economic policy; rather, it is an ideology. It is the dominant paradigm and in policy terms it frames what is done and can be done, and it also determines what is included in the development discourse and what is excluded. Its key elements are the notions of individualism, of a limited role for the state and the need to allow markets to operate 'freely'. Key policies under SAPs included the removal of subsidies, privatisation of goods and services, the opening of economies and removal of barriers such as tariffs to allow 'free' trade, and diversification of what is produced, replacing subsistence goods with goods that could be exported. What should be clear from this collection of policies is that the poor would be particularly hard hit as the provision of free or subsidised goods and services are cut. The middles classes working in over-large state bureaucracies were also hit, as many jobs were lost. The intense competition for jobs meant salaries were low and working conditions poor. The focus on production for export further impacted on those already feeling poorer through reduced income, as food prices increased due to limited supply and the removal of subsidies, compounded by having to pay for health, education and basic necessities, such as water. While this may be a way to bring economic 'development', it highlights the fact that although this 'development' is all encompassing, occurs at both the social and individual levels, and is a continuous and cumulative process – that is, it fulfils ideas of what is 'development' (Thomas 2000) – it does not always bring positive or 'good' change.

Overall, the social and human cost of SAPs has been recognised as being high (Cornia et al. 1987), in particular, the price was high for women as there was a transference of services from the market to the home, and related costs from the paid to the unpaid economy (Afshar and Dennis 1992; Beneria and Feldman 1992; Elson 1989, 1991; Moser 1989a, 1992). SAPs were important for demonstrating that women's labour is not 'infinitely elastic' and they are not able to stretch during times of crisis to cover all shortfalls in state or public provision of goods and services (Elson 1991). This is an important lesson to learn and pertinent when considering household coping strategies during post-disaster crises, to ensure projects for reconstruction do not merely burden women further and stretch them to breaking point (see Chapter 6).

While the high human costs of SAPs could perhaps be justified if growth rates had been high and the debt burden substantially reduced, this was not the case. In the early 2000s there was implicit acceptance by the IFIs that SAPS had not led to the growth hoped for and moreover that they had a significant negative impact on income distribution. In particular, a positive relationship between the implementation of SAPs and increases in inequality had been noted (Lopez 2002). Increased poverty, continued high debt and little sustained economic growth caused a shift in thinking in 2000 and a new priority being placed on poverty reduction by the World Bank and the IMF via the Poverty Reduction Strategy Papers (PRSPs), in line with the wider shift to a poverty focus as witnessed by the United Nations Millennium Development Goals (MDGs) (see Chapter 9). The extent to which the PRSP initiative should be seen as a new era in development thinking, marking a real change from SAPs, has been debated. The alternative view is that they represent not revolution but an evolution of neo-liberal thinking, whereby the critiques of SAPs have been absorbed within the dominant paradigm (see Bradshaw and Linneker 2003). For example, the imposition of policies on the Third World was one critique of the IFIs and SAPs. Writing a PRSP remains a 'condition' for obtaining World Bank/IMF funds but the condition is not about content but about process (Booth 2003). The contents are not dictated by the IFIs but countries must go through a participatory design process. The extent to which countries are free to design their own PRSP, however, has been questioned. The World Bank's PRSP 'Sourcebook' acts as a guide for those writing PRSPs and suggests a number of areas that should be considered, and these do include 'new' elements such as human capital, good governance, gender and the environment. However, the World Bank and IMF continue to stress that economic growth is the 'single most' important factor influencing poverty reduction (World Bank 2002).

World Bank economists have sought to demonstrate that economic growth is (still) good for the poor (see Dollar and Kraay 2000) and in light of this have looked to highlight ways in which economic growth initiatives can be improved or enhanced. Gender has been found to be one such economic growth enhancer (see Chapter 3). The relationship between economic growth and poverty reduction has been contested, however, and analysts suggest that while the poor do benefit from economic growth, so do the rich. The rich may benefit more, given their bigger asset base, and at the very least if both benefit equally, while the poor get richer the rich do also, meaning that the gap between the rich and the poor does not change and the poor remain 'poor' in relative terms (Oxfam 2000). What is largely accepted is that countries with high inequality have a harder time reducing poverty through economic growth since higher inequality tends to mean that the poor have a lower share of the gains from any growth (Ravallion 1997, 2001; Deininger and Olinto 2000). This suggests that the main factor influencing the impact of growth on poverty is the initial level of inequality, and that large inequalities may explain continuing poverty in countries where some economic growth has occurred, such as in countries of Latin America (Killick 2002).

While inequality is not tackled, poverty will remain, and as inequality and poverty are at the basis of vulnerability, economic growth in itself will not necessarily be able to reduce the vulnerability of nations and groups of people to natural hazards. Economic growth focused development, then, in itself may not reduce the risk of disasters. This suggests the need to tackle both poverty and vulnerability directly. The next section will explore the notion of poverty in more depth, including gendered experiences of poverty, and consider its links to vulnerability, risk and disasters.

CONCEPTUALISING WELL BEING AND GENDERED WELL BEING

Poverty as a concept has risen up the policy agenda since 2000 and, given its perceived link with vulnerability and as a factor in allowing hazards to become disasters, it is important to discuss what is meant by the concept.

The now famous presentation by MacNamara to the World Bank in 1973 initiated debates about the best way to define and measure poverty and from this date there has been wide discussion around the different conceptualisations of the term 'poverty' among people and organisations working in the field of 'development'. At the outset it is important to stress that the meaning of poverty is highly contested and no consensus has yet been reached (see McIlwaine 2002 for further discussion). Although the poverty discourse has accepted that income or consumption based poverty metrics are limited, and much of importance is left out, these metrics remain dominant and continue to establish levels of global poverty and trends in poverty reduction (Ravillion 2001, 2002). At the country or macro level key indicators of development that are used to classify countries according to their high or low-income status include Gross Domestic Product (GDP), Gross National Product (GNP) and more recently Gross National Income (GNI), usually expressed in terms of Purchasing Power Parity and as a per capita measure. This notion of the per capita wealth of a nation does not, of course, reflect the actual distribution of resources, and the key defining measure of inequality, the Gini Coefficient, is seldom used as a measure of development, despite the apparent importance of inequality in limiting economic growth gains. 'Alternative' measures, such as the UNDP's Human Development Index and derivatives such as the Gender Empowerment Index, while taking into account quality of life measures, such as longevity and education, still include in their calculations some notion of income. Perhaps the most used, and most critiqued, poverty metric is the poverty line and the notion of a 'dollar a day' as defining poverty has become an accepted standard. The numbers below the line, and the amount they are below the line, tells us which countries and which people are the most 'poor'.

Such simplistic measures of poverty have been criticised both on methodological grounds and in terms of their explanatory value. Income measures, for example, tend to use the household as the unit of analysis. As such, it is not possible to compare the situation of a woman with that of man in a comparable household. The only comparison possible is between female-headed households and male-headed households. Differences in gender are 'forced to be differences across households in which the genders live' (Kanbur 2002: 9). This suggests a fundamental problem in that measures of wealth and poverty are not adequate to capture gender difference.

Considering the specific causes of women's relative poverty or the basis of the gendered experience of poverty, it is possible to isolate three key contributing factors

- That women have fewer possibilities for translating work into income. This stems from women's exclusive responsibility for reproductive work, the conceptualisation of their productive activities as 'helping' men and their concentration within sectors which are either an extension of their reproductive roles (and thus lower paid) or within the 'informal' economy (see Scott 1986 for discussion).

- When women do have an income they find it more difficult to transform this income into decision-making capacity or to decide how it is used. Perceptions around the value of the contribution to the household, social norms and self-esteem and relative autonomy influence their capacity to have a voice in decision-making processes (see Sen 1987, 1990; Agarwal 1997 for household models).
- When women do make decisions, they are less likely to be ones that will improve their own personal well being and more likely to improve the well being of all or others. This supposed 'altruism' of women while it seems to stem from their 'natural' attributes as carers and mothers is a socially constructed conceptualisation of what it means to be a woman (see Dwyer and Bruce 1988; Folbre 1994 for evidence and discussion).

The causes of women's poverty operate at different levels and there are different sites or spaces that contribute to it: the community; labour market; the household (Bradshaw 2002a). All these spaces need to be taken into account when understanding and addressing women's relative poverty. However, the household is often overlooked by policy makers. These same sites also help to explain women's relative vulnerability to hazards and why they may experience disasters differently from men. The basic unit of analysis in disasters, as with development, is often the household, yet the household is a contested site and cannot be assumed to be a place of unity and solidarity, especially in times of crisis.

The conventional idea of a household is of the nuclear unit (a couple with their children) but in the Developing World extended households (the nuclear unit plus other family or friends) and single parent households (most usually female-headed units) form a significant proportion of all households. In terms of female-headed households, it has recently tended to be assumed that they not only represent a significant minority of all households (estimates are that they represent between a third and half of all households) but that they are significant also for the conditions under which they occur and which they perpetuate, that is, they arise in situations of poverty and they are poorer than other household units (see Chant 2003 for discussion). However, many who work on households, and in particular female-headed households, have questioned the idea that they are the 'poorest of the poor' and have called for a re-consideration of the relative poverty of women within male-headed units (see Chant 2008b for debates). While women heads may have less access to resources (earn lower wages than men and do not have access to a male partner's income) they control the resources they do have. Women who live with a male partner may (in theory) have access to a larger pool of resources (the male's higher earnings as well as her own) but, given notions of male 'headship', the woman may not have control over these resources. The fact that research suggests that male heads withhold income from the household income pool to spend on themselves means that the resources women partners have access to may actually not be any larger than for female heads. The problems with understanding the relative situation of women heads and women who live with a male partner stem largely from the understanding or, better stated, the meas-urement of poverty. Traditional measures of poverty tend to 'stop at the front door', that is they take the household as the basic unit of analysis and compare household to household, and do not consider differences within households. How women live and experience poverty is not captured, is not measured, and thus is made invisible.

Measuring Well Being

One person who has greatly advanced understandings of poverty and influenced the development discourse is Amartya Sen. Sen's original ground-breaking work actually focused on a 'slow onset' disaster – famine. Contrary to the usual analyses of the time that explained famine in relation to crop failure, he suggested that starvation was a product of a failure of entitlements to available foods, not a lack of food *per se* (Sen 1981). His work was built around the ideas of endowments (or what could be described as the bundle of potentially productive assets an individual has) and entitlements (the ability to command resources, such as food, that this bundle brings through various market, social and moral relations). Sen's work demands a shift away from ensuring that people have a good, such as rice, as a fundamental policy aim. For Sen, the importance of having a good is that it influences the capacity of a person to function: rice provides an individual with the capacity to live without calorie deficiency. In turn, a person's capacity to function determines what they can and cannot do, can and cannot be: the idea of positive freedoms (Sen 1999). This approach suggests then the focus should be on capabilities rather than vulnerability, an approach that underpins the adoption of the concept of resilient communities in the disaster context (see Chapter 1).

Perhaps one of the broadest conceptualisations of well being has been provided by Nussbaum (1995), who developed the idea of 'basic human functional capabilities', which included a consideration of those elements that define a human being (such as cognitive capacity – the ability to think, perceive and imagine). They are far ranging and extensive, ranging from being able to live to the end of a human life of normal length, have good health, adequate nutrition and shelter, through being able to avoid unnecessary and non-beneficial pain and as far as possible to have pleasurable experiences, to being able to laugh, to play, to enjoy recreational activities. While this is a very broad understanding of well being compared to the 'dollar a day' definition, and although enumerating well being presents great difficulties in terms of understanding vulnerability to hazards, it may be a more useful concept than income poverty. Elements such as being able to avoid 'non-beneficial pain' apply to the 'disaster' event, while being able to laugh and play are important issues for psychosocial reconstruction post disaster (see Chapter 7). However, for many donors and policy makers these 'capabilities' are not seen to be priorities, particularly for the income poor, and instead are seen as something to be considered, if considered at all, only once basic needs are satisfied. Well being pre- and post disaster is often conceptualised only in economic, not social or cultural, terms and this has implications for other notions such as vulnerability.

Vulnerability and Risk

The concept of vulnerability emerged within development in the 1990s as one attempt to encompass more subjective elements of well being within official poverty discourses. It arose from criticism of defining poverty as income or consumption, and in recognition that the relationship between income or consumption levels and other forms of deprivation, such as environmental risks, crime, and violence, is often weak.

However, the World Bank still adopts a rather narrow definition of vulnerability (Sabates-Wheeler and Devereux 2008), despite the work undertaken by Bank employees (see Chapter 1), which had widened discussion to include elements such as social capital. In its social policy discourse, it draws on Lipton and Ravallion's (1995) definition: the likelihood of being harmed by unforeseen events; or, as susceptibility to exogenous shocks. It notes that the poor are especially vulnerable since they are typically more exposed to risk, while they have limited access to appropriate risk management instruments.

Risk emerged as a key concept for the World Bank during the late 1990s as an important element within the Bank's new policy focus on social protection. In 2001 the Bank published its first Social Protection Strategy (World Bank 2001a) underpinned by a conceptual framework of 'Social Risk Management' (Holzmann and Jørgensen 2000). As Haddad

(2007: 14) has noted, despite the title 'Social' Risk Management, the SRM has an 'almost exclusively' economic focus. This is perhaps not surprising given it is the strategy of the World Bank, essentially an economic-oriented institution. Understandings of risk within the Bank's social protection discourse mirror those of the naturalist or technical approach within the disasters discourse: informed by Bernstein (1996) it sees risk as something to be 'mastered' (cited in 2001a: 9). However, while there has been technical 'mastery' over nature, the strategy notes that industrialisation and urbanisation have brought the introduction of new risks, most importantly, work-related accidents and unemployment. This is used to justify the focus on economic risks, and the Bank suggests 'risk and its measurement is *traditionally* related to variability of income or consumption, typically measured by its variance or standard deviation' (World Bank 2001a: 13, emphasis added). Despite this assertion, their so-called 'traditional' understanding of risk and its measurement is not one shared by the wider risk literature (see Chapter 1). The World Bank's conceptualisation of risk is interesting since, in contrast to the disaster discourse, it (re)constructs risk not only as a problem for the poor, but also as a potential solution to their poverty, as it notes the need to provide the poor with the opportunity to adopt 'higher risk-return activities' or to take (good) economic risks (Holzmann and Jørgensen 2000: 3).

Within this World Bank rhetoric, disasters are constructed as a development 'risk', using data demonstrating an increase in disasters as evidence of the world becoming more risky, and climate change as 'increasing risk' to individuals and families. However, the disaster discourse on vulnerability and risk does not seem to inform development risk rhetoric.

DRAWING THE LINKS: DEVELOPMENT AND DISASTERS

Post the Second World War has seen the notion of 'development' emerge as a planned, professional process focused on promoting economic growth. During the 1980s and 1990s, in particular, the neo-liberal policies of Structural Adjustment saw the focus on growth eclipse other elements of development. The lessons learned from SAPs, which are of interest here, are not so much about economic growth but about how people respond to the hardship that a focus on economic growth can bring. The academic response to SAPs saw advances in understanding poverty, moving away from narrow definitions of income poverty to wider notions of well being. These ideas of well being may also be useful for a better understanding of the disaster context. While those working on disasters can learn lessons from development, an opportunity for people working on development to learn from disasters presented itself with the new focus on risk within the World Bank's social protection discourse. In the social protection discourse, disasters are used to contextualise risk but are not apparent within the conceptualisation of risk, which remains a narrow economic conceptualisation, justified through efficiency arguments and with a focus on risk management. While the Bank's social protection strategy uses the increase in 'disasters' as evidence of the world becoming more risky, and 'climate change' is mentioned as 'increasing risk' to individuals and families, disasters are not discussed within the strategy. Despite recognition of the relation between disasters and development, this key development strategy, which utilises the language of risk and vulnerability, has not 'mainstreamed' disasters within the strategy. Instead, disasters are an explanatory factor rather than a policy issue – something that will be returned to in Chapter 9.

Yet the World Bank has begun to focus its work on disasters and, in 2006, the World Bank, in conjunction with the ISDR, launched the Global Facility for Disaster Reduction and Recovery (GFDRR) to finance initiatives aimed at reducing vulnerability to natural hazards. This interest in hazards and disasters is echoed by other development agencies, such as the UK's Department for International Development (DFID), who have increasingly sought to 'mainstream' disasters into their development work, or recognised the need to 'disaster-proof' development (DFID 2004). At the same time that the World Bank has adopted the rhetoric of disasters, UN initiatives to design a global agenda focused on disasters resulted in the 2005 Hyogo Framework for Action (HFA), which notes on page 1 that 'there is now international acknowledgement that efforts to reduce disaster risks must be systematically integrated into policies, plans and programmes for sustainable development and poverty reduction'.

There seems, then, to be a convergence in the official disaster and the official development discourse around the need to 'mainstream' disasters into development. However, while disasters are presented as a development risk within the development discourse, the disaster discourse calls for disaster risks to be integrated into development. This difference in approach may be expected, given the different priorities of the sets of actors, yet it is important since it highlights that the World Bank and other development actors still see disasters as extraordinary events that 'set back' development and not as part of development. That is, risk is not seen as something in the development discourse that is systematically produced as part of the modernisation process (Beck 1998) and something then systematically produced through the development model that the Bank is promoting in the developing world. Instead, disaster is understood as an exogenous threat rather than an endogenous risk, and this informs the discourse around 'disaster-proofing' development. The result is that there is a lack of importance given to disasters as events in themselves. Instead, they are conceptualised as harming economic development gains and it is these gains that need 'protecting'. Thus, reducing the impact of disasters is seen as a means to an end, rather than a goal in itself, and is justified on efficiency not equality grounds.

Issues of equality and efficiency will be further explored in the next chapter, which considers how gender has or has not entered the development and disaster discourses.

3. Gender, development and disasters

INTRODUCTION

Having explored the notions of disasters and development, and related ideas such as poverty, vulnerability, and risk, attention now turns to how gender has been incorporated into development and disasters. In this chapter, the evolution of thinking around 'engendering' development is discussed. The disasters field has lagged behind somewhat in incorporating gender into its discourse and practice so the focus is on development. The discussion seeks to serve as a framework for understanding how gender might be incorporated into discussion of disasters, and the problems that engendering the disasters discourse might meet. However, first some basic gender concepts and theories need to be presented.

GENDER AS CONSTRUCT

> Gender relations as well as natural disasters are socially constructed under different geographic, cultural, political-economic and social conditions and have complex social consequences for women and men. (Enarson 2000: 1)

There are some notions which are basic to gender studies. First, is the term 'gender' itself. While now in common usage, gender is a relatively new term and has only been widely used in relation to differences between men and women since the 1970s. Until then, discussion of differences between the two groups was based on sex, that is biological difference based on the sexual organs present at birth. Whilst this construction denies the existence of those people who are born with an indeterminate sex, with neither sexual organs or with both, such binary opposites pepper Western thinking and understanding. In general, the construction places one group, in this case the male, as central, and the opposite, in this case the woman, is 'other' to this, known through their difference from the dominant 'norm'. Simone de Beauvoir's famous 1940s text, *The Second Sex,* highlights this construction of women as 'other' and, more recently, post-modernist thinkers have developed the idea (see below).

To suggest there is a 'construction' of women as the second sex, highlights the fact that, while biological differences are natural, the meaning given to them is not, and depends on society. Drawing parallels with disasters: while a hazard is a natural event, a disaster is only what society understands or constructs it to be, and this can change. This notion of change is inherent in ideas of gender. The term 'gender' seeks to capture how biological differences are interpreted, or seeks to understand social constructions of what it means to be a man or a woman (ideas of masculinity and femininity). This is usually captured by the notion of gender roles and relations. It is important to remember that the study of gender is not then the study of women, but rather the study of the (unequal) relationships between men and women, why and how they are produced and reproduced and how they can be changed. To recognise these differences or to work to change them is usually what is meant by the notion of taking a 'gender perspective', sometimes also presented as analysing an issue through a 'gender lens'.

The term 'gender' will be used throughout this book but, as with all academic concepts, it is not without its critics. The main problem with 'gender' is that, much like the phenomenon it seeks to describe, it is a construct in that the usage of the word, if not the word itself, is new. It also does not translate well in many languages. While 'sex' and biological difference is something we see and understand from an early age, the idea of gender has to be taught: its meaning is not given and known but rather is constructed, and thus is contested. Staudt (2002) describes gender as 'obscure terminology' and by definition elitist in activist terms. Concerns about what the adoption of the term 'gender' would mean for activists working to promote women's rights were compounded when organisations such as the World Bank adopted the term (World Bank 2001b). Given the 'fuzzy' nature of the term, what the World Bank means by a 'gender perspective' may be very different from what a feminist means by this (see below). Yet both may now be seen to be 'doing gender'. For those working in organisations such as the World Bank, the term 'gender' offered a convenient compromise language (Staudt 2002), a more neutral and rational term than 'woman' that suggested a more 'technical' approach, and which was easier to use to convince economists of the need to address the issue (see Saunders 2002 for discussion). Ultimately, therefore, for some the term 'gender' and related ideas such as 'engendering' and 'mainstreaming' are depoliticising in that they move the focus from where it should be – on women and an understanding of the situation and position of women.

Despite the criticisms, the notion of gender difference is useful as it highlights that while differences are often based on biology, they are not 'natural'. For example, it is a biological fact that women give birth and can breastfeed. This has evolved to make women the primary carer of children; and evolved further to make women the primary carer for others, moving from the natural function of women as child bearers to the social construction of women as 'naturally' better at ironing and cleaning. Thus women tend to work in the home (undertaking reproductive activities in the private sphere) and when they work outside the home (undertaking productive work in the public sphere) their jobs may be extensions of this reproductive work, for example as teachers and nurses. Women are seen to be 'naturally' better at this and, again, while there may be some basis in biology, gender experts would suggest that rather than being born that way, girls from a young age are brought up to behave that way. That is, women's 'natural' skills are actually taught in the home but this skills training is invisible, as are the skills themselves. The construction of women as naturally more caring means that when they work outside the home they can be paid less – theirs is not a skill acquired through schooling or training that should receive monetary recognition, but something that comes 'naturally' to them.

These distinctions – between men and women, public and private, productive and reproductive – are important because of how they relate to relative power. One argument is that women and men each have their own sphere of influence and women have power within the home. It is true that the household may be a refuge from a hostile world that discriminates by race or religion for example, but it can also be a site of oppression for women in that it produces and reproduces inequality between men and women (see Chapter 6 for a discussion of households). On the simplest level, in a capitalist economy women's roles leave them economically dependent on men, and thus in a less powerful position than men.

Ideas of gender inequality are captured in the concept of patriarchy. Patriarchy has a history of usage among social scientists and has a whole variety of different meanings (Beechey 1979: 66). Here, patriarchy will be defined as the set of social relations between men which, although hierarchical, establishes an interdependence and solidarity between them which allows them to dominate women (Hartmann 1981: 14). This definition rejects the notion that every man is in a dominant position and every woman in an oppressed one. It also places the emphasis on the social structures that construct these relations, not individual men and women. Finally, it is important to note that the form patriarchy takes can change but not necessarily lessen, as Walby's (1990a) work on the UK highlighted. For example, women entering the labour force may not reduce patriarchy but, rather, reflect a shift in sites from private to public patriarchy, as women move from the control of their fathers, brothers and husbands in the home to the control of their male bosses in the workplace. The extent to which patriarchy is seen as an important explanatory of women's subordinate position defines to a large extent the differences in feminist theorising. While quite fundamental differences in understandings of what brings about women's oppression exist within feminism, a commonality is that women are understood to be oppressed, and there is a desire to change the subordinate position of women relative to men. Feminism then is a political movement and is a lived experience, that is, it stems from personal experience as much as academic learning.

FEMINISMS

Feminist theory has evolved over the decades, and there is not the space here to discuss these theories in full (see Tong 1989). Only a brief introduction to the ideas will be provided here. At least a basic understanding of how women's oppression has been explained is important to the discussion that will follow about how best to address gender issues post disaster.

At one end of the spectrum are the ideas of liberal feminism, which suggest that women's situation stems from the aggregate of numerous small-scale individual deprivations. Change is seen to come about by ensuring the equal access of women to the 'public world' through women's education and employment. Liberal feminists then seek equal rights with men and argue that women and men should be rewarded in accordance with their talents, not their sex. It has been critiqued for not challenging the position of men or the existing organisation of society and through campaigning to remove discriminatory practices it has been charged with responding to the symptoms not the 'disease' itself. The lack of challenge it represents to existing power relations means, perhaps not surprisingly, that liberal feminism is favoured within the dominant or official development and disasters gendered discourse.

By contrast, patriarchal relations are central to understanding women's subordination for radical feminists, who suggest that men as a group oppress women by calling on the 'naturalness' of men's domination. While this inequality is institutionalised, each individual, intimate relationship is a power relationship – thus arose the notion of the 'personal as political', which saw women re-examine their own relationships with men. As all women are universally oppressed, the commonalties of oppression are seen to be greater than the differences between women, suggesting a common 'sisterhood' of struggle. While radical feminism places the focus on patriarchy, Marxist feminism sees patriarchy merely as a manifestation of a wider oppression and struggle. The universal oppression within this thinking is that of class oppression and women's oppression arises from this, that is patriarchy is a product of the capitalist system. The capitalist classes exploit (male) labour in the workplace, but men oppressed by capitalism can in turn exploit women in the home. They are socialised into their role and are both oppressed and oppressor; and thus the system continues unchallenged.

A later wave of feminist thinking embraced post-modernism (see, for example, Derrida 1976, 1978; Lacan 1977; Lyotard 1984; Foucault 1976, 1980) which, rather than focusing on commonalities and seeking universal truths and explanations, instead focused on difference, and the deconstruction of socially constructed knowledge (Marchand and Parpart 1995). Its focus on a local, specific historically informed analysis of different realties, and its emphasis on difference was appealing to some feminists, but not others. For some, the focus on individual perceptions and experiences of power means that systematically unequal relations of power ultimately vanish from accounts of power (Hartsock 1990: 165) and it leads to a political fragmentation and the dissipation of feminist consciousness and activism. As Walby suggests (1990b: 2): 'Postmodernism in social theory has led to the fragmentation of the concepts of sex, race and class and to the denial of the pertinence of overarching theories of patriarchy, racism and capitalism … is a denial of significant structuring of power …'. By contrast, Fraser and Nicholson (1990: 34) suggest 'post-modernist incredulity toward metanarratives' paired with the 'social-critical power of feminism' was a way to 'affirm feminist politics as plural, ever changing, and made up of many different voices'. They suggest it leads to a stronger solidarity, which is essential to overcoming the oppression of women in its 'endless variety and monotonous similarity'.

Whatever the view on post-modernist feminism, ideas of difference have emerged as a key theme in feminist thought over the last few decades and are reflected in the feminisms of women of colour and 'Third World women'. This thinking recognises that concern with female 'otherness' from men has meant differences among and between women have been ignored. It also suggests the omission of any mention of non-Western women, or of race and ethnicity and the Third World in the dominant feminist discourses was not a mistake, but rather reflects those who were constructing the discourse – white, educated and Western women. Feminist theory was charged, initially by women of colour in the United States, as only explaining, and only trying to explain the situation of white, middle class women (see hooks 1988, 1991). Development

Alternatives with Women for a New Era (DAWN) emerged as an influential movement of activists, policy makers and researchers in the Third World that questioned the notion of a shared sisterhood built on First World understandings of oppression (Sen and Grown 1988). Women from the developing world accused Western scholars of creating Third World women as an undifferentiated 'other' oppressed by both gender and underdevelopment (see Mohanty 1991, 1997, 2003). Women, like countries, were constructed as needing to be 'developed'. Feminism was charged with presenting Third World women as universally poor, power-less and vulnerable, and presenting Western women as a reference point for 'progress'. These charges of treating 'Westernisation' as progress were also charges levied against Modernisation theories designed to develop the Third World, as discussed in the previous chapter, and remain visible within the disaster discourse focused on 'managing' disaster risk.

INTEGRATING WOMEN AND GENDER INTO DEVELOPMENT

The evolution of how women and gender have been integrated into the development process is much better documented and more 'advanced' than the same processes for disasters. However, as later sections will show, there are overlaps between the two, and the disaster discourse has seemingly borrowed from the various manifestations of 'engendering' development. This section will introduce the main ways this engendering of development has occurred, both in theory and in practice.

The two main theories of development – Modernisation theory and Dependency theory – make no explicit mention of women or gender, and their ability to improve the situation of women has been questioned (Jaquette 1982; Moghadam 1992). During the 1970s, gender did become part of the development agenda, however, particularly for the United Nations. Prior to this time, policies aimed at 'developing' the Third World were considered to be 'gender neutral' – there was no explicit mention of women but the inherent assumption was that policies and projects that help men would also help women. The turning point came in 1970 with the publication of Boserup's landmark text 'Women's Role in Economic Development', which effectively demonstrated that 'devel-opment' or rather processes of modernisation can harm women. While critiqued in turn (see Saunders 2002), her work was ground breaking at the time since it illustrated that policies were not gender neutral but based on assumptions that were gendered.

Far from gender neutral, all policies have a gendered aspect, since they are based on assumptions about the world that may ignore gender difference or gendered realities, and also because they seek to change the behaviour of people – people who are either male or female. All policies, even supposedly neutral macro level economic policies, work by influencing how people behave through markets (prices), institutions (such as laws) and through changing social norms. Men and women are different, have different access and control over resources, different wage rates and different consumption patterns, so any policy that attempts to change individual behaviour will have gendered consequences. They may be indirect rather than direct. For example, during Structural Adjustment measures the most obvious impact might have been male state employees being laid off, but the indirect costs may actually have been borne by women, if they were forced to seek productive work as well as continuing with their reproductive activities, activities which may have increased as they were forced to seek out the cheapest produce and make, rather than buy, food, clothes, and so on (see Chapter 2). Since the cost is in time and women's health, and is hidden, the differential gendered impact is often not recognised. However, an economic crisis allows gendered lessons to be learnt about how households operate under crisis and reveals the inequality in time burdens placed on men and women through the adoption of household coping strategies. Rather than being gender neutral, the economic policies that place households in crisis are gender blind – they do not recognise the impact on women. The question then is, Why not? Is it because the cost to women is hidden, or because women's time and health is not valued? If the latter is the case, then it could be said that policies are gender biased in that they intentionally or unintentionally favour one or a dominant group and do not value (the negative) impact on another group (see Elson 1991).

Boserup's work made clear the negative impact development could have on women and instigated a movement to integrate women into development. This movement continues today and is generally seen to have two key ideological threads – Women In Development (WID) and Gender And Development (GAD), these and some more recent moves to 'engender' development will be discussed below. Once again the ideas contained within WID and GAD are well documented, as are the debates around them (El Bushra 2000; Kabeer 1994; Moser 1993; Ostergaard 1992; Saunders 2002; Young 1993), and so only a brief discussion will be provided.

Women In Development (WID) is an approach that emerged in the 1970s and set out to deliberately target more development resources at women. It has its roots in liberal feminism and was, and is, the acceptable face of engendering development and also, more recently, disasters. Women's subordination was seen as having its roots in their exclusion from the market sphere, and limited access to and control over resources. The key, then, was education and employment by means of laws and legislation to effectively place women 'in' existing processes. That is, it aimed to maximise women's access to the modern sector. While women's significant productive contribution was made visible, their reproductive role was downplayed. Women's 'problem' was diagnosed as insufficient participation in a benign development process, through an oversight on behalf of policy makers. As the name suggests, it sought to integrate women into existing development processes. However, this integration did not stretch to integration into development agencies and, instead, WID set up separate offices and officers (Rathgeber 1990).

For many, WID interventions have made women more visible within development but the way this has been done is problematic (Bandarage 1984; Jaquette 1982; Parpart 1993). Critics questioned whether you could, and more importantly should, just try and integrate women in a process, or 'add women and stir'. Those who questioned the dominant development discourse of Modernisation also questioned the benefits for women of being more integrated into this process. There was also a suggestion that the focus on women constructed them as 'the problem', rather than the unequal gender roles and relations that are at the basis of gender subordination.

A second, little known, tradition is Women And Development (WAD). While seemingly a small difference, the change of one word from 'in' to 'and' is quite important. It could be suggested that if WID was a reflection of Modernisation theory then WAD is a gendered Dependency theory. WAD located gender struggle within the structure of capitalism so, as with Marxist feminists, it privileged capitalism over patriarchy. For this reason, the extent to which it actually had an explicit aim to 'engender' development or the extent to which it was 'properly feminist' was questioned (Saunders 2002: 7).

The more usual counterpoint to the Women in Development school has been Gender and Development. Here, there are two changes, from 'in' to 'and', and 'women' to 'gender', which may be seen to be in response to the criticisms levelled at WID above. The change to 'gender' reflects the fact that it is not women that are the problem but the gendered relations between men and women, while 'and' suggests the need to explore both gender and development. That is, it is not sufficient to add women into to existing processes of development but that there is also a need to problematise that development. The focus on gender means that, rather than looking at women in isolation, the focus should be on addressing the imbalance of power between women and men. Gender and Development projects are more holistic and not just about income and education. This approach includes giving special attention to the oppression of women in the family and highlighting the need to enter into the 'private' sphere. While attractive in theory, GAD has its origins in academic thinking and it may be seen as a more theoretical understanding than the practically oriented focus of WID. Initially, it was NGOs that embraced GAD but more recently institutions such as the World Bank have had a stated GAD approach. However, while many say they have a GAD approach what they often do in practice is WID (Rathgeber 1990).

Those working with grass roots women's organisations and Third World gender activists became disillusioned with both WID and GAD, both of which for them represented Third World women as 'benighted, overburdened beasts, helplessly entangled in the tentacles of regressive Third World patriarchy' (Parpart 1995: 254). Linked to the Third World feminist tradition discussed above, which highlighted diversity and difference, there was a call to consider inequalities of power on many levels – not just male or female, but rich or poor, First World or Third World. It suggested the need to recognise that women occupy multiple sites of oppression and what is seen to be a key issue for a low-income woman may be as much class-based as gender-based discrimination. As there are multiple sites of oppression there is also a need to address multiple inequalities of power. The 'empowerment approach' places a consideration of power relations at the centre.

'Empowerment' is a complex and contested notion (see Rowlands 1997), which is now rather freely used, but in its grass roots origins it encompasses the notion that the idea of development interventions is not to change others but to facilitate their ability to bring change for themselves. There are generally three stages to empowerment interventions and these are generally practised by feminist activists working at a local level. First, to expose oppressive power relations, second to challenge them as social not individual problems, and third to work together to shape different social relations. This is the most radical and thus least mainstream of all the approaches as it is a clearly feminist and political project that challenges the global system, not just gender or development, and seeks far-reaching change at a societal not just individual level.

While the empowerment approach has a focus on changing women's position in society, the WID approach focuses on improving her situation, and there has tended to be a disjuncture between what feminists see as a priority and what those working from a development perspective see as key. Feminist demands tend to be 'strategic' or political demands while development has a 'practical' focus, for example providing women with services (Molyneux 1985; Moser 1989b). Thus, while feminists call for the rights of women, such as sexual and reproductive rights, to be recognised and fulfilled, development seeks to ensure that all people, including women, have enough food to eat, a home, employment, and so on. Similarly, post disaster, there is often the suggestion that there is no space to consider women's rights, as the more important task of providing material relief takes precedence. However, while, for some, practical needs must be met before more strategic concerns can be broached, for others, meeting women's practical needs can only reinforce their subordinate position, not overcome it (see Box 3.1).

BOX 3.1 WOMEN'S PRACTICAL AND STRATEGIC GENDER NEEDS AND INTERESTS

While the inclusion of women's needs is fundamental, focusing on basic needs alone runs the risk of confusing women's needs with family needs. Many of the needs defined as the basic needs of women are also needs of all male and female members of the family, such as the provision of water, health, housing and basic services and food. They are identified as the practical needs of women because it is they who assume the responsibility for them (in their reproductive role). Williams et al. (1994) suggest women's practical needs:

- Derive from the position of women within the gendered division of work
- Mainly arise from the gendered roles of women and reinforce them
- Are a reaction to an immediate perceived need
- Are formulated from the existing concrete conditions
- Do not question the subordinate position of women, although they are a product of this position.

Focusing exclusively on the practical needs of women could result in:

- Focusing on women as the most efficient providers of services. This actually constitutes a focus on the family concealed within a focus on women.
- The lack of recognition of women as anything more than just mothers and housewives. It does not take into account the different activities carried out by the women or their triple role – reproductive, productive and community work.
- The reinforcement of women's traditional roles and stereotypes inherent in society.

- A lack of recognition of the basis of women's responsibility for reproductive activities and the consequences of this. In other words, a lack of recognition of the unequal power relations that exist within a society.

A gender perspective does not just focus on the practical needs of women, it also focuses on women's and men's responsibilities, on the relations established between them and on what are known as 'strategic' needs or interests. It is formulated on the basis of an analysis of the subordination of women in society.

Women's strategic interests (Williams et al. 1994):

- Question the nature of the relations between men and women
- Are aimed at overcoming women's subordination
- Include access to credit and other resources, the elimination of institutionalised forms of discrimination such as the right to land ownership, measures against intra family violence, and alleviation of domestic work, for example.

It is perhaps easier to think of strategic gender interests as the transformations necessary to change the unequal situation between men and women. The idea of post-disaster reconstruction programmes with a gender perspective is that they recognise not only the needs of the people involved but also the strategies and actions people use in order to help themselves. They also recognise the existence of unequal relations of power between men and women, which form the basis of the differences in their needs and capacities, while working to transform such relations into more equal ones.

Despite its 'gender' focus, academic literature around gender and development became more self-conscious about its tendency to focus primarily on women and from the late 1980s there was a rise in studies that mentioned or explicitly focused on men. Until that time men had been a rather vague category. Mohanty's (2003) critique that 'Third World' women were being constructed as a homogeneous group remains valid but there was also increased recognition that men were even more open to this. It was suggested that 'gender roles and relations' had become shorthand for inherently oppositional relations constructing men as 'lurking' in the background and imagined as 'powerful and oppositional figures' (Cornwall 1998: 46). Conversely, and simultaneously in the gendered development discourse, men have been constructed as lazy (Whitehead 2000), sitting round talking while women work. This negates the fact that much male socialising is focused on planning community and productive activities as well as engagement in local politics. This image of the idle man and hardworking woman is also present in post-disaster images and reports (Mishra 2009).

By the end of the 1990s, there was recognition of what has variously been defined as 'men in crisis' or 'troubled masculinities'

(Chant 2000: 7). This crisis arose from, or manifested itself as, girls 'over achieving' compared to boys in education, global changes in production that saw the rise of women's employment and men's under or unemployment and, related to this, women assuming decision-making roles within households. This was fuelled, or at least reinforced, by a policy focus on women as more efficient providers of social services. From the start this 'crisis of masculinity' was questioned as labelling threats to people's livelihoods, brought by changing global structures of production, as a crisis for men, and thus shifting the focus from the underlying problems of international capitalist patterns of dominance (see Chant and Gutmann 2000).

In practical, if not in ideological terms, the case has been presented that men need to be included in development, because men have problems or because men are a problem (because of their sexual practices (as transmitters of HIV for example)). The focus of many projects has been on male subjectivities – the personal constructions and understandings of 'maleness' and the implications of this for relationships with others. While this is laudable, critics have noted there is a tendency to forget the political and the vested interest men have in resisting change, or that projects ultimately aim at 'empowering men to dis-empower themselves' (Redman 1994). The focus constructs men as self-reflecting subjects and complex individuals, while the 'Third World woman' remains positioned as an object of subordination. Ironically, despite this, women's projects tend to have a practical needs focus and rarely provide women with the luxury to reflect on their subordination and 'femaleness'. A luxury even less accessible when men's projects provided competition for limited funding from the 'gender' funding pot. As Pearson (2000: 44) notes, the focus on men, and at that particular point in time, might be seen ultimately as aiming to dilute the radical women focused agenda, not enhance it.

Another process seen as de-politicising the gender agenda was a movement within donors and large agencies in the late 1990s and early 2000s for engendering development through gender mainstreaming.

ENGENDERING DEVELOPMENT

While agencies such as the World Bank announced its gender mainstreaming strategy in 2001, the initial calls to mainstream gender into development had come much earlier, and from feminist circles, at the Beijing conference in 1995. The resultant Beijing Platform for Action now acts as a framework for annual sessions to review progress. The

United Nations World Conferences on Women had begun in Mexico in 1975, followed by meetings in Copenhagen (1980) and Nairobi (1985) with the fourth, and last full meeting, in 1995 in Beijing. During this time the concepts of reproductive health, reproductive rights and sexual rights became popularised (Petchesky 2000). Reproductive health, as promoted by the International Conference on Population and Development (ICPD) Platform of Action (POA), focuses on ensuring 'complete physical, mental and social well-being' in all matters related to the reproductive system, including a satisfying and safe sex life, the capacity to have children and, freedom to decide if, when, and how often to do so. Related reproductive rights are generally discussed in relation to the ability and knowledge of couples and individuals to decide 'freely and responsibly' the number, spacing and timing of children. There is a less universally agreed definition of 'sexual rights' but this generally relates to freedom to express sexuality, enjoy sexual relations and enjoy sexual health. Those who see the purpose of sexual relations as being for procreation rather than pleasure may, of course, contest the idea that the ability to 'pursue a satisfying, safe and pleasurable sexual life' (WHO 2002) is a 'right'. Herein lies an issue with women's rights – they are highly contested as 'rights'.

The 1990s witnessed the 'rise of rights' (Eyben 2003) as many organisations and international development agencies adopted some form of 'rights based approach' to development (Molyneux and Lazar 2003; Piron 2005). However, the rights-based approach has not been without its critics (IDS 2005; Molyneux and Cornwall 2008; Tsikata 2004) and rights are not a straightforward concept.

The 'right' to land highlights the complex and contested nature of rights. There are multiple rights – the right to travel across land, the right to farm land, the right to sell land – and multiple actors to consider when looking at just one parcel of land. Some actors will enjoy multiple rights. Rights are not all equal, however, and there exists a hierarchy of rights, ranging from limited, short-term rights to extensive long-term rights to future benefit streams (Schlager and Ostrom 1992). Rights are ordered and gendered (Razavi 2003: 23) and women's rights tend to be the lesser rights, for example, indirect rights to access or use land. Women's land rights also tend to be nested in the land rights of the family. For example, even if women own land they may not be able to sell it without the consent of their husband.

While land and property ownership is often considered to be a relationship between people and things, actually the main relationship is between people and people. Granting women the 'right' to land, while important, is not sufficient to ensure access to, and control over, land for women. The extent to which an individual is seen to have the 'right' to use land rests with an analysis of the extent to which they have fulfilled the obligations necessary to make this claim, not only the legal framework supporting the right. Claims can be built through the fulfilment of social obligations of, for example, a wife to her husband or other relatives. Alternatively, the right to make a claim may lie with an ability to work the land. Women may be less able to work land and thus claim rights to land, due to biological differences, such as strength but, more usually, cultural norms that limit what it is acceptable for women to do, and hence learn to do. Obligations may not only be those fulfilled in the past but to be fulfilled in the future. For example, even if they can inherit, sisters will often give up land to brothers not only because this is often socially expected of them but also because through such actions they hope to be able to secure the ongoing support of their brothers in the future. This suggests, as Cornwall (2002: 204) notes, that the relationship between sister and brother may be vital in understanding patterns of resource allocation and household dynamics, yet these are often not seen as 'gender relations'.

The potential of rights for increasing recognition of women's demands as legitimate claims has made them particularly attractive to women's movements, and some of the most effective organising over the past twenty-five years has been around rights-related claims (Antrobus 2004a; Ruppert 2002). Despite the advances made, questions have been raised more recently over the sustainability of gains made in women's rights, which is well illustrated by the Millennium Development Goals (see Chapter 9). While they contain a goal focused on gender equality, they make no mention of sexual and reproductive rights and ending violence against women is also missing from the MDGs. While the 'exclusion' of gender within the MDGs has raised concerns, elsewhere the inclusion of gender has also been problematised, and nowhere more so than within the policies and projects of the World Bank and its plan to engender development through gender mainstreaming.

The latest evolution in how to incorporate gender into development has seen processes of engendering through gender mainstreaming (see Mukhopadhyay 2004; Porter and Sweetman 2005; True and Mintrom 2001; Woodford-Berger 2004; Walby 2005).

Walby's (2005) analysis suggests that for gender to be effectively mainstreamed there needs to be a tripartite approach

- An inclusion approach, which entails the equal treatment of women (and men) in interactions with them, including within development projects and programmes

- A participatory approach, which suggests listening to and including women in planning and policy processes and incorporating their perspectives into the products of that process
- A gendered approach, which would mean analysing gendered power relations and how these are affected by particular work in particular contexts in order to address gender imbalances.

In practice the gendered approach has rarely been part of the analysis and is most resisted since it challenges the vested interests of men, who remain the majority of those working in and for development, especially within large and influential institutions such as the World Bank and IMF (Stevens 2007).

The approach most usually adopted to mainstreaming by the big institutions is what has been termed the 'integrationist' approach, which seeks to add women in to all stages of the existing policy process. It tends to take a technical approach to the 'problem' for example, providing skills training, and has justified women's inclusion in projects on efficiency grounds, promoting this through the promise of the gains in economic growth that it will bring (see below). The outcome of this has been much like that for WID programmes: women have been included and women's practical needs met, but this has not challenged the basis of women's exclusion. The technical approach does not question why these practical needs are constructed as women's needs. The alternative approach is more radical and based on a desire for transformation, not only of women's lives but the agencies and institutions that make policies. To illustrate: if the small number of women involved in agriculture is seen to be a problem, then the integrationist 'solution' would be to set up training programmes and provide women with the technical skills necessary to farm. This addresses the practical need for women to have the skills to farm, but does not address the question of why they are not farming now. One reason women are often not agriculturalists is that they do not have the right to own land, or do not have the resources to do so. The transformative approach would seek to address this strategic issue, and to challenge the social norms that deny women's rights to own land. It is easy to see why it is the technical 'integrationist' approach that has gained ground within development institutions.

It is the approach to mainstreaming, rather than mainstreaming *per se*, which is the basis of the key criticisms of this attempt to engender development. The technical approach to engendering makes gender just another category to be included in policies with little thought or analysis and, as such, its inclusion poses little challenge to the existing status quo.

Mainstreaming may actually make it more difficult to ensure women's concerns are addressed since, once mainstreamed, gender becomes the responsibility of all, or the responsibility of no one, to ensure it is carried out (see Mukhopadhyay 2004). As long as the box is ticked, gender has been 'done'. Mainstreaming then has been critiqued as being de-politicising, not least since institutions can say they have included gender, tick the box with little real gendered engagement, and pre-empt any criticism of their policies on gender grounds.

How gender is mainstreamed into policy processes and projects, be they development or disaster focused, seems to matter. Why gender is being mainstreamed is also important, as an examination of the World Bank demonstrates.

THE WORLD BANK ENGENDERING DEVELOPMENT

In 2001, the World Bank launched its 'gender mainstreaming' strategy, backed up by a policy research report, *Engendering Development*, which examined the conceptual and empirical links between gender, public policy, and development outcomes. It had one clear conclusion: societies that discriminate by gender tend to experience less rapid economic growth and poverty reduction than societies that treat males and females more equally. This and earlier research suggested that improved gender equity can bring economic growth gains (see Dollar and Gatti 1999; Klasen 1999).

The World Bank Gender and Development Group (WBGDG 2003: 6) highlighted, in particular, the benefits that investment in human capital, especially girls' and women's education and health brings, suggesting that if the countries of Africa had closed the gender gap in schooling between 1960 and 1992 as quickly as East Asia did, this would have produced close to a doubling of per capita income growth in the region (WBGDG 2003: 12). The logic is that 'educated, healthy women are more able to engage in productive activities, find formal sector employment, earn higher incomes and enjoy greater returns to schooling than are uneducated women ...' (WBGDG 2003: 6). While seemingly logical, this does not take into account the unequal relationships of power within the home and the fact that that male control may limit women's ability to engage in productive activities outside the home or lead to conflict if they do so, especially if they earn higher wages than men. It also ignores the fact that women still tend to be responsible for domestic work in the home and will face a double day of reproductive and productive work. The suggestion that girls' attendance at school could be enhanced through providing a source of clean water close to school for them to carry home after their school day is complete (WBGDG 2003: 12) further demonstrates that 'engendering' does not seek to challenge gender roles, let along gender relations, and may actually reinforce gender stereotypes.

The fact that recent World Bank documentation states that 'gender-sensitive development strategies contribute significantly to economic growth *as well as* to equity objectives' (World Bank 2001b: 3, emphasis added) suggest that for them, gender equity or women's empowerment is a secondary concern, a by-product of policy designed to promote economic growth gains. Moreover, women are seen to be an efficient means to bring about wider economic goals. For example, it has been suggested that while increases in household income are generally associated with reduced child mortality risks, 'the marginal impact is substantially greater, almost 20 times as large, if the income is in the hands of the mother rather than in the hands of the father' (WBGDG 2003: 15). Similarly, the World Bank has noted that social gender disparities result in a reduced ability to manage risk (World Bank 2001a: 27) and thus produce economically inefficient outcomes. It has been suggested that improving women's access to risk management tools will bring efficiency and equity gains (Holzmann and Kozel 2007).

It seems the Bank's focus on economic growth remains strong. The difference is that the focus is now on achieving efficiencies in fulfilling economic growth goals and using a range of social policy tools, including risk reduction measures, as a means to that end. Women appear to be the favoured means to operationalise these new initiatives and to deliver economic growth.

In the 1970s, the battle was to ensure women were included in development but by the mid-2000s this had changed to a questioning of that inclusion. The use of women as the efficient provider of economic growth gains has lead gender activists and feminists to suggest that at times the inclusion of women in development processes is as problematic as their exclusion. A discussion of engendering development illustrates that how women are included, or gender is mainstreamed, is as important as whether or not it occurs, and it cannot be assumed that women's inclusion is necessarily, or always, a good thing. The extent to which the same issues apply to the gender and disaster discourse will now be considered.

DRAWING THE LINKS: ENGENDERING DISASTERS

Attempts to engender disasters appear to be a number of decades behind processes to engender development. One of the main disasters journals, the *International Journal of Mass Emergencies and Disasters of the International Sociological Association*, published its first special edition dedicated to women and disasters in 1999. A ten-year anniversary edition of the journal marking this event was planned, while the original has been revised and re-published (Phillips and Morrow 2008). In the interim decade, there have been a number of edited texts focused on gender and disasters, starting with *The Gendered Terrain of Disasters* (Enarson and Morrow 1998). In 2009, Fordham edited a special edition of the journal *Regional Development Dialogue* entitled 'Gender and Disaster Manage- ment', in the same year that an edited collection, *Women, Gender and Disasters* (Enarson and Chakrabarti 2009), was published. The latter book includes contributions from a wide range of scholars and practitioners from a diverse range of countries, including scholars from 'Third World' countries, demonstrating how the field has expanded. Toward the end of the century, events such as Hurricane Mitch in Central America saw advances in terms of understandings of how gender roles, relations and identities are constructed and re-constructed in the disaster context (Brad- shaw 2001a, 2001b, 2002; Cupples 2007). High profile events during the early part of the new millennium, including the Indian Ocean tsunami, meant an upsurge in case studies and survivor narratives (see for example Oxfam International 2009), and accounts from field workers (see for example Clarke and Murray 2010) that focused on women as well as men. Research post Hurricane Katrina allowed new voices to be heard (see for example David and Enarson 2012) and brought new directions in gen- dered research (see for example Fothergill and Peek 2008; Gault et al. 2005; D'Ooge 2008), and advances in theoretical discussion of the meaning of disasters (see for example Brunsma et al. 2007).

While advances have been made in terms of research on gender and disasters, gender concerns are less evidently a part of current disaster planning and policy. Tierney (2012: 245) suggests the field of disaster research has been characterised by a series of 'critical disjunctures', discontinuities in research and the systematic neglect of some topics and even the collective resistance to the introduction of new ideas. Until recent years, gender might have been seen as one such topic. By the late 1990s, despite the best efforts of a small group of women dedicated to advancing understanding of the topic, Fordham (1998) noted that the incorporation of a gender focus into disasters work had still not advanced much further than revealing the situation of women. In 2000, Enarson highlighted that if addressed at all, gender has been integrated into disaster research and practice as a demographic variable or personality trait and not as the basis for a complex and dynamic set of social relations. Boserup's work has been identified as the moment that a movement toward integrating gender into development emerged but there is no such one moment that can be identified within gender and disasters, and no such defined movement to integrate gender into disasters within global agencies and agendas or official disaster discourse.

The most coherent 'movement' within the gender and disasters field is the Gender and Disasters Network (GDN). Conceptualised in 1997 in response to a gender gap in disaster analysis and practice, it is unique in its 'strategy of engendering Disaster Risk Reduction by taking advantage of the virtual space created by the World Wide Web' (Sanz et al. 2009: 15) and it has become a 'legitimate and respected voice for gender and disasters issues and a repository of gender and disaster knowledge' (ibid.). The GDN represents a virtual community that reacts to events, by disseminating research, and by sharing findings and good practice – as exemplified by the Gender and Disasters Sourcebook (2006) – and on an international level by calling for this practice to be put in place. While existing primarily as a virtual community, the initiative has been reinforced by face to face meetings at international conferences: the 'Women and Disaster' conference in 1998 in Vancouver, followed in 2000 by a meeting in Miami with the theme 'Reaching Women and Children in Disasters'. In 2004 around a hundred women and men met to discuss 'Gender Equality and Disaster Risk Reduction'.

The change in titles from 'Reaching Women and Children', at the 2000 conference to 'Gender Equality' at the 2004 conference parallels the shift in language witnessed in the gender and development field. For the first time, during the 2004 meeting, a breakaway discussion was held largely consisting of men. It identified the current practice of focusing discussions on identifying and mitigating women's vulnerabilities as 'limiting in the long run' and called for engaging with 'men and boys in equal measure' (Mishra 2009: 35). This move toward reasserting masculinities demonstrates parallels with the changing and contested gender and development discourse, and the rise of masculinities within gender work.

The 2004 conference led to the 'Honolulu Call to Action' (see Anderson 2009), which suggests the need to

● Include gender issues and social equity in assessment, design and implementations and monitoring as a compulsory element for all development projects

- Ensure that dynamics of disaster risk, gender, social equity and environmental analyses are considered in an integrated manner
- Highlight gaps in the Millennium Development Goals in terms of Disaster Risk Reduction (DRR) and gender
- Guarantee representation of grass roots and wider civil society organisations by ensuring that they receive adequate resources to be active participants.

The Call for Action also called for efforts in a number of directions: to build the capacity of women's groups and community-based organisations; to improve communication, training and education; to increase gender perspectives in science and technology for risk reduction; to recognise the specific challenges in engendering complex emergencies; to improve the capability and response of organisational structures and to ensure increased participatory approaches toward DRR. Under each item recommendations were made on how to achieve these outcomes.

The GDN has since gone on to seek to influence the international policy dialogue, for example, through a delegation being invited to make an oral and written statement at the Global Platform for Disaster Risk Reduction in Geneva in 2007. However, despite these advancements, as Enarson and Meyreles (2004) note, we are yet to see gender fully mainstreamed in humanitarian relief, to see it integrated into research and field projects from the major disaster centres, and to see it included in disaster training courses. We might add to this that it is yet to be fully integrated into global DRR initiatives, such as the Hyogo Framework for Action (HFA). Where it has been included, the disaster discourse has borrowed from the discourse of gender and development. It has seemingly borrowed many of its limitations also. For example, the Hyogo Framework for Action makes a call to 'mainstream' gender into disasters (see also Chapter 9) yet makes no attempt to mainstream gender into the policy document, suggesting a lack of political will to put such ideas into practice.

While the engendering of the dominant disasters discourse has advanced slowly, what has advanced is the inclusion of women in post-disaster activities. The following chapters will consider how this has occurred, and, in the light of the understandings of processes of engendering development, seek to critically examine what this has meant for women and men impacted by disaster. It begins with a discussion of the relief period and the actions of those involved, the people affected and the responders, and the key conceptual and theoretical discussion this raises around humanitarian relief.

4. Internal and international response to disaster

INTRODUCTION

This and the following chapter will focus on the period during which a disaster is unfolding and the emergency phase immediately after an event occurs. This phase is generally referred to as 'the relief period' and is characterised by 'humanitarian' giving designed to save lives and alleviate suffering, or to provide relief to those who have survived the crisis. In the developing world context, much of this relief aid will originate from outside the country, and often outside the region. While the idea of humanitarian relief is based on ideas of universalism and neutrality, this and the following chapter will highlight that neither are necessarily characteristics of the relief period. This chapter will emphasise that, right from the beginning, the outside response is framed by wider political and cultural considerations around giving, fuelled by the media and media reports of the crisis. Not all events of the same magnitude receive the same amount of giving, and the response is not necessarily related to need. Moreover, it is important to remember that, while international agencies are important in major incidents, in most cases the first responders are not outside agents but are in fact the 'victims' or 'survivors' of the event. Thus, before a consideration of the international and external response, this chapter begins with a consideration of women and men's own actions for relief and recovery.

RESPONSE AND RESCUE

When a natural or man-made hazard threatens a population, the potential for a 'disaster' arises. In some cases there is due warning that an event is about to occur and those who may be affected can respond accordingly. However, this is not always the case for a variety of reasons. Some events such as earthquakes have a rapid onset and there is little chance of warning the population. Others, such as hurricanes, can be tracked, monitored and their impact predicted with at least some degree of certainty. However, even when a hazard can be predicted, the extent to which a population can respond depends on their having been warned of the event. The Indian Ocean tsunami illustrated that an event may be predicted, but if it is not communicated to those who may be affected, or not communicated in time, they will not be able to respond. For example, Sri Lanka was deemed a country safe from natural hazards and thus a tsunami early warning system did not exist. Yet, in the hours it took for the first wave to arrive on the shoreline, people could have been evacuated to safety. In fact, Sri Lankan radio reported on events in Indonesia but still did not issue a warning (Dumroes 2006). As part of Sri Lanka's development plan, tourism had been promoted and many of those affected were tourists, with little idea of how to react and no advice on what to do once the wave started to advance. The lack of knowledge meant also that when people saw the sea retreat they did not realise what was going to happen next, and did not respond immediately. Once the first wave started to encroach on land, many panicked and lives were lost when people did not run to higher ground, or did not know that they should do so. Since the event, signposts have been erected highlighting evacuation routes. As this case shows, early warnings, which include information on what to expect and what to do, can save lives.

Even when early warning systems exist, an individual's ability or willingness to respond to the warning will determine the outcome of the event for them. The ability to respond is linked to the capacities and vulnerabilities (see Chapters 1 and 2) of individuals but, in general, low-income countries and low-income people may have less capacity to react to warnings. So, for example, warnings of Hurricane Katrina's approach were not sufficient in themselves to ensure a response. Some people could not leave the area as they lacked access to private or public transport and some did not want to leave their homes. In some cases, people, who wished to leave, returned home on being told they could not take their pets with them (Enarson 2012). Such seemingly minor considerations, as whether a person is a devoted pet owner or not, can determine how an event is experienced and can even determine if an individual survives or not.

The ability of authorities and rescue organisations to help the population respond is in part determined by the conditions in a country or region or the level of 'development', but it is also, in part, determined by the nature of the event, with rapid onset events once again leaving little time for preparation or evacuation. However, while slow onset events may allow time to prepare, those that take a relatively long time to build to crisis, such as drought and famine, are often ignored until the crisis actually occurs. They are also rather ignored by the academic literature on disasters, and our understanding of these events may be less than for rapid onset disasters (Wisner et al. 2003). While events that are not rapid onset, such as hurricanes, for example, do allow time for evacuation, they do present logistical problems once they impact. Hurricanes can lead to widespread flooding, and they can knock out bridges and roads, hampering initial rescue services and leaving those affected to save themselves.

Contrary to how it is often portrayed in the media, the real 'first responders' are individuals themselves as threats and losses elicit strong and rapid responses by the 'victims' (Kaniasty and Norris 2004), rescuing themselves by moving to safety, for example, and also helping to rescue others. Local Non-Governmental Organisations (NGOs), community, and Church groups may provide an early response, using whatever resources they have to hand to help those they work with and work for. The first set of official responders on the scene tends to be local services, such as the fire service, police, military and Civil Defence and the local Red Cross, if applicable. It is important to remember that international agencies only arrive once a state of emergency has been called, that is, once a country states it cannot cope alone. Thus, it is important to bear in mind that when national and international agencies talk of rescue operations, rather than saving lives they are actually working to keep people who have 'saved' themselves alive. This is, of course, crucial work. People who get themselves to safety should be able to expect to receive help that arrives in a timely and coordinated manner. However, there is still the need to recognise that people have saved themselves – are survivors – rather than having been saved – and labelled as victims. It is not just semantics: it may be important for the longer-term psychological well being of survivors (see Chapter 7). Language also matters in referring to people. For example, the fact that those who fled hurricane Katrina were called 'evacuees', a term which has no basis in international law, rather than 'internally displaced persons', meant they were not afforded the legal rights and protection which the latter status brings (Ross 2012).

It is not only the actions of international agencies that may construct survivors as victims, but also the media. Media portrayal of events which focus on international rescue efforts may help construct people as passive victims waiting to be saved. This imagery not only helps 'sell' the disaster to the viewers, but also helps 'buy' relief, because helpless victims may be more likely to provoke donations (see below). In particular, the media may focus on the plight of women after an event – men and the painful experiences they have suffered are rarely shown on mainstream media reports (Mishra 2009). The media use imagery of women, or better mothers, trying to care for their sickly and hungry children in terrible conditions in its coverage, and this 'appropriation of suffering' serves as a powerful strategy to convince donors, both international and individual, that their compassion is justified (Kleinman and Kleinman 1997). Images of crying and inconsolable women, often clutching one or more young children to them, are the ones most often used. Such images not only render men invisible but also, and may intend to, construct women as helpless victims and, through carefully chosen images, reinforce ideas of women as mothers first and foremost. The media rarely focuses on the role women have played in rescue efforts or show them as active responders. However, women do respond actively to save themselves as do men, and households adopt coping strategies to alleviate their suffering immediately after events.

GENDERED ACTIONS FOR RESPONSE AND RESCUE

While women are constructed as a 'vulnerable' group, care is needed in assuming this will always be the case. It is more appropriate to recognise, not that women will always be vulnerable, but that events will always be gendered – that is, how an event is experienced will be different for men and women, and will also be experienced differently by different women.

If women are the more vulnerable, it could be assumed that more women than men would die during disasters. While this is often asserted, it is difficult to say that it is the case with any certainty since accurate records of deaths often do not exist, and records disaggregated by sex are seldom kept. The 'tyranny of the urgent' may help to explain this – the idea that there is no time for such things. However, more practical issues may explain the lack of records, such as the fact that bodies may be buried or swept away and never recovered. Rather than being 'dead' people are recorded as 'missing'. Bodies may also be disposed of where they lie, or in mass graves, without identification or records being kept. It is is often not known who has died in a disaster and it is difficult to say with any certainty who is more likely to die in any particular event, since this will depend on its character, its timing, as well as local culturally specific gendered characteristics. Moreover, individual responses are dependent not just on vulnerability but also on notions of risk and these too may be gendered (see Chapter 1).

Response is subjective and will be framed by individual understandings of appropriate behaviour, which in turn are shaped by cultural norms, including gender norms (see Enarson and Chakrabarti 2009). This can influence fatalities. For example, the Indian Ocean tsunamis are a well-documented example of women's greater vulnerability due to a factor as simple as clothing – women's clothing made it difficult for them to run and to swim compared to men (Ariyabandu 2006, 2009). The fact that boys were more used to running and climbing trees than girls, due to socially constructed ideas of what is appropriate behaviour, meant they were better able to protect themselves.

Just as it has been suggested that more women than men die, there is also the suggestion that more women, and children, are adversely affected: women and children often make up the majority of those in refuges and camps. This may suggest they are more vulnerable or have suffered greater impact than men. However, as noted in Chapter 1, while gender differences may explain the relative vulnerability of women and their presence in refuges, it may also be due to how gender intersects with other characteristics of vulnerability, such as poverty, that explains this. A synthesis of data on women affected by Hurricane Mitch, who ended up in shelters in Honduras, demonstrated that the majority of the women were in the low-income bracket and over half of the women were heads of household (51 per cent), which is significantly more than the national percentage (26 per cent) of households headed by a woman (Tábora 2000). However, care needs to be taken about assuming that women's presence in refuges suggests they were more vulnerable to events. It may instead highlight that they took action to reduce their vulnerability, by evacuating, for example. Female heads may be more able to take such action than married women because they may have more autonomy in decision making in the home. Women's presence in the refuges may demonstrate not their vulnerability but their self-protective actions as care givers. However, while these actions may have saved lives, these same roles seem to hamper women's ability to leave refuges and return home (Willinger and Knight 2012). Women's presence in refuges may actually be indicative of men's vulnerability, or the fact men may make themselves vulnerable by taking more risky action during and after an event.

A study post Katrina explored the response to the calls for evacuation from New Orleans and found that the preferred response for the agencies seeking to manage the event – for the whole family to evacuate together (unison evacuation) – was not the preferred response for some residents (Haney et al. 2007). The study found that, instead, there was 'evacuation by division' in that some family members left while one or more stayed behind. Those that left tended to be women and children, while men stayed, which suggests an amplification of traditional gender roles during crisis. The characteristics of those men that stayed as Katrina approached included being Afro-American. Those who stayed were also more likely to be employed (not unemployed) but in low-income jobs, suggesting men were concerned about losing their jobs if they left the city. They were also more likely to be religious. That is, the 'stayers' could actually be characterised as hard-working black men with a strong belief in God's will, fulfilling their socially prescribed protector and provider role. An image very different from that constructed by the media after the event (see below).

This socialised behaviour of men in many societies as brave, fearless and strong may lead men toward riskier behaviour than women. This, coupled with the construction of the male as the protector of 'his' wife and family, may mean men are more active in rescue and recovery during events. However, this being said, although the male protector role should mean a man would seek to save his family first, if the event strikes while he is out at work then he has only himself to save. Instead, women may be those 'protecting' the family and their carer role may make them more vulnerable to events as they are slowed down in their own response through helping children or the elderly to leave the home. It is estimated that 40 per cent of those that did not evacuate during Hurricane Katrina were physically unable to leave or were caring for a person with a disability (Davis and Rouba 2012).

During an event, individuals not only seek to save themselves but also others. How they do this and the extent to which this occurs may again be gendered. While it is culturally constructed that men are the protectors, both men and women may help others when it is needed as the following narratives from men and women affected by Hurricane Mitch demonstrate (Bradshaw 2001b, 2002b). The following quote from a Nicaraguan male discussing how the people in the community reacted as the river began to rise and flood the area illustrates a number of points: 'not until the river started to rise more quickly did we start to get organised and we helped out those who had more things to lose, to get the kids and goods out, to evacuate them. The women were helping by rescuing other women'. The first thing this illustrates is that people obviously did not respond until the danger to them and their belongings became very evident, that is the rain and swelling of the river initially was not perceived as a risk. Second, it illustrates that people will prioritise even at such a time – helping those 'with more things to lose'. The next comment suggests that children are seen quite literally as more 'things' to be rescued. However, of greatest interest in this context is the comment that 'women were helping by rescuing other women'. Thus women's activities are seen only as 'helping' the men, and even then there is gender segregation with women helping by rescuing other women. It raises the question of what would happen if a woman tried to rescue a man? Would she? Would he let her? For instance, in Middle Eastern cultures it is shameful for men not to actively participate in dealing with the impact of natural hazards (Saad 2009) and, presumably, women taking on, or taking over, this role would be even more shameful. While few studies or narratives of rescue exist (a notable exception being David and Enarson's 2012 edited collection), one description of women's experience of training for evacuation suggests that women rescuing men may occur (Fordham 2009b). A woman notes how during the exercises she had to carry a person to be saved, a man, noting she had not known that she could do that, and commenting 'sometimes women don't know about our strength. In emergencies we have the opportunity to test ourselves and become "not just women"'(Fordham 2009b: 184). It might then be that women do not rescue men as they do not know they are able to do so, and have no experience of it. It might be that women do rescue men, but as it is seen as exceptional, being more than 'just women', it is seen as a one off. It might also be that, in such circumstances, such actions, because they are exceptional, are 'forgotten'. The extent to which gendered norms are ingrained in a society or psyche helps decide who rescues whom, how this is perceived, and if it brings about lasting change.

Women in the Nicaraguan study continued to 'help' men after the hurricane had passed over, as first responders, seeking to clear roads to allow people out and aid in. However, again there appears to have been gender segregation, as one man notes: 'She went with the women looking how to repair the road ... . The men in front and they (the women) coming behind with rocks'. The interviews with men after the event highlighted the way that not only was the response gendered, but how this response was understood was also gendered. That is, what women saw to be positive actions were not necessarily read this way by men. For example, when asked what the women did immediately after the event, one man notes: 'Nothing, the poor things, they just tried to attend to their children who were in the mud and sick with temperatures.' That is, women's traditional caring roles were seen as inactivity rather than activity. Women also organised to help each other, going house-to-house cleaning patios to make them suitable for production, and organised to help the wider community in digging out wells and replacing fences (Delaney and Shrader 2000). Yet, one man notes of women's collective activities: 'The women on their own haven't done anything more than get organised to carry out some censuses.' This highly important task of documenting deaths, injuries and losses was not valued, perhaps, because it had no immediate, visible benefit to the community or, perhaps, because it was initiated and carried out by women. Many women noted that men did not value their contribution, as one woman notes 'the men say that women work less, "you don't work equally to me, women can't work, they don't know how to'", while another suggested, 'men recognised our contribution at the time. Some have now forgotten'.

Women worked alongside men to help themselves and others in collective action and the study suggests that there may be some diversification in gender roles during and immediately after an event. However, there may also be some amplification of traditional roles as well. While the diversification is recognised, at least in the short term, women's traditional roles are given little recognition or value even at the time (Bradshaw 2001b). The roles adopted to alleviate suffering after an event will not only include clearing rubble and looking to repair property and rehabilitate land but, as time goes on, will also include strategies to earn an income and survive in the short term, or to rebuild livelihoods.

LIVELIHOODS AND COPING STRATEGIES

Livelihood is a concept that has its roots in the work of Robert Chambers (1995, 1997) and, while largely developed in relation to rural areas, it is now seen to be applicable in urban areas. It refers to the capabilities and assets and activities (including material and social resources) required to ensure a means of living and seeks to reflect the multiple activities in which households engage to ensure their survival and well being (Rakodi 2002). It has traditionally been understood as comprising different strategies: accumulation (improving the means of production); betterment (improving consumption); adaptive (to ensure continued levels of consumption or wealth); and survival or coping strategies to deal with exceptional circumstances (Dietz et al. 1992). Coping strategies are those activities adopted by individuals and households to respond to crisis. The resilience of people's livelihoods during a crisis is largely determined by the resources or assets available to them, and how these have been affected by the event. Their coping strategies are the creative means people find to use their existing or remaining resources to respond to their changed circumstances, generally focusing on income generation.

A range of coping strategies are adopted during times of crisis, ranging from insurance mechanisms, through the disposal of productive assets, to destitution (Byrne and Baden 1995). These three stages have also been categorised as: non-erosive coping; erosive coping; and non-coping (de Waal 1989). Initially people choose coping strategies that are not damaging to livelihoods, for example, the sale of some small livestock, labour migration and the collection of wild foods but, as more people adopt the same strategies, they become less productive. For example, prices of livestock may fall, if the supply increases, given that demand may be limited. Households then have to resort to more damaging strategies that can undermine their long-term livelihood viability, for example, selling off key assets, or re-mortgaging land. The coping strategies that communities, households or individuals adopt can make a difference between survival and destitution. However, coping strategies can also be destructive to long-term livelihoods and are not necessarily 'developmental' in that they do not always increase long-term productivity or survival (Davies 1993). They may also be environmentally destructive, leading to the depletion of natural resources.

While coping strategies are often thought of as household strategies, there are differences between people within households in terms of their control over available resources, and how use of these resources will affect them. Coping strategies are clearly affected by class and age as well as gender, as they are related to the social and economic resources available to a given individual or household. Those with greater resources are likely to have more options in times of crisis or to be able to pursue them more effectively. For example, young men who are mobile and can pay for transportation are able to get to the areas where work is – or where wages are higher – quicker than those without money, and therefore get the better jobs (Brown 1991). In general, men, who tend to have greater resources under their control and greater mobility than women, will have a wider variety of options to fall back on. In crisis situations, women may be forced to adopt survival strategies for which they are ill equipped, or untrained. Female-headed households, in particular, are likely to have fewer options available to them due to the lack of adult, able-bodied men on whose labour they can call. The way different classes are affected by crisis may differ by gender also. It may be assumed that a woman within a wealthier household will have more resources available to her but gender norms may mean she has no control over household resources, and may have less experience of working to generate an income than a woman from a low-income household, and less ability to do so due to the stigma attached.

Migration is a common strategy for coping with crisis. Large-scale abandonment by whole families of their places of residence is often expected, and feared, post event. However, this is usually seen to be a strategy of last resort and it is more common for one or several members of the family to migrate rather than the whole family. Following Hurricane Mitch large-scale migration of male heads of households was reported (Delaney and Shrader 2000). While the decision for a male head to migrate may be based on an economic rationale – that they can find work and send money to their families – the decision to leave may also be based on socially constructed gendered roles. Male heads may seek to migrate because they are no longer able to fulfil their role as the providers or heads of their household. Leaving is one means of coping with the loss of standing that the disaster brings. While the idea is that men send remittances back to their family, the general literature around migration suggests some men may never actually send money or may not continue to send money to their family. Some men, after migrating, will actually start a new life and new family elsewhere. Given that a disaster may highlight the inability of a man to protect and provide for 'his' family, starting a new family elsewhere may seem an attractive 'coping strategy', post event.

There is little information about the impact of migration on men and women post disaster but it has been suggested that women who are left behind when men migrate may suffer a double impact from male migration. Not only are they left waiting for money that may never arrive, but also the household may have sold what little they had to finance the migration, leaving the woman without any means of survival. However, research from Nicaragua highlights the dangers in assuming it is men that leave (Bradshaw 2001b). Women may also migrate, perhaps because they may more easily find work in the service sector, for example. However, the study demonstrated that while both men and women migrated, for both, this tended to be temporary and most returned due to the lack of economic opportunities outside the community.

Migration by one or more members of a household may seem a good coping strategy but is dependent on jobs being available outside the area impacted by the event. This may not always be the case and this 'coping' strategy may actually deplete the resources of the household, rather then adding to them. Other strategies may also have negative effects, and the impact of the strategies adopted by a household may have a differing impact depending on the gender, age and status of different members of the same household. Coping strategies are often examined at the level of the household without consideration for the differential gendered impact or for the processes of negotiation through which different strategies are adopted. As noted above, migration will have an impact on those that migrate – often men – and those left at home – women and sons who have to take over their roles. Other strategies, such as selling domestic animals may also be gendered. For example, the small livestock that may be sold first are usually the livestock women tend to care for. In some cultures, wealth is held in jewellery, and its sale means the sale of the only asset a woman has. Other strategies have time rather than money implications. For example, collecting wild products may mean more work for women and children, and reducing consumption costs may involve women spending longer buying and preparing food as they shop around and make everything from scratch.

From a gender perspective, the coping strategies adopted by households may place particular burdens on women's time, energy and resources that are not sustainable or desirable in the long term. Thus, whilst coping strategies may be successful in ensuring short-term survival, they may increase long-term vulnerability, particularly if what was a coping strategy gradually becomes an adaptive strategy, used for day to day survival (Eade and Williams 1995). The literature refers to the creativity that people demonstrate when finding ways to rebuild their lives post event (Das and Kleinman 2000) but there are few real examples of such actions. More generally, the way people react tends to be derived from previous experience (Oliver-Smith 1992). For example, Samuels (2010) found that women had coped in post-tsunami Aceh by setting up small kiosks at the front of their (rebuilt) houses to sell small goods to the local community, such as foodstuffs, sweets and cigarettes. Similarly, the strategies adopted by individuals and households in response to Hurricane Mitch did not differ much from normal, everyday strategies to deal with repeated crises, both small and large scale (Bradshaw 2001b). In more recent years, the notion of 'normal' times has been questioned, in that large numbers of people live in a context of permanent crisis, living through a succession of blows that limit the options available to them and makes 'coping' strategies a part of daily life. However, one 'creative' form of coping was noted post tsunami, and that was marriage. The large number of women who died during the tsunami left a large number of widowers, often with small children to care for. In the short term, a strategy for men to cope with this new 'carer' role might be to take daughters out of school but in the long term marriage might be a better livelihood strategy. It may also have played a therapeutic or healing role (Samuels 2010). After the event, there were fears that, given the gender imbalance, very young women would be forced to marry older men (Oxfam 2005). However, no systematic study exists to show the extent to which this did occur.

While households adopt their own strategies based on the available resources, they are not bounded entities, but rather units of social interaction (see Rosenhouse 1989; Roberts 1991 on debates on the concept of household). The social relations adopted by households may be informal, creating links with other households, the church, women's groups, and so on. The importance of such informal relations or networks of reciprocity, exchange and mutual support has been recognised in situations of economic crisis (see Moser 1996). Social relations may also be more formal, such as those with Local Authorities and NGOs, and they also constitute an important resource when faced with crisis situations. The notion of social capital has emerged as a key concept to explain how these relations operate (see Chapter 2).

SOCIAL NETWORKS AND COMMUNITY RESPONSE

Social capital is most generally seen to have its roots in the work of Putman (1993). However, a large number of authors have written on the concept, including in the development context (Collier 1998; Dasgupta and Seregeldin 1999; Hulme 2000; Harriss and Renzio 1997).

Social capital is best thought of as a potentially productive asset built over time as a by-product of other activities and social processes. Social capital is considered to be a feature of both 'government' and 'civil society' that facilitates collective action for the mutual benefit of a group, where 'groups' may be as small as households or as large as the nation (Knack 1999). 'Governmental social capital' focuses on those institutions that influence people's ability to cooperate for mutual benefit, and includes elements such as civic engagement, civil liberties, rule of law and enforceability of contract (Collier 1998, Almond and Verba 1963). A large-scale natural hazard reveals the levels of governmental social capital and puts social cohesion to the test, as well as the honesty of public administration and people's willingness and ability to cooperate for mutual benefit. The limited research that does exist tends to highlight the shortcomings of governments post event.

In contrast, at an individual level, the disaster literature does suggest that, after an event, there is a 'heroic' phase, or a period of post-disaster utopia. For example, Phillips (2009: 52) talks of the 'stunningly compassionate' efforts of individuals and organisations after Katrina. A study by Loker (2009) in post-hurricane Honduras suggested there exists a 'moral economy of disasters', highlighting how those affected not only help themselves during and immediately after the event but prioritised helping others, and how quickly and extensively they sought to do this. However, this positive stage may not be as altruistic or egalitarian as assumed (see Kaniasty and Norris 2004). While initial outpourings of help may be based on a perception of need and loss, some people may enjoy a relative advantage – giving may follow established social patterns, suggesting a pattern of neglect or concern. These patterns of neglect may reflect existing patterns of inequality, but inequalities may also be heightened. In particular, some groups may not be seen as worthy of help because they are seen to be somehow to blame for their situation (see also Chapter 5). African American women impacted by Hurricane

Katrina, for example, may have suffered from being constructed as undeserving recipients of benefits long before the event (Sterett 2012). Notions of deserving or undeserving victims may also be related to peoples' actions or inactions in the face of events. This is a particular issue in slow onset technological or 'man made' toxic hazards, which may create high levels of blame and recrimination (Tierney 2000). Blame may also be gendered – for example, the earthquake in Pakistan in 2005 was not seen by some (men) as a 'natural' event but rather as one brought on by the 'sins of women' who had transgressed cultural norms (Sayeed 2009).

Having access during a disaster to social support and social networks may be important at a number of points. First, in terms of responding to the actual event, research suggests that interpretation of warnings may be influenced by their interpretation by others within an individual's network. Individuals will seek confirmation from their networks (Mileti 1995) and social networks are critical resources for confirming the personal relevance of the message (Phillips and Morrow 2007). Katrina highlighted that interpretations of warnings may differ between communities. This is reinforced through social networks: people seek confirmation of the need to act (or not) from those similar to themselves, that is, of the same race or ethnicity (Haney, Elliott, and Fussell 2007). The second period when social networks are important is after an event as people call on them for help as part of their coping strategies to find friends and family as well as shelter and basic needs. While people may have large stocks of social capital, what is key is that in times of crisis they are able to transform or translate social relations or 'goodwill' into tangible resources such as cash, food or accommodation. Research post Katrina highlights how some groups were able to do this effectively through ethnic and kin networks (see Nguyen 2012 on Vietnamese and Rosenbaum 2012 on Jewish women). However, for others, this transformation was not possible (see Barnshaw and Trainor 2007) and their stocks of social capital proved to be of little use.

Research in Nicaragua highlights the way that the geography of social capital is important in terms of transforming goodwill into usable resources (Bradshaw 2001b). In a community study post Mitch almost one in three households in the communities studied noted that before the event they relied for support on people who lived in the same community. There were few opportunities for using support networks during the crisis since all had been affected. Events with a large geographical coverage, such as Hurricane Mitch, which touched all five countries of Central America to a greater or lesser extent, may similarly make transformation of capital into resources more difficult. Even when others in a social network have not been affected by the event, they may show themselves unwilling to help those who have been. Hoffman's (1998) study after a firestorm in California notes that some women found that some of their friends did not, or could not offer aid. It is important to recognise that a woman's ability to help may be tempered by her ability to access household resources if she has limited personal resources; that is, her ability to negotiate with men. Thus, while women may have better and wider social networks than men, their ability to transform good networks effectively into tangible resources may be less than a man's. Hoffman also notes that while help in the form of donations of used clothes and household items may not always be welcome or liked, they cannot be refused, as much for social reasons as from need. Even when friends, family and social networks are not affected and are happy to transform their goodwill into tangible resources, and these resources are wanted and welcomed, those affected may not be able to access the resources. For example, the lack of access to transport to go to a friend's house in the next town may mean a person cannot call upon their stocks of social capital or transform this into tangible coping resources. Lack of transport might be important in terms of re-establishing social networks in the medium term. More generally those without transportation are isolated from activities to rebuild communities (Willinger and Knight 2012).

Coping strategies that involve calling on social networks may not see the conversion of goodwill into cash, but rather into the provision of temporary accommodation. Many of those who evacuate prior to events such as hurricanes may seek shelter with friends and family. There are also examples where strangers have taken in others just after events, such as the earthquake in Haiti. After the storm has passed or the tremors have stopped, the destruction of housing and infrastructure may mean that a short-term response to the event becomes a medium-term coping strategy as families are unable to return home, often for a relatively long period of time. This puts strains on familial relations and perhaps even more so on non-kin relations. Studies suggest that the initial stage of social mobilisation of social support may quickly deteriorate, as the needs of those affected are understood to be greater than the resources available. The victims and responders become disillusioned and the harsh reality of grief, loss and destruction sets in. A decline in 'altruistic' behaviour may occur over time. As with other coping strategies, living with friends and family brings potential 'costs', in this case social rather than economic costs, not least for women forced to live with in-laws. One consequence of coping strategies that call on familial networks may be the re-establishment or re-enforcement of familial power relations, which further remove agency and control from women in particular (Hoffman 1998).

Post-disaster coping strategies are therefore influenced by what stocks of physical assets a person or household has, and what social networks and relations they can transform into assets. While they allow short to medium-term survival, they often come with economic and social costs. They may also not be sufficient for the reconstruction of livelihoods: outside interventions may be the key to re-establishing livelihoods.

There are three main elements to rebuilding livelihoods during reconstruction

- Livelihoods provisioning. Direct provision of essential needs (e.g. food, water, shelter), usually during the emergency stage
- Livelihoods protection. Activities to prevent a further decline in household livelihood security (e.g. cash and food for work, providing seeds and tools)
- Livelihoods promotion. Activities to improve household resilience to events in the future (e.g. through savings and credit programmes, crop diversification and marketing, improved health care).

The main idea behind interventions aimed at reconstruction is that they should contribute to the coping strategies of the people affected (see Chapter 6). However, as this discussion has highlighted, while some strategies adopted by people and households improve the situation in the short term, they can have high and negative costs in the long term. Furthermore, the strategies adopted by 'a household' can have positive effects on that household's overall welfare, but negative consequences for one member or several members. In particular, the strategies adopted by women may benefit the household but have a negative effect on the women themselves.

While many stories post event demonstrate how people help each other and stress that disasters can produce pro-social responses indicative of a 'therapeutic' community, this is not always the case. Moreover, an event may promote the opposite response: instances of anti-social behaviour and 'corrosive' community responses have been noted in the literature. Looting is perhaps the most often documented example of anti-social behaviour and is recorded in many countries and contexts, the most visible recent example being from New Orleans post Katrina (see Bowden 2011). At the outset, it is important to note that it is difficult to distinguish a 'looter' from someone looking for food and clothes for their family, who may have been left with nothing and who would, in other contexts, be labelled a hero perhaps (Ross 2012). There were also reports of 'looters' coming to the aid of stranded people, and rescuing those who the official rescuers seemingly had forgotten (Davis and Rouba 2012). There were, of course, those who did use the hurricane as an opportunity for personal gain yet, while this behaviour was constructed as unusual or an aberration, and given a highly racialised spin by the media, there are documented cases of looting in a variety of events in the US prior to Katrina. Looting will more usually occur after civil disobedience than disasters, where people see looting as a means to redistribute resources from rich to poor. However, as Frailing and Wood Harper (2007) suggest, Katrina occurred within a set of historically evolving socio-economic conditions that had seen high socio-economic inequality and rising crime rates before the event. As Barton's key 1970s text noted, disasters lay bare the social problems of a society, that is, they reveal existing problems and issues. Understanding the hurricane as a socially con-structed catastrophe rather than a 'natural' disaster allows the 'social disturbance' that followed Katrina to be better understood within the discourse of redistribution. However, it is also important to note that the perception of high levels of crime, including robbery, sexual assault and murder, reported by the media, was not backed up by the final statistics. For example, when the authorities entered the two largest refuges they did not find bodies 'stacked' up as had been expected. In fact, murder rates for the month in which Katrina occurred were not higher than usual. The perception of disorder was then as much related to how the media portrayed the, predominately black, people and events, as associated with actual high rates of crime (Dynes and Rodríguez 2007). The 2010 earthquake in Haiti and Hurricane Katrina both demonstrate how media reports can be gendered as well as racialised, with black men constructed as violent and anti-social, in comparison to women who are presented as the 'deserving' victims of events. Journalists and the media are increas-ingly important to how events are perceived and are important in determining how people respond to an event, including levels of giving.

DETERMINANTS OF THE LEVEL OF EXTERNAL RESPONSE

In terms of international actors, it is important to note that, officially, there cannot be a response until a state of emergency has been called. That is, international humanitarian actions cannot begin until a country states that the event has had an impact it cannot deal with alone. It might seem that all leaders of countries would wish to call a state of emergency as soon as possible so as to receive aid but this is not always the case. A state of emergency suggests that the country cannot cope alone and some countries may not wish to make this admission. Katrina was interesting because offers of relief aid and assistance flowed, this time, from the Third to the First World but some offers of help, most notably from Cuba, were declined. Refusal of outside assistance may be based on ideological issues but it may also have an economic basis. Countries may be worried about how the outside world might see them as a trading partner, for example, or what this might mean for confidence in them as a loan holder. On the other hand, debt relief may be one part of the international response, as was the case in Central America after Hurricane Mitch. Another reason for not wanting outside help may echo Bankoff's (2001) concerns (see Chapter 1) that international governments may use such events to establish a foothold in the country. The national government may fear losing control once the doors are open to the international community. Events in Haiti after the 2010 earthquake illustrate how just such a situation may occur, where reports suggest many aid agencies bypassed local and national authorities in the delivery of assistance, and donors did not adequately consult with key government ministries when taking decisions that would affect Haiti's future (Oxfam 2011). The Interim Haiti Recovery Commission (IHRC) that was established by the Haitian government under pressure from the international community also illustrates this point, given that once established it has been under 'considerable US influence' (Oxfam 2011: 3).

Governments with a political ideology that is different from that prescribed by the dominant neo-liberal paradigm may be especially concerned to keep outside intervention to a minimum. On the other hand, corrupt governments of whatever ideology may not welcome outside interventions that may reveal their corruption. An interesting reason was given by the then president of Nicaragua, Arnaldo Alemán to explain why he delayed calling a state of emergency after Hurricane Mitch. He told journalists that it would lead to 'a river of profits for many fishermen', suggesting that NGOs would 'take advantage' of international aid if an emergency were called. This is ironic given he was later found guilty of embezzlement of aid monies. In contrast, the reaction of the president of Honduras to the same event was to call a state of emergency immediately and as the international relief operation moved in, so too did the world's media. Honduras was portrayed, and thus perceived by the public, as harder hit than other countries and it received more aid more quickly than Nicaragua.

The Role of the Media

The amount of money received by a country may be dependent on the media (Bennett and Kottasz 2000; Olsen et al. 2003). This is increasingly so and it does not just determine individual giving but also influences NGO and governmental response. Brown and Minty (2006) found that a typical 700-word article raised donations by 18.2 per cent. Just an additional minute allocated to coverage on the evening news increased that day's donations by 13.2 per cent for the average agency. How an event is presented in the news is of course important in increasing giving. Owen (2008) used six spoof news articles that described the same disaster to explore what influences aid giving. The news articles actually presented the same death toll and suffering, but gave the events different names or locations and edited them to highlight different aspects as 'causing' the disaster. He found that almost two thirds of participants would prefer to give in those scenarios where the population was portrayed as more 'innocent' or less to blame for events or their impact.

While the media may be highly influential in determining response, the item still has to get on the news in the first place to have an impact. Even major international disasters can be knocked off the top of the news by quite insular national news stories. For example, in July 2011 the drought and famine in East Africa had to compete in the UK for news time with riots across England and a newspaper 'phone hacking' scandal. It seemed to be losing the contest, given that, in August 2011, UK donations per person to the crisis were reported as just £4.50, compared with eventual totals of £58.89 for Haiti and £196 – 45 times higher – for the Indian Ocean tsunami (Ball and Xan 2011). However, there might be other factors that also help to explain this. A study by Bennett and Daniel (2002) highlighted that the bigger the event and the more destruction, the more likely it is to be reported. Despite claims that, rather than the scale of an event, the scale of the expected economic impact on Western markets is what determines media coverage (CARMA 2006), greater destruction does tend to make better TV. However, this destruction needs to be packaged, and a 'granny up a tree' shot, recreated if necessary, is needed to ensure extensive coverage (Bennett and Daniel 2002). Once again, women and children are presented as the helpless victims of the event.

Dynes and Rodríguez (2007) suggest four 'framing themes' when considering coverage of Hurricane Katrina – the first event to hit the US in the era of continuous 24 hour cable TV. The first was the idea of 'finding damage' or capturing catastrophe through extensive and diverse images. Of course, little context is given to these images: half destroyed housing looks dramatic but it needs to be put into the context of having been sub-standard prior to the event. Finding death is also a concern, not so much in terms of presenting images of the dead, but in terms of producing and reproducing estimates of the numbers of dead – generally underestimated in the Third World context but overestimated during First World events such as Katrina. News reports also seek to find the 'bad guys'. In the case of Katrina, they displayed images constructed as looting, and reported high levels of crime and murder in the key refuges, which were later proved wrong. This was also the case in post-earthquake Haiti, where reports focused on men trafficking children, with little discussion of the high levels of trafficking reported prior to the event. Local reports in Sri Lanka post tsunami suggested high levels of sexual assault and rape, most shockingly said to have occurred during the rescue period (Fisher 2009; Nobel de Silva 2006). While not to question the existence of such attacks or their severity, other than local news reports, little evidence exists to demonstrate an increase in attacks on women by unknown males post disaster (see Chapter 7). In all these cases, the media constructs men as the 'bad guys' while women are presented as either protectors or as needing protection. However, if women have not been 'protected' they may become less of an appealing image for the media to portray since, as the former president of MSF notes, 'the raped woman rarely represents the ideal victim' (Le Pape and Salignon 2003:11 cited in Ticktin 2011). This being said, in conflict situations women as victims of war allow a construction of good versus evil that is hardly reflective of the complexities of the situation. While attempting to 'humanise' war, media coverage may actually dehumanise all involved (Hume 1997 cited in Chandler 2001).

The final 'framing theme' focuses on a response – finding authority and finding help. The former relates to the press's search for someone or some organisation to be 'in charge', which is rarely if ever the case, while the latter highlights a lack of response or lack of rescue efforts. Acts of individual heroism make good news stories, and British person-nel 'rescuing' victims overseas was found to be a factor that helped get an event news time in the UK (Bennett and Daniel 2002). More generally, the presence of nationals in a country as victims of the event increases media interest. Media will often give a disproportionate amount of coverage to their nationals caught up in the events (CARMA 2006). Where no nationals are present, the likeness of those affected to the giving population is important, making stories on Africa more difficult to 'sell' to European countries, compared to events affecting largely white populations (Zagefka et al. 2010). Some developing world countries may find it difficult to gain coverage, whatever the nature of the event, as they are seen to be old news, e.g. famine in Ethiopia. While some may be favoured for their historical or colonial links to a Western nation, and because of the large migrant population resident in the country, others may struggle. India, where media coverage of events in the UK tends to be both extensive and positive, can be compared to the case of Pakistan, for example. Media coverage, in turn, may be an important factor in influencing individual giving patterns.

Factors Influencing Individual Giving

While a story on the TV news or in the newspapers can have a large impact on giving by the general public, this is not the only factor that is important. Gender may be an important variable but there are no studies to date that focus on gendered giving post disaster. A study in 2010 used panel data to explore the differences between male and female giving, generally, focusing on single males and single women heads of household. It found that women across all income categories were more likely to give than men and that in the majority of cases they were also more likely to give more than men (Mesch 2010).

Studies of post-disaster giving highlight the fact that, as well as media coverage, giving is positively associated with the number of people affected, and the level of political and civil freedom in the country affected (Fenney and Clarke 2007). Developing world nations, in general, are more likely to elicit a response than the 'Developed World' (Bennett and Kottasz 2000) but giving is more likely if identification with the victims is high and 'victim blame' is low (Zagefka et al. 2010). The extent to which identifying with those affected is important has been found to vary by nationality, with this being more important for German givers than those in Spain, for example (Flint and Goyder 2006). It has even been suggested that something as simple as a donor sharing the same initials or name as a hurricane may increase willingness to give (Chandler et al. 2008). Brown and Minty (2006) summarise the reasons why people respond to media appeals, post event, as being related to the 'warm glow' it brings (citing Andreoni 1989,1990). However, giving to a media appeal also allows people the opportunity to partake in 'impact philanthropy' (citing Duncan 2004) through conspicuous giving (citing Glazer and Konrad 1996). It may also be influenced by the simple fact that so many others are also giving (citing Sugden 1984), and this may be important for, and fuelled by, the increased use of internet sites. The Indian Ocean tsunami was said to offer ideal conditions for giving – the extensive media coverage had a role to play but so did other issues: the fact that it was perceived as a sudden-onset 'natural disaster';

constructing the victims as blameless; its timing just after Christmas; and the number of Western tourists killed (Telford and Cosgrave 2006).

Dramatic and destructive events such as the tsunami, where it is easy to see how money would provide a 'solution', may obtain more donations than complex events such as famines, where money may not be seen to provide the answer. That being said, while the 2011 drought in East Africa had a slow start, as noted above, by November, the Disaster Emergency Committee (DEC) had announced record giving by the British public of £72 million, which at this time was the third highest appeal total in its 45-year history. That this was a DEC appeal may in itself be important, since more money is raised when the charity is well known and is part of a wider international appeal (Bennett and Kottasz 2000). However, not all events provoke an internationally coordinated response and the response patterns of international actors are also determined by a range of factors.

Factors in Determining International Involvement

It is important to bear in mind that, while aid given by the international community may be seen to be given on 'humanitarian' principles, it cannot be seen as apolitical. At the very least aid arrives within a political context since, as discussed in Chapter 1, disasters are not extraordinary, external events but are a product of a (lack of) development, or the nature of development to date, which has left the population vulnerable to a natural hazard. Disasters, by definition, demonstrate an inability to respond to an event and are often accompanied by high levels of blame, usually pointing to the failure of the national government to predict, warn and protect. As such, when aid enters a country, it is in a highly charged political context. The aid-giving government may also not be beyond politics when determining what to give and how. Just as the way a population responds to a particular country may be determined by historical ties, so too may aid given by governments. Aid may be based upon moral judgements about former colonies, upon economic judgements about strategic trading partners and upon political judgements about either wanting to isolate or to build alliances with 'rogue' nations. Aid may also become a political tool, especially at election time and used to elicit votes. This may be at the national level. For example, Tony Blair's promise to match the funds donated by the general public after the Indian Ocean tsunami was seen by some to be a 'vote-winning' action in the run up to the General Election. It may also have a more international element. For example, there were suggestions that the Spanish and

French used post-tsunami donations to gain favourable publicity for their campaign to host the Olympic games (CARMA 2006).

In order for the giving of aid to fulfil these wider political goals it needs to be visible, that is, reported by the press. It also needs to be 'flagged' with the country name and flag being clearly marked on grain sacks and rescue vehicles and, later, included in name plates on new bridges, for example. A recent report for the British government (Select Committee on International Development 2006) noted that there were good reasons why the Department for International Development (DFID) usually chooses not to 'fly the flag' over the programmes it has funded, often related to promoting a sense of ownership of the programme by the local community or national government. However, it notes that, if partner agencies put their own 'flags' on such programmes, these gains are lost. The report concluded that there are some circumstances in which it would be appropriate for DFID to identify its contributions to human-itarian assistance in the Third World, as this could have a 'positive impact on perceptions of the UK in the countries concerned'. That is, those affected will have a positive view of the donor country with implications for trade relations in the future.

While it may seem that the governmental response is at least in part based on its own needs, as much as the affected country's needs, the public tend to assume that international NGOs and charities are more altruistic in their response. What follows is not intended to deny the good work done by NGOs across the globe and the fact they help keep survivors of events alive, fed, clothed, housed and disease free. However, it is important to problematise their role also and recognise that they also get involved for good and bad reasons (see Anderson and Woodrow 1998). Many NGOs get involved post event due to a commitment to humanitarian principles (see Chapter 5) and compassion for those affected. This includes NGOs that have no experience in providing relief, particularly those that are working in and around the area where the event occurs. NGOs may also feel compelled to get involved because they feel they are the best at delivering aid, particularly to what they may see as an under represented group, such as women, the elderly, or children who might otherwise be ignored. However, there may also be a certain amount of pressure on organisations to respond. This may come from the government in the country where they are based, which may be looking for a means to channel its aid. It may come from the fact other NGOs have reported that they are going to respond, from the general public asking about how they can give, or from their staff in the area asking if they can divert available funds to provide relief. Once again, the media will have a role to play, since their portrayal of suffering will encourage the public to donate, and governments and NGOs to respond. The availability of funds is an important consideration and a cynical view would suggest this may be a determining factor. As Anderson and Woodrow (1998) point out, it is a fact of life that development funds are harder to raise than relief funds and this may influence an NGO's willingness to become involved. Organisations may feel that their survival depends on them responding, since not doing so might be questioned on compassionate grounds, while doing so will keep them in the public eye and help raise further funds in the future for development work.

Thus there are multiple pressures on international NGOs, as well as international governments, to respond and not all these pressures stem from compassion and notions of humanitarianism. Moreover, the notion of 'humanitarianism', and its continued relevance in itself, has been critiqued and traditional principles of political neutrality and universality called into question, as will be explored in the next chapter.

DRAWING THE LINKS: WOMEN'S (IN)VISIBILITY WITHIN RESCUE AND RESPONSE

Research suggests that during a large-scale natural hazard people are driven to respond quickly and often collectively. How people respond, and why people respond, is relatively well documented in the literature but a missing element is an understanding of the gendered differences in response. What is usually documented, as in the Indian Ocean tsunami, is that women cannot respond as well as men due to their socially constructed roles and gendered socialisation. In contrast, the acts of men to save themselves and others are either taken as a given in the literature, or portrayed by the media as acts of bravery. Women's rescue efforts are largely invisible. It is assumed that women will be slowed down in saving themselves through seeking to carry or help young children, the infirm and the elderly in their care. Women may also help other women to save themselves and their possessions, but this may be constructed as women helping men in the (male) rescue efforts, rather than women rescuing women (and men). Women, then, are constructed as 'helpers' rather than 'rescuers'. Women may indeed be helpers rather than rescuers, since in many cultures a woman would not think of undertaking actions to 'rescue' a man. If such an act cannot be imagined by women, or men, then men are unlikely to accept the act even if offered.

Women's actions are often invisible to those involved during an event, or made invisible by those involved immediately afterwards. When they arrive on the scene, the world's media both make women visible through its coverage but also invisible through the nature of that coverage. Media coverage of events such as the earthquake in Haiti and Hurricane Katrina involved racialised constructions of men as violent aggressors involved in looting, sexual assault and trafficking. By contrast, media coverage of women constructs them as blameless and helpless victims seeking to protect their children while in need of protection themselves. Such images not only help 'buy' news time but, in turn, help to ensure that the disaster 'sells' to the general public, governments and international agencies, provoking the giving of aid. Aid is more likely to be provided when the event occurs in the developing, rather than developed, world but politics rather than need may drive giving by individuals and governments alike. Giving is not only driven by NGOs' altruism either: post-disaster funding may be more accessible than funding for 'development' and may also help ensure access to future development funding by raising the organisation's profile. Thus, the post-disaster or 'humanitarian' response may be as much a political as a moral response. It may depend on the donor's own interests and also how the 'victims' are perceived. In particular, the idea that those affected are blameless seems to be important in determining how an event is covered and in determining the extent of giving after the event, as the next chapter will explore.

5.   Humanitarianism and humanitarian relief

INTRODUCTION

Relief aid given immediately after an event aims to save lives, keep those saved alive, and alleviate extreme suffering. It is usually constructed as driven by some notion of a moral duty to respond to the suffering of humanity, that is, to respond to all sufferers, regardless of how distant, and regardless of nationality or politics, religion or culture. As the politics of aid discussed in the previous chapter highlights, the idea that the response immediately after an event is apolitical and equal for all is questionable. Yet notions of neutrality and universalism are what inform the idea of humanitarianism, which underpins the relief period. While the idea of humanitarianism has a long tradition, events in the 1990s, in particular, highlighted problems with the traditional or classical view of humanitarian aid, which led to changes in how aid giving is practised on the ground. The changing face of humanitarianism has allowed it to emerge as an extremely valuable public relations tool for international actors involved in conflicts, and can either be read as suggesting a move to a more ethical or moral foreign policy (Chandler 2001) or, conversely, as embedding humanitarianism on the margins of contemporary war (Mills 2005).

This chapter will explore the changing conceptualisation of human-itarianism and consider what this means for relief efforts post disaster in the developing world. Much of the debate on humanitarianism has related to the post-conflict context but, as this chapter will demonstrate, not only do 'natural' disasters and conflicts combine to produce complex political emergencies, but also post-disaster relief is at times used to promote conflict resolution. Some of the key issues related to debates over humanitarianism, such as the involvement of the military and notions of deserving versus undeserving victims, are common to both conflict and disaster contexts.

It should be noted at the outset that there has been little discussion of gender issues in debates around the meaning of humanitarianism. How-ever, the issues raised by humanitarianism and humanitarian actions do raise gender issues (see Dijkhorst and Vonhof 2005), which will be highlighted where appropriate. The practice of humanitarianism will also be considered, since gender issues are clear within the practicalities of relief aid.

CLASSICAL HUMANITARIANISM

> Part of the appeal of humanitarianism is that it exemplifies moral certainty: it purports to save lives and alleviate suffering. How can one argue with this kind of moral imperative? (Ticktin 2011: 253)

The roots of humanitarian relief lie in religion and missionary work although the majority of faith-based organisations see relief operations as deriving from their faith rather than as opportunities to promote that faith. Catholic organisations such as CRS, Caritas and CAFOD represent some of the largest and most visible faith-based aid organisations. Islamic organisations are increasingly important on the global stage and also have a long heritage of humanitarian giving based on the fundamental belief that the act of helping someone in distress is not a choice but an obligation in the same way as prayer or fasting during Ramadan is (Krafess 2005).

Contemporary humanitarian thinking has evolved from two strands of thinking: the Wilsonian tradition, named after US President Woodrow Wilson; and the Dunantist tradition, named after Henry Dunant the founder of the Red Cross. The Wilsonian tradition sees US values as a force for good in the world, and humanitarian giving as being in line with US foreign policy objectives. This tradition characterises large US-based NGOs such as CARE. By contrast, the Dunantist tradition is associated more with European organisations, good examples being Save the Children UK, Oxfam and MSF (Médecins Sans Frontières or Doctors Without Borders). The NGOs associated with each tradition differ in terms of their financial structures, with Wilsonian organisations more reliant on government funding, as well as having divergent political histories and philosophical traditions (see Stoddard 2003). The European Dunantist organisations take a more long-term view of humanitarian response and see advocacy as having an important role to play, compared to US organisations, which tend to focus on providing aid quickly and efficiently. Perhaps more fundamentally, European organisations have more independence from the state in terms of funding and in terms of their relationship to the state, which is often adversarial. Thus NGOs that seemingly share the same humanitarian aim have very different philosophies about that aim, especially in terms of how it, and they, should relate to states and governments. More generally, there are also divergent views on the notion of humanitarianism.

For a long time, the meaning of 'humanitarianism' seemed clear and straightforward. What is now known as 'classical humanitarianism' has limited and short-term objectives, which aim to provide assistance to save lives and alleviate suffering, and a mantra of 'do no harm'. The basic principle of humanitarianism is expressed by the Red Cross as 'the desire to prevent and alleviate human suffering wherever it may be found'. All victims of disaster or conflict are seen, then, as having a (moral) right to support, and as such giving aid is seen as obligatory, based on ideas of 'universalism' and the aid given is unconditional. This notion of 'universalism' may help to explain why humanitarianism is considered to be gender neutral or as not needing 'engendering', since it is constructed around the equal rights of all to a response regardless of sex, as well as nationality, politics, culture, religion, and race, and more recently sexuality and other defining characteristics of an individual or group of individuals. This notion of universalism poses a dilemma or paradox for those seeking to ensure the involvement of women in humanitarian actions, however. On the one hand, it is possible to draw on 'universalism' to promote women as 'equal subjects/objects of humanitarian aid, indistinguishable from other types of victims'. However, this may hide the specific issues women face and the alternative is to highlight women's difference from other victims, for example their experience of a conflict not through combat but through rape, in order to ensure they receive the same attention as other victims (Ticktin 2011: 250). This dilemma illustrates one of the 'paradoxes of feminism' – the need to emphasise difference (of women) in order to claim sameness (as equal human beings) (Scott 1996).

Universalism reflects the humanitarian principles of neutrality, impartiality and independence. The idea is that humanitarian organisations act independently from all governments and politics and do not take actions that advantage one group affected by an event over another and, more particularly, one side of a conflict over another. It is humanitarian organisations' lack of politics that has ensured their access to crisis zones, and their security within them, over the years. As far back as the Nigerian-Biafran war, these humanitarian principles have been questioned, and it was the growing incompatibility between the kinds of problems being addressed at the end of the 1990s and the kind of the humanitarian responses being put forward by the international community (Hendrickson 1998) that lead to the emergence of what became known at the UN World Summit in 2005 as 'new humanitarianism' or what Weiss (1999) refers to as 'political humanitarianism'.

COMPLEX POLITICAL EMERGENCIES AS GENDERED CONFLICTS

The post-Cold War geopolitical context was characterised by a growing number of intra-state conflicts in Africa and Eastern Europe, in part brought about by changing notions of the First/Second/Third World. It brought, on one hand, a blurring of the distinction between combatants and civilians and, on the other, the construction of civilians as targets. This blurring of the distinction between combatants and civilians was further exacerbated by the events of 11 September 2001 since, as Mills (2005: 165) notes, 'terrorism by its very nature obscures such a distinction'. This blurring has included women being increasingly seen as combatant civilians, especially with the use of female 'suicide bombers' and with male terror suspects using female clothes to disguise themselves. However, in gender terms, it is the construction of civilians as targets that has perhaps been of most importance and especially the widespread use of rape as a 'weapon of war' during conflicts in the 1990s.

The use of rape as part of military operations is not new, but the attention it now receives from the media and peacekeeping institutions is, and so is its aim. Rape falls within the notion of 'Gender Based Violence' which is defined as physical, sexual and psychological violence against both men and women, and is not a 'accidental' side effect of war but 'a crime against the individual and an act of aggression against the entire community and nation' (Bouta, Frerks and Bannon 2005: 33). As Card (2002: 125) notes: 'if there is one set of fundamental functions of rape, civilian or martial, it is to display, communicate, and produce or maintain dominance'. During the Rwandan and the Bosnia-Herzegovina conflicts, for example, the aim of martial rape was not just to show domination but was also part of a wider strategy to destroy the ethnic identity of the opposition, through destroying social relations and cultural norms. In the Darfur and Sudan crises, Fadlalla (2007) suggests that rape was understood not as a private matter, a crime against individual women, but as a 'political violation' seen as dehumanising an entire group or population. So widespread was rape in Rwanda that the UN Special Rapporteur noted that 'rape was the rule and its absence the exception'. In 1998, the International Criminal Tribunal for Rwanda made the landmark decision that war rape in Rwanda was an element of the crime of genocide.

However, while widespread, the survivors of sexual violence have generally been 'neglected in standard models of humanitarian aid delivery' (Le Pape and Salignon 2003, cited in Ticktin 2011: 250). In part, this relates to how sexual violence is seen within societies – both by those affected and those charged with providing aid to those affected – and how it is seen by both men and women.

On the one hand, mass or martial rape may be used to highlight men's (collective) inability to protect 'their' women, thus de-masculinising these men and calling into question their socially prescribed gender roles as protectors. In some cases, men themselves may be the victims of sexual assaults and men during the Rwandan crisis were targeted with attacks that often included the mutilation of genitals (de Brouwer 2007). On the other hand, there is a question about what rape means to men who rape. Rape violates international rules on combat and while it might be assumed soldiers are ordered to rape, this may not be the case. Men may rape out of fear of what will happen to them if they do not do so or through revenge for what they believe the opposition forces have done to their families. A study of the Bosnia-Herzegovina conflict also found rape might be a 'reward' from superior officers, who provide wine, food and women to rape in order to build camaraderie among the forces (Stiglmayer 1993). While men who commit rape are transgressing cultural norms, it is not clear how this changes, or if it changes, the way that they are seen in society, since it is constructed as part of combat 'duties'. However, rape and sexual violence does change the way women, at least, are seen within society and within their marriages, leaving many as outcasts, despite the fact they are not to blame for what happened to them. This feeling of shame may mean that women do not report the event but if rape is understood by the women themselves as being a political act, as an act of war, as a collective happening, then women survivors may be much more open to talk about their experiences (see Ticktin 2011).

Rape that results in pregnancy also means that the future generation of the ethnic group is 'diluted', since children born through martial rape will be of mixed heritage. Turshen's (2001) conceptualisation of the 'political economy of rape' suggests the need to understand 'women as property' and 'women and property' as explaining the strategic reasons for rape. In the former, women as men's property when raped and impregnated are both made to bear children for the enemy community and cannot bear children for their community due to stigma or injury. In the latter, forced 'marriages' mean their attackers have rights over their property and possessions. Of course, how society, and the women themselves, respond to children born of rape is also an issue. Many women will reject the pregnancy, choosing abortion where this is an option, or reject the child, abandoning newborns (Lorch 1995 cited in Card 1996). Reports suggest some women may decide to take their own lives rather than carry through pregnancies or live with the shame. The Organisation of African Unity (2000) has concluded of Rwanda that 'we can be certain that almost all females who survived the genocide were direct victims of rape or other sexual violence, or were profoundly affected by it'. Despite this, the 'profound affects' of rape on women have received little attention in the longer term, perhaps due to the short-term goals of humanitarian interventions, which means international reporting of rape seeks to expose the identities and tactics of the perpetrators rather than ensure women's well being (Fadlalla 2007).

The construction of civilians as targets, including women as targets of sexual violence, meant that the protection of civilians became a real challenge during the 1990s, as did ensuring that aid itself did not become part of the problem. Kent (2004: 220) suggests that the absence of political solutions to crises such as that in Rwanda meant international donors saw the 'humanitarian bandage' as more convenient and accept-able than political engagement. Humanitarian aid became a strategy for political containment rather than problem solving (Mills 2005). This also led to the proliferation of responders, including UN responders, and a changing understanding of response, which linked the short-term goals of saving lives to the longer-term goals of reducing future vulnerability. Consequently, the notion of humanitarianism became more ambiguous and ambitious (Rieff 2002). The changing nature of conflict and, more recently, the repackaging of security as a development concern, along with the lack of development being seen as an international security threat, helps explain this politicisation of humanitarian actions (Curtis 2001) and the rise of 'new' humanitarianism. While welcomed by some, others see the humanitarian framework as being under 'assault' (see Macrae 1998). At the same time, as there has been an increase in humanitarian interventions, there has been a decrease in respect for humanitarian norms (Mills 2005) and it has been suggested that, while there are now more actors involved in humanitarian work and in many ways it has become more institutionalised, understandings of what humanitarianism means have become more ambiguous (see Chandler 2001).

'NEW' HUMANITARIANISM

The Rwandan crisis, perhaps more than any other, highlights the perceived problem with classical humanitarianism. The 1994 Rwanda crisis
is a good example of what came to be known as a 'complex emergency',
whereby political and ethnic conflict forced a mass movement of people
fleeing the violence, placing them within an inhospitable 'natural'
environment. The response saw large numbers of NGOs converge on the
camps set up in Zaire or the Democratic Republic of Congo. On the one
hand, the humanitarian interventions faced issues around the lack of an
international military response that put those in, and working in, the
camps at risk. On the other hand, it became evident that aid was being
used to fuel the fighting and to feed those who would then go on to kill
again because aid, according to humanitarian principles, was being given
to all in need, regardless of who they were or what they had done. As
evidence of what was occurring grew, MSF were one of the first agencies
to decide to withdraw 'humanitarian' aid, based on an understanding that
this aid was being given to and used by people who were committing
genocide. While they later returned to the camps, MSF instigated a
programme of 'witnessing'. In the face of an international refusal to
acknowledge the slaughter in Rwanda as genocide, they chose to speak
out against what they saw occurring and against the perpetrators of these
crimes. This idea of a 'duty to bear witness' within the new humanitarian
discourse, of course, goes against the idea of neutrality as presented in
classical humanitarianism, an ideal still upheld by some humanitarians
such as the International Committee of the Red Cross (see Rieffer-
Flanagan 2009). For those who question the classical ideals of humanitarianism, the notion that there can be neutrality is naïve. Neutrality in
cases such as Rwanda can be seen as demonstrating, at best passivity
and, at worst, complicity with the genocide being committed. The events
led to a debate within humanitarian circles around the meaning of that
term, which left humanitarianism as a contested notion.

The debates around what humanitarianism is, while seemingly theoretical, have important consequences for action on the ground. Events such
as Rwanda led to the construction of the 'undeserving victim' (Stockton
1998). More recently, the 'war on terror' has further embedded this idea
within the sphere of humanitarian interventions through evoking feelings
of unknown others as 'evil', and thus not deserving of humanity (Mills
2005). This results in aid being made conditional on the receivers being
able to show no blame for their plight and also, increasingly, a need to
see some longer-term, positive, impact from the aid. Withholding aid

today for supposed future political gains is based on a perhaps misguided confidence in economic, political and social forecasting (Stockton 1998: 356); not least because the idea that it is possible to distinguish 'the bad man from the good woman and child' can also be called into question (Macrae 1998: 314). This gendered language is not accidental: historically there has been a feminised construction of civilians, while aggressors are masculinised. While having its roots in the realities of the 'formalised' conflicts fought between armies of (men) during the First and Second World Wars, it does not necessarily reflect post-war patterns of conflict, which have largely occurred within national boundaries. It needs to be noted that women have taken up arms in many conflicts and have become leaders of armed groups. It has been estimated they make up around 10 per cent of combatants (Bouta, Frerks and Bannon 2005) but it has also been noted that their presence does not change the character or culture of conflict nor does it necessarily lead to equity (Cockburn 2001). If not as fighters, women may be engaged in activities to support those involved in combat, such as cooking and washing and, of course, providing sexual services. Women may also act as guards for female captives and many will have witnessed the rape of other women and done nothing to intervene. Women may also sexually assault other women using objects, or encourage their men to perform acts of sexual violence (de Brouwer 2007). That is, as women are part of a society so too will they be influenced by, and conform to the norms of that society, and may, like male soldiers, have little real choice other than to do so. During periods of conflict this may include colluding in atrocities against other women. The popular conception of women as victims and civilians compared to the male aggressor – of men as being to 'blame' for conflict while women are blameless – is, then, rather misleading. The increasing use of sexual violence against women in both the conflict and post-disaster contexts adds to this, in that women who have experienced sexual assault cannot be easily identified with the images of innocence required to designate sufferers as worthy aid (Ticktin 2011: 259).

Those against withholding humanitarian aid from some people in need, for fear they are perpetrators rather than victims of violent acts, suggest that aid organisations cannot know with any certainty who these 'non-deserving' people are. They do not have the knowledge or foresight to say with certainty what will happen, nor do they have the moral right since withholding aid on the basis that those in need may be criminals is the 'arbitrary application of punishment before trial' (Stockton 1998: 354). However, the lack of political intervention by outside governments left both the political and humanitarian problem in the hands of the humanitarian community (Eriksson 1996). NGOs had to undertake the tasks that the international community were, and are, unable to fulfil (Kaldor 2006). Given the restricted mandates and limited power of humanitarian organisations it has been suggested that this meant organisations were merely left 'throwing food at political problems' (Prendergast 1996: 8–9). In Rwanda, the unresolved political crisis was 'dealt with' by aid. The post-conflict evaluation concluded that humanitarian aid could not be a substitute for political action.

Kosovo raised similar issues but here it was not the lack of protection that was the key issue but the way that victims and aid givers were protected, as military intervention went side by side with humanitarian action, not least using armed military convoys to protect those delivering aid. Humanitarian work has traditionally been disassociated from military operations, yet this may have been a false dichotomy since, for example, an airport may need to be seized before aid can be landed and distributed. The military also often have a role to play in policing, during and after events. As Hurricane Katrina demonstrated, militarisation is not confined to the developing world (Tierney and Bevc 2007). The fact that humanitarian space cannot be opened up or maintained by the humanitarians themselves suggests benefits from thinking politically and collaborating with diplomatic and military institutions. This may come more naturally to those humanitarian organisations with their roots in Wilsonian rather than Dunantist traditions. Actions coordinated by military and civilian organisations are political and humanitarian and as such they are not impartial, neutral or consensual (Weiss 1999). For example, the Indian Ocean tsunami saw a strong US military presence seemingly responding to the need for rescue and relief yet the deployment of troops on a massive scale also allowed the US to pursue political aims in Indonesia and to make advances against Tamil held regions in Sri Lanka (Bello 2006). Protecting aid distribution may require a military presence but Woodward (2001) suggests that the 'humanitarian bombing' in Kosovo marked a crossing of the line between the humanitarian and the political. Over and above the moral questions such actions raise, on a practical level there are also problems. For example, the UN's High Commission for Refugees (UNHCR) could not prepare to deal with the consequences of the military actions since this might jeopardise the action and undermine the strategy for coercive diplomacy.

While the UN entered the field of humanitarian action rather late and with 'some reluctance' (Kent 2004) it has emerged as the key coordinating body for international responses to large-scale events. This being said, while it was assumed the international response post Tsunami would be led by the UN, in fact the World Bank emerged as the key donor and the key manager of donations. World Bank involvement raises issues around what is being promoted and why, and has been critiqued as allowing them to more easily push through neo-liberal priorities such as privatisation as 'conditionalities' of aid (Bello 2006). UN engagement in humanitarian actions also raises issues since it pits humanitarian notions of impartiality and neutrality against the more political ideas of peace-keeping forces, and raises issues around the sanctity of sovereignty. It also raises questions about the 'peacekeepers', not least in the light of charges that in Guinea, Liberia and Sierra Leone, and also the Democratic Republic of Congo, some UN personnel sexually exploited women and children and exchanged cash and resources for sexual favours (Willits King and Harvey 2005: 23). Involving the military in humanitarian activities made humanitarian intervention a very contentious issue, because any military intervention by one state in another state was traditionally called a war (Nan 2010). Sovereignty, once a cornerstone of humanitarianism, became 'sovereignty with responsibility' and the flip side was the concept of 'Responsibility to Protect' or R2P. The R2P framework is based on the idea that sovereignty is not a privilege, but a responsibility. If a state fails to fulfil its responsibilities to protect its people from harm, the international community has the responsibility to intervene, including a military intervention. Thus, the new humanitarianism saw humanitarian relief as part of an integrated political strategy, more controlled by governments, often partially militarised and with giving as conditional.

New humanitarianism then 'is "principled", "human rights based", politically sensitive and geared to strengthening those forces that bring peace and stability to the developing world' (Fox 2001: 275). It has served to 're-legitimise' an arena of aid that has been blamed for fuelling conflicts, prolonging wars and standing neutral in the face of genocide. Its aim is short-term relief but with long-term positive consequences for 'development'. Compared to when classical humanitarianism emerged, the current context requires analysts and practitioners to question orthodoxies and offer a thoughtful analysis (Hilhorst 2007), in particular resisting the urge to act ahead of reflecting. Weiss (1999) suggests the need for 'reflective humanitarians'. We might add to this, the need for reflective gendered humanitarians, as an analysis of humanitarian relief in practice demonstrates the gendered pitfalls of 'humanitarian' giving, as will be explored below.

RELIEF AID IN PRACTICE

It is impossible to really do no harm. (Rieff 2002: 22)

Relief aid is aimed at saving lives and alleviating suffering. It seeks to provide food and clean water, protection – clothes and shelter – and also to attend to injury and sickness and prevent the spread of disease. As such, it is seen to be a straightforward response to need and it is often assumed that any help is better than none. However, time and again events have shown this is not necessarily the case and increasingly the potential longer-term negative implications of short-term relief aid have been recognised.

The first issue for relief aid is the idea of the need for speed. The notion of the 'tyranny of the urgent' sums up the issues raised – that the need for urgent action is the driving force and overrules all else. This 'myth of speed' means that organisations feel they must rush to the disaster scene to be helpful. Yet, more than speed, what is needed is timeliness – to be there when needed (Anderson and Woodrow 1998: 49). The tyranny of the urgent means that, for example, the initial response is often driven by politics and funds rather than assessment and need, as evaluations post the Indian Ocean tsunami demonstrated (Telford and Cosgrave 2006). Needs assessments are often not carried out and allocations may instead be based on what the respondent perceives to be the needs of those affected. This is often based on previous experience of similar events. Although useful, relying on experience may lead to a 'checklist' response where the same items are distributed regardless of where the need is and who is impacted, and also regardless of what other agencies and responders are providing. Such an approach does not allow gender or culture to influence existing plans and processes (Hyndman and De Alwis 2003). Such responses can also lead to culturally inappropriate items being provided, such as canned pork being distributed to Muslims, for example. It can lead to geographically inappropriate items, such as summer clothing being provided to countries perceived to be hot, despite them experiencing extreme temperature drops in the evenings. It can also lead to some requirements not being provided at all: women's sanitary items are a good example of things that for a long time were not include on checklists. Even as late as 2005 and the Indian Ocean tsunami, 'hygiene kits' for women, while provided, were under resourced. The UN were able to provide around 25 000 but had to appeal to donors to provide 100 000 more (Nobel de Silva 2006). In this instance, the contents of the kits were locally sourced but products

supplied from overseas may not be culturally appropriate, since manufactured sanitary towels may not be used in some cultures, for example.
Women's hygiene needs are also an important consideration in the design
of evacuation camps and refuges, especially in terms of the number and
location of toilets and washing areas. Obviously, segregated areas are a
necessity in most cultures. However, simple issues such as whether a
door has a gap at the bottom, rather than closing completely, can make
the difference between women being able to use facilities or not. The
location of the facilities is also much written about. If they are on the
margins of a camp, they may provide greater seclusion but may also put
women at risk walking to and from them. This problem can be compounded by poor lighting and lack of policing.

The sourcing of goods is a key issue in post-disaster responses. While,
often, relief aid is flown into Third World countries, drawing on existing
stocks (or surpluses) of goods in the US and Europe, this is not seen to
be the best response. Often food is still available within the country, in
areas not impacted by the event, or in neighbouring countries. Flying in
foods for protracted events may lead to a change in diet or, at the very
least, to dependency on this aid. That is, by providing aid the local
markets become further de-stabilised and over time foodstuffs imported
from the West may take over from local home-grown produce, reducing
the ability of farmers to re-establish their livelihoods in the long term and
undermining development. A second key issue lies in how to distribute
the food and goods. While the media often portrays distribution as
chaotic, especially in the developing world context – showing officials
throwing resources to unruly people who surround the trucks clamouring
for food – it actually tends to be more orderly and planned than this. One
question is around who to give food to, and it is increasingly recognised
that providing food to women is more likely to mean that the food stays
with the family (rather than being sold for cash to spend on other goods)
and to be distributed 'fairly' within the family. What is meant by a 'fair'
distribution is that women will feed children, the ill and infirm, ahead of
themselves. They will also favour men, either as a rational decision (if
the man is the main income earner), through social norms, or at times
due to lack of choice. However, Haiti demonstrated that distributing food
to women is not without problems.

The World Food Programme conducted 'women-only' food distribu-
tions in Port-au-Prince after the earthquake in Haiti. This was explained
as being not only about efficiency, but also power, with the Executive
Director of the World Food Programme recognising that 'in situations of
desperate poverty, access to food is power' and noting that the decision to
allocate family food vouchers to women was aimed at changing the

balance of power and also seen as a means to help protect women against violence (cited in Uwantege Hart 2011). Only women were allowed to enter the distribution points and they were policed by male military escorts to 'protect' them from the men, who were presumably, if not their husbands, brothers or sons, at least members of their own community, and who were held at the entrance gates without any chance of access. The environment surrounding distribution points entailed a real risk for many women, and there were reports of women being robbed of their food, and also of them being coerced to engage in sexual acts in order to receive extra food coupons. As such, the aims of empowering women and protecting them from violence were not fulfilled. In fact the very nature of the asymmetrical power relationship within which assistance is bestowed from First World to Third World, from male aid workers to female 'beneficiaries', aims or expects to illicit their gratitude, and 'symbolically disempowers' women (Hyndman and de Alwis 2003: 218). Accepting aid may not come easily, especially for middle class women more usually involved in charitable giving than receiving (Rosenbaum 2012).

Over and above being 'beneficiaries' of aid in general, as pointed out by Delaney and Shrader's (2000) study post Mitch, women often appear to be busier and more involved than men in the daily work of short-term emergency and rehabilitation. However, care must be taken not to construct men as idle, given that their activities may be less visible, less tangible or less discernible as being a response to the events, involving discussion and planning as well as activities outside public spaces such as camps or distribution centres. That is, in contrast to 'normal' situations, where women's actions are private actions, they may now become the ones in the 'public' domain, especially since men's (productive) activities may cease. Women easily incorporate themselves into the multiple activities in shelters, undertaking actions such as organising themselves not only to clean and maintain the shelters and the areas affected, but also to care for the people under their responsibility and coordinate with the aid-distribution bodies. That is, women's 'reproductive' roles as carers continue and, indeed, are essential for the running of the camp but men's productive roles are usurped by the camp authorities and donors, who effectively become the household 'provider' or head. Men may then suffer a 'crisis of masculinity' while for women, their elevated status as the receivers of resources may not represent 'empowerment' or bring a decline in patriarchal relations but only a move from private to public patriarchy (see Chapter 3).

While the important work being carried out by women in camps is public and thus visible, it still tends to be ignored. This may occur since men's (more limited) actions may carry greater authority as they include decision-making roles. For example, of a sample of 281 shelters in Honduras post Mitch, 190 (68 per cent) were coordinated by men (Delaney and Shrader 2000). A case study from post-Mitch El Salvador highlighted that although women were participating in the physical distribution of relief aid, they did not have a presence when it came to taking decisions about how it should be distributed. It was the community's executive council – made up of men – that decided who was going to receive the aid (see CEPAL 2003). Women's work may also be actively ignored since men's actions are given more value by those involved and by those documenting actions. For example, while studies have registered the sex of the people coordinating shelters, they have failed to register those people working to distribute food and clothes, and to provide health care and other services. These activities are mainly carried out by women.

While who receives food and other resources is a key issue for a fair distribution process, a further issue with distribution is ensuring fairness not between individuals but between communities, locations or camps and ensuring all have all they need. The coordination of activities to ensure aid is not replicated in terms of goods provided, and to ensure a fair geographical distribution, is a key problem identified by the literature and post-event evaluations. How to resolve the problem is less clear. Each new 'disaster' brings new reports of some villages receiving funding from three or four organisations while others receive nothing, or the same goods being provided by a number of different organisations, such as housing and latrines, while potable water is supplied by no one. Replication may stem from the simple fact that agencies may not know what others are doing. This lack of coordination between agencies is a recognised problem, and one that it seems agencies are unable to resolve (see Chapter 6). However, the replication may also reflect competition to give – to give to the apparently most needy, and to give quickly – in order to ensure they remain visible to the media and to the public and to aid funding for their 'development' projects in the future.

An internal issue facing agencies is how to ensure there are the human resources on the ground to respond. This is a problem that arises because during 'normal' times agencies do not need high levels of staff but, when an event strikes, they need to be able to quickly employ and deploy staff. This lack of 'surge capacity' has again been noted repeatedly and its outcome is either a lack of staff on the ground or a lack of appropriate staff. Individuals with experience but without the appropriate language skills may be sent, or those with the language skills but with little training may be deployed. Each brings its own problems. This, of course, suggests Western agencies will fly in experts from their home countries, as many still do, but it is recognised good practice to employ those from the country itself, which circumvents the language issue but may mean a lack of experienced staff. Alternatively, experienced staff may be recruited, but often they are already working with local small-scale organisations and NGOs and are 'poached' by the big international agencies, who can offer better salaries, conditions, and career prospects, as well as seeming to be the best way to ensure help reaches those needing it.

Events such as the Indian Ocean tsunami highlight the fact that while it may be assumed that agencies cannot mobilise sufficient resources due to lack of money, too much money may also be an issue. The generosity of giving post tsunami highlights the fact that funding bears little correlation to real needs on a global level. It also highlights that international agencies will continue to accept money even if they do not have the resource to use this money effectively. Few agencies sought to halt fundraising when limits were reached (Flint and Goyder 2006). Limited 'absorption capacity' will mean funds cannot be used effectively, while excess of funding might be a disincentive to coordinate with others since there will be little need to share resources. It may also be a disincentive to assess the impact of projects, which is important since the impact of projects may be negative as well as positive.

DRAWING THE LINKS: LONGER-TERM IMPLICATIONS OF SHORT-TERM RELIEF

The relief period is often characterised as a short period of intense activity immediately after an event, which aims to save lives and alleviate suffering. The interventions are portrayed as being based on a 'human-itarian' impulse to respond and the notion is that all help is good help. Responses, however, may be as much driven by politics as morals, and more recent events have highlighted that it is often easier to do harm than to do 'no harm' and the very notion of 'humanitarianism' has come under attack.

Practical interventions can have short-term implications for the crisis, for example fuelling conflict, and have longer-term implications for recovery. While presented as neutral, the practical application of human-itarian aid is not only political but is also gendered. Women are often constructed as blameless victims, as protectors (of children), or as needing protection (from men). As such they are increasingly targeted for relief actions and their 'natural' roles as mothers and carers make them efficient vehicles by which to distribute aid. Studies from refuges highlight how women are quickly able to resume their gendered roles through relief aid but that traditional divisions of roles and responsibilities between men and women continue during the emergency period, meaning that, for example, while women assume multiple 'extra' activities this does not necessarily translate into their inclusion in decision-making processes. However, targeting resources at women is not only about efficiency but also about power, and an attempt to address power imbalances or to 'protect' women who are constructed as 'powerless'. Such targeting may have implications for the emotional well being of women and men, potentially increasing violence against women in the short term, while having a psychosocial impact in the longer term (see Chapter 7).

In summary, short-term relief projects may have longer-term implications for the material and emotional well being of those receiving the funding and those denied the funding. The impact may be compounded by what happens as projects turn from relief and towards recovery or the reconstruction phase, as will be explored in the next chapter.

6. Reconstruction or transformation?

INTRODUCTION

The period immediately after an event sees relief efforts to keep people alive, to keep them healthy, and to alleviate suffering. In time, this is replaced by a period of reconstruction. While the relief period is seen as short term, reconstruction involves medium to long-term plans to rebuild infrastructure and livelihoods. The practical elements of reconstruction are generally agreed to be activities such as rebuilding houses, schools, hospitals and infrastructure, and rehabilitating land for agriculture. However, the notion of 'reconstruction' has come under scrutiny. The notion of 're'-construction suggests building back what was once there but, given that what previously existed could not withstand the force of the event, the utility of just 'building back' has been called into question. While survivors may talk of returning to 'normal', the academic, NGO and governmental discourse focuses on notions of 'building back better' (Kenny 2010). Thus government plans now talk of transformation rather than reconstruction. Following Hurricane Mitch, for example, the region's governments produced reconstruction plans with titles such as 'Transforming El Salvador to Reduce its Vulnerabilities' and slogans such as 'The government invites you to reconstruct and transform Nicaragua together'. Not only has the need to improve on what existed been recognised within this change in terminology, but also what is included in reconstruction has been widened to include building back 'better' livelihoods as well as infrastructure.

The idea that opportunities for transformation exist after a disaster is largely based on the profound changes that such an event may produce in the lives of the people involved (Byrne and Baden 1995; IFRC 2006). It may also be related to the fact that disasters tend to reveal existing national, regional and global power structures (Enarson and Morrow) 1998), throwing into sharp relief the inequalities and vulnerabilities within countries (Blaikie et al. 1994). Thus, it is now largely agreed that reconstruction provides a 'window of opportunity': not just to transform the physical landscape, but also the political and socio-economic landscape; and not only transform the material conditions under which the majority of the population live, but the context in which these conditions were being produced and reproduced. Just as the destruction of old buildings provides an unique opportunity to start anew so, too, disasters are seen to at least temporarily destroy existing social structures and relations, suggesting an opportunity for new ones to develop in their place. Disasters reveal the 'normal' order of subordination and inequality (Hewitt 1983). They reveal unequal power at all levels, including within intimate relations (Enarson and Morrow 1998: 2) and it is suggested that there exists also an opportunity for the transformation of gender roles and relations (IRP 2009). At the very least, the loss of day to day gender roles means alternatives can be more easily introduced. The logic is that, through changing gender roles, gender relations can also be transformed.

However, this optimistic view of the transformation of society and societal roles has not always been realised in practice and, while disasters reveal inequality and open the door for a change, this does not always lead to a decrease in disparities. Instead, they may deepen (Anderson 2011). Analysis post Katrina, for example, suggests that the rebuilding of New Orleans had the overall effect of worsening the status of women and children (Willinger and Knight 2012). As Blaikie et al. (1994: 210) point out, social, economic and political vulnerability are often reconstructed after a disaster, thus reproducing the conditions for a repeat disaster. In the late 1990s, Anderson and Woodrow (1998: 2) suggested that, too often, disaster responses had not contributed to long-term development and, worse, they had actually subverted or undermined it. In particular, the majority of plans for reconstruction, both governmental and non-governmental, have tended not to include gender roles and relations as part of their vision for transformation (Bradshaw and Arenas 2004).

These next two chapters will consider the reconstruction period more closely to explore the extent to which it can and has brought transformation in practice, using post-Mitch Nicaragua as a case study of the possible gendered impacts of reconstruction. This discussion will build on discussion in Chapter 4 around the response of individuals and households in the immediate aftermath of the event and, in particular, the coping strategies those affected adopted to reconstruct their livelihoods. The focus here will be on the role of international agencies and NGOs in reconstruction and how this impacts on the lives and livelihoods of women and men.

PROJECTS FOR RECONSTRUCTION

When communities are impacted by a natural hazard, people do not have the ability to decide what is destroyed but they do have the ability to decide what is reconstructed after the event (Miller and Rivera 2007). This notion of agency suggests that those aspects of society that are not reconstructed are those that society wishes to forget, while what is reconstructed reflects social and political ideals or a society's values (Baker 2003). The idea that post-disaster societies have a choice in what is reconstructed, however, is open to question since at times external agencies may have more say than the internal population on the nature and extent of reconstruction. External actors involved in reconstruction may have their own agendas (see Chapter 4) and established plans and projects for reconstruction.

Although projects for reconstruction take many forms, the most usual use of reconstruction funds remains using money raised to physically reconstruct a community or nation. For individuals, the focus is on the rebuilding of housing. This is often accompanied by rebuilding social infrastructure, such as schools and hospitals, and on making these more accessible to more people and more able to withstand future shocks. However, rebuilding the economic infrastructure, such as roads and bridges, is often the priority for governments as this helps re-establish trade links and promote economic recovery. If local people impacted by the event are employed in the rebuilding process, it provides a source of much needed revenue. An evaluation of the Indian Ocean tsunami noted that rapid cash assistance, through programmes that employ local people within reconstruction, could prevent people selling off precious assets (at low prices) as a coping strategy (Oxfam 2010). The report highlighted that one lesson was the importance of economic recovery, based on re-establishing the livelihoods of poor people, such as small-scale agriculture, construction, and the informal economy. However, a review of reconstruction initiatives coordinated by the Disasters Emergency Committee in post-tsunami Aceh (da Silva 2010) showed not only the tendency for government, donors and the media to focus on the rebuilding of houses, but also to see the number of houses constructed as a measure of achievement. It noted that the rebuilding programmes that focused on rebuilding houses and community infrastructure did help reduce vulnerability to natural hazards and achieved a widening of access to services, but it also noted that more could have been done to generate local economic activity, develop skills and create employment opportunities. That is, the physical reconstruction of communities still tends to account for the major part of reconstruction, compared to the reconstruction of community and household livelihoods.

Where livelihoods are a focus of reconstruction, that focus is often on re-establishing income generating activities through providing the necessary tools of the trade, such as fishing boats and nets, seeds and agricultural machinery. This aid is often targeted at men and their activities. It presupposes that the beneficiaries are able, with the right equipment, to return to their former trade, and want to return to it. Neither may be the case. After the Indian Ocean tsunami, studies noted how people's relationship with the sea had changed, now seeing it as something to fear rather than a provider of food and income. This had implications for those formerly engaged in activities on the sea and sea shore, in fishing (men) and drying the fish (women), making them reluctant to return to their former activities (Domroes 2006). Some, who do want to return to their former activities, may not be able to do so since, even with new tools, they are no longer located close to their former income generating site. This occurs when people are not allowed to return to the site of their former homes and livelihoods and are relocated instead to 'safer' areas. Access to land is a key issue, and a limiting factor, in post-disaster reconstruction.

Access to Land and Land Rights

Hazards, such as tsunamis and floods, earthquakes, fire and volcanic eruptions may directly impact on land, physically reducing the amount of habitable or farmable land available through the erosion of coastlines and changing water levels, but also through leaving land either under ash or saline. Events also change the landscape, destroying natural boundaries that marked out individual land holdings, making land effectively unidentifiable to those who 'owned' it but who do not have legally drawn deeds locating it. Lack of 'legal' ownership, or proof of this ownership, is not uncommon in the Third World. For example, only around 25 per cent of land in the tsunami-affected areas of Aceh was registered (Fitzpatrick 2007: 15). In the developing world, the idea of 'ownership' may rest on perception rather than legality. Perceived tenure can be based on a number of things, such as illegal occupation of a dwelling over a long period of time, the fact the land is not required for any other purpose or is deemed unsuitable for habitation, the provision of basic services to the area by a local authority or support from a local politician. By comparison, formal tenure is established through state legislation (laws, codes and regulations) and through designated state institutions. A third important type of tenure system exists that is legitimised not through the state's authority but through a different set of community institutions and authorities, and is generally referred to as a 'customary tenure system'. Under this system, although land is usually individually owned, communities regulate how the land can be transferred and how community members can receive rights to new plots of land (Oxfam 2006). Changes in communities, or loss of community elders, may see a change in how 'ownership' and rights to land are understood and managed.

Questions over who owns what land emerge post disaster with missing or non-existent land deeds, erosion of physical land boundaries and changes in community leadership. Questions over who owns land encourage the phenomenon of 'land grabbing', where individuals and groups take over land previously 'owned' by others. This occurs frequently post event when the owners do not have legal title and are less able to return quickly, through fear, culture or economy. They find land has been taken over by others when they do return. It is not only individuals that are guilty of land grabbing, but governments also. For example, post Katrina, it has been suggested that poor women of colour did not lose their homes to the levees failing, but lost their homes to city planners (Henrici et al. 2012). The Indian Ocean tsunamis also provide a good example of institutional land grabbing. Governments in the countries affected 'discouraged' those who had once occupied the shorelines from returning by making compensation dependent on not going back or preventing this return through the creation of 'buffer' zones (Action Aid 2006). In Sri Lanka, the introduction of buffer zones post tsunami effectively meant no rebuilding 100 metres (South) or 200 metres (North) from the shore. However, existing buildings that were built well enough to stand the impact of the tsunami could remain. Moreover, those seeking to invest in the tourist industry were also provided with exemptions from the zoning (Shanmugaratnam 2005). The justification for this was that the zone needed to exist to protect those who cannot build dwellings to the required standards. While there is a building logic to this argument, the fact remains that those who can 'build back better' are more usually the rich, and are often external investors looking to build hotels and leisure resorts (Williams 2005). Governments may support such investors, since the development of tourism may be a key aspect of national development plans. The tourism industry may find they can actually benefit from the opportunities disasters bring and managing 'natural' disasters is becoming an important element of tourism management (see Ritchie 2009; Glaesser 2006; Henderson 2006; Lynch 2007).

Given this, moving to a new settlement may at first sight be an attractive proposition for the poor. Housing will generally be of a higher standard than that destroyed, and services will be provided that may not have been formally or legally available in the destroyed settlement, including in a developing world context, electricity, water and sanitation. In larger new settlements, a school, perhaps a medical practice and community centre may be available. The higher standard of building coupled with the 'safer' geographical location will mean the people who move there will be less vulnerable to future events. However, new communities seldom reconstruct the old community. They are often constructed without consultation or participation. Instead they tend to be physically constructed from blueprints of ideal housing or community types, and socially constructed out of families from various communities and different social networks. Research from Nicaragua highlights, in this context, the trade-off between, rather than a reduction in, vulnerabilities (Bradshaw 2001a, 2002b). When women living in a new community constructed post Mitch were asked about changes in their well being since the hurricane, many noted the positive benefits of the new community – they now had better houses, built further away from the river – yet, at the same time, they noted the lack of work or opportunities to grow their own food that the move had entailed. The women noted that they felt safer but hungrier. However, even greater safety might not be an outcome, as a study in post-hurricane Honduras demonstrates (Barrios 2009). Here, relocating communities, without the full participation of those to be relocated to a newly constructed settlement in a 'safe' place, not only split communities and took them away from their economic and social roots, but also allowed gang culture to dominate the newly constructed post-disaster landscape, rendering it unsafe. Thus while physical vulnerability may have declined, economic vulnerability may have been increased, as may 'social' vulnerability through loss of networks and an increased (fear of) crime. Policies designed to reduce the poor's vulnerability to disasters therefore may not necessarily be pro-poor in the longer term.

LESSONS NOT LEARNT

Despite continued critical evaluations of post-disaster reconstruction, the same mistakes continue to be made. Based on evaluations of reconstruction after hurricane Mitch in Central America, and taking into account evaluations of more recent events, such as the Indian Ocean tsunamis and the Haiti earthquake, suggests the following to be key issues (da Silva 2010; Bradshaw and Arenas 2004; Bradshaw 2004a; CEPAL 2003; Lloyd-Jones 2006; Oxfam 2010).

Lack of reliable information on which to base interventions, especially limited participatory processes on which to determine needs, priorities and design

Many international organisations continue to initiate reconstruction activities based on existing national-level information, which is often limited. The data is rarely disaggregated by gender. Many continue to provide a standardised response including standardised housing design. There seems to be a continued reluctance to listen to the survivors of events, often justified through reference to the time this would take (Kenny 2010). Where participatory processes occur they may be superficial – consultation rather than participation.

Lack of coordination between donor organisations and their concentration in the same communities and the same people

At the national level, the international media's extensive coverage of certain communities immediately after an event can result in a concentration of resources in these communities (see Chapter 4). At the community level, lack of coordination may mean that some services are replicated, while others are lacking. Despite the fact that communities may not need the aid being offered, or may know it is being replicated, they may not feel they can reject all or any offers for help. Those that are selective about who they allow to 'help them', however, may have a better experience of reconstruction (Fanany 2010). At an individual level, there may be a concentration of resources in particular households or individuals. This may occur because various organisations working in the same community may use the same community leader as their way in, and that leader may keep identifying the same people as those most in need. There may also be systematic exclusion of some groups. For example, post tsunami, it was found that those who were renting housing before the tsunami were not targeted by housing projects, while the limited housing stock meant that finding somewhere to live was more difficult and rents had increased substantially (Fitzpatrick 2007).

Problems over how projects are delivered, financed and monitored

It is generally agreed is that it is better to use local materials, wherever possible and, in terms of construction, the advice is to also utilise building debris when possible (ProVention/Alnap 2005). However, while sourcing goods locally may be advisable, it may not be feasible where sufficient supply does not exist or because of the time involved to produce and supply goods on a large scale. The provision of fishing boats in post-tsunami Aceh demonstrates the continued problems related to sourcing goods locally post event. The lack of sufficient people trained in the skills needed for reconstruction activities is an issue in a number of areas, including the construction of housing. Training programmes providing skills in building and carpentry are often initiated by organisations alongside their housing projects, and some organisations see this as a chance to train women in 'non-traditional' skills. In the short term, this provides labour for their programmes, but in the long term it is questionable whether local markets can support the number of newly trained women and men. Training and subsequent work on the housing may not be paid; instead, housing projects often rely on some element of 'self-build', which may be part of the eligibility criteria. The idea of 'self–help' or 'self-build' housing has a relatively long tradition, being popular with development organisations in the 1970s. However, the issues it raises around the skills, time and money needed, as well as the nature of the housing produced, meant it became a contentious issue that sparked the so-called 'Turner-Burgess' debate (see Conway 1982 and Burgess 1978, 1982; Turner 1976). The fact that it remains the preferred option for providing housing post disaster is interesting, given that at other or 'normal' times it is no longer favoured.

For some men and women working on reconstruction projects means that they cannot dedicate enough time to rehabilitating their land or seek income generating activities. This means that they take longer to re-establish their livelihoods. The housing may also be provided via loans rather than as a 'gift', the financial burden of which may leave beneficiaries, who may not have been able to re-establish livelihoods, more, not less vulnerable. Similarly the provision of services, such as water and electricity, may mean that the targeted beneficiaries cannot afford to live in the housing in the long term. Often, new communities, particularly if the housing is built to a high standard, quickly become 'middle class' settlements. The fact that many international agencies still do not employ follow up and monitoring systems means that many do not know what the real impact of their projects on the beneficiaries has been in the longer term, or even if the intended beneficiaries did in fact benefit. This may help to explain why they continue to repeat the same mistakes again and again.

The exclusion of some groups from the reconstruction agenda

While, as will be explored below, women are increasingly included in the reconstruction process, not all women are recognised within reconstruction plans. The intersection of gender and life stage, in particular, is important for determining inclusion or exclusion. Women with young children and economically active women may be targeted as mothers and as 'workers' respectively. The very old will be a target, as will the very young. However, unmarried adolescent women will be defined as daughters and dependents rather than as women in their own right. Being neither very young nor very old, neither mother nor worker, means they may be made invisible within the reconstruction process and their needs are seldom addressed.

While the exclusion of women generally from reconstruction has been an issue in the past, it is less so now and with the rise of gender mainstreaming and engendering development a 'gender perspective' is standard within many international NGOs and agencies and increasingly applied in the disaster context. What this means in practice will now be considered.

GENDER ISSUES IN RECONSTRUCTION

In the contemporary post-disaster context, studies suggest women are included in the reconstruction projects being targeted as beneficiaries and participants. For example, an evaluation of projects post Mitch financed with funds through DEC (ECA 2000) concluded that the projects 'tended to favour women and children in the distribution of products and services' and that women were included as

- Beneficiaries of the self-construction of houses with the title issued in the woman's name
- Participants in construction projects (roads, houses, bridges), which helped break certain stereotypes concerning their capacity to work
- Beneficiaries of productive programmes in order to reduce their economic vulnerability. These included: chicken rearing, agricultural projects, the manufacturing of cement blocks for construction and agricultural aid.

Women were also recipients of direct economic aid when, within a packet of cash given to each household, an amount was allocated directly to women. Some evaluations mentioned this as marking 'a step forward for the women' and that the money was spent effectively in the case of 'consolidated' marriages. However, it was also recognised that such packets of economic aid for women do not help the women free themselves from the 'oppressive power structures' in the household and in the community (ECA 2000). The evaluation suggests the focus of reconstruction overall was on employment and equality, or very much a WID approach, while the power structures at the base of women's lack of equality of access were not tackled. Tackling these would have a required a different 'Gender and Development' (GAD) approach to gender and reconstruction (see Chapter 3).

While the majority of projects have a practical focus some do appear to have a more 'strategic' component. However, even projects that seem to be explicitly promoting women's strategic interests – ensuring their right to own property, for example – on closer examination may not have women's empowerment as their intended outcome, as the following quote from an NGO employee working in Nicaragua post Mitch illustrates: 'Assigning the title deeds of the new houses to the women within the community assembly has been a new experience … We explain that it is a way of protecting the children' (Bradshaw 2001b: 74). Providing title of housing to women was in this case a means of ensuring security for children – security of children was the aim and women were the mechanism by which to achieve this. Post event, it is not unusual for international organisations to grant title to new housing to women but even such a seemingly good idea is not without problems. For example, when women have title to the house, men may see women as having financial responsibility also, including responsibility for household bills, and they may withdraw their economic and physical support in the home. Providing title in both names, another option, leads to problems should the couple choose to separate, not least since patriarchal legal and moral systems will rarely support women's claims, if a woman feels she can make the claim in the first place. Rights to land and property are a complex issue and issuing a title does not change the underlying social factors that determine who is seen to have the 'right' to title, which is decided through fulfilling socially determined obligations.

Disasters that impact on the amount or quality of land available raise issues around land rights and how these are governed. In many developing world nations 'customary law' has a greater relevance in determining land rights than statutory or state laws. While often perceived to be 'backward', customary tenure systems are as diverse as the property relations they embody (Cornhiel and Garcia Frias 2005). As they tend to be premised on land as a social relationship, rather than a market or exchange relationship, they can actually afford women greater room for manoeuvre in negotiating access to land than market-based systems (Action Aid 2006). Indirect rights that women may have under customary laws may be eroded through processes that see land become a marketable asset. Processes post disaster may hasten this move to market-based land systems and represent a key challenge to women's livelihoods and land rights.

Those without land are generally those without power in a society, and those without power are those without land, whatever the land tenure system. This helps explain why women, who typically have less power, have less 'rights' to land. Although no reliable figures exist, it is estimated that land ownership by women is less than 10 per cent worldwide (FAO 2002: 14). This is in contrast to estimates that 50 per cent of the total workload in planting and in care for domestic animals in Sub-Saharan Africa is carried out by women, while in Asia an estimated 50 per cent of food is produced by women (GTZ 1999). Women, then, work the land but do not own it. This lack of landownership has important consequences for them and the household. There is an opportunity, post disaster, to question who owns land, why and how, and on improving women's ownership rights.

However, promoting women's rights to land, especially by international agencies, often meets with resistance and, more generally, conflict commonly arises over land post disaster (FAO 2006). An implicit assumption within the arguments against women's land rights is that women are less efficient farmers than men. While women may lack the technical knowledge men have, due to gender discrimination in education and training, women do have knowledge of traditional process and may farm in a more environmentally efficient manner. Moreover, women already contribute to agriculture but their work often goes unrecognised and unremunerated. Giving women an incentive to improve agricultural output through ownership would improve the efficiency and productivity of land use, not reduce it. Another argument, put forward by those who oppose women inheriting land, is that land is a finite resource and inheritance leads to the fragmentation of land and may lead to plot sizes too small to be efficient. To confer title on women is seen to jeopardise the sustainability of rural families and family life. It is interesting to note that land owned by the male head is presented as being the 'family plot' but, when land is discussed in relation to establishing women's independent rights to land, it is often presented as if it were a move toward 'individualising ownership' and it is opposed on the grounds it will take land away from the family (Deere and León 2001). This is, of course, not backed up by research and it is women who are found to use disposable resources for the good of the wider family, or display altruistic behaviour, more than their male counterparts. Since any resources, when placed in the hands of women, are generally used to improve the welfare of the household overall and particularly children in the household, establishing women's rights to land could reduce women's and the household's risk of poverty and deprivation. Studies suggest that even access to a small, unviable piece of land, when used in conjunction with other livelihood strategies, may improve the situation of a poor household. Moreover, resources, such as land, held in the name of the woman improves her bargaining position within the household, and thus her ability to influence the use of household resources more generally. Studies then do suggest there are benefits to be gained from women having independent rights to land (see Agarwal 2003; Deere and León 2001) and these are both efficiency and equality gains, or practical and strategic benefits.

Finding funding for addressing strategic rather than practical needs, post event, tends to be difficult. Women leaders in Honduras, Nicaragua and El Salvador all agreed that following Mitch it was even more difficult to obtain financing for 'strategic' gender projects than before the event (Bradshaw 2004a). Moreover, as one women's organisation notes, 'we have found that the training (conscious-raising activities) is not the women's priority right now. Their priority is survival, being in business, looking for a penny to live off, and no matter how interesting the training might be, it will always be last on the scale of priorities' (Bradshaw 2001b: 75). Reconstruction raises questions about the extent to which women want to, and are able to, engage in projects that do not produce a real benefit in terms of providing resources for the household. On the other hand, while the inclusion of women in reconstruction efforts is to be welcomed, a question is raised about the extent to which a focus on women's 'practical' needs can bring about a transformation in gender relations. It is also important to note that, if practical resources are provided to women without attention to how gender relations operate within households, this allocation to women may not bring any more benefits to them or the home than giving the resources to men: women may hand the cash allocated to them to the male head, or they may be coerced into doing so. There is a real possibility that such programmes may generate conflicts within couples over the use of the resources, as has been found when funds have been targeted at women in social protection programmes such as Conditional Cash Transfer programmes (see Bradshaw 2008; Bradshaw and Quirós Víquez 2008; Molyneux 2006). Merely handing cash to women does not change the patriarchal structures that dictate who controls it within the household – it provides access to, but not control over, resources. Thus gender relations remain unchanged. To understand post-disaster gender relations demands an understanding of household functioning and how this may be affected, and affect, projects for reconstruction.

Although popular at one time, unitary models of household functioning (see Becker 1981, 1991) have generally been replaced by non-unitary models based on bargaining and the ideas of cooperative-conflict (see Agarwal 1997; Sen 1987, 1990a). The members of a household seek to improve both their own situation and the household's collective 'welfare' but household resources are finite, and there exist differing preferences among household members for how resources are used, so there is underlying conflict between those cooperating. The resolution of differences is the result of the each member's negotiating capacity or 'bargaining power' which, in turn, is based on the perceived relative contribution to the household of each. Income is often the key contribution valued by the household and consequently women are often in a weaker bargaining position than men. Blumberg's (1991) 'Gender Stratification Theory' suggests that the greater women's relative economic power, the greater their control over their own lives. However, as Mies' (1982) classic study highlighted, women do not always benefit as much as might be expected from their income generating work, if the work they do is considered to be an extension of their reproductive activities or as merely supplementing the male earnings. Even when women take on traditionally 'male' jobs, the outcome might be to reduce the 'worth' of that occupation rather than increase women's value in the household (Deere and León 1982).

Post disaster, the extent to which changing gender roles, for example, by women being trained to construct houses, will bring about changes in gender relations is open to question, and will depend on how these jobs and the resources they generate are valued. It is the relative value attached to what each member brings to the household that is important. Although each person's perception of his or her own contribution is important, other people's perceptions, both inside and outside the household, also have an influence. Social norms such as prejudice against women being in public spaces, for example, or factors such as external support systems, may be important in how women perceive their contribution and how others perceive it. Social norms may mean that men undervalue women's contribution, while women may place a higher value on the contribution of the male than on their own, even when their economic contribution is similar or even higher. To Bruce (1989: 988), it is not women's income *per se* that is important but the extent to which they can, through this, move out of confined roles and see themselves differently.

Any changes in women's roles, which change positively how women are seen and valued, may be important in terms of bargaining power, and thus change positively their status within the household. Post disaster, these changes may come from coping strategies adopted by households or from formal and informal aid programmes and projects. Such projects can influence coping strategies and can also change the distribution of resources within and among households. Donor organisations, while recognising the importance of the strategies adopted by the households, have not tended to consider the impact that their own programmes have in terms of the process of negotiating roles and relations within households. They, as with other policy and project evaluations, have tended to stop at the front door.

Disasters set in process a chain of events that may impact not just on women's practical life but also gendered identities or what it means to be a woman. The following case study, drawing on collaborative studies by the author in post-Mitch Nicaragua, including a national level survey (CIET/CCER 1999a, 1999b) and an in-depth study of four communities (Bradshaw 2001a, 2001b, 2002b), seeks to explore the gendered household processes set up by post-disaster reconstruction.

THE IMPACT OF RECONSTRUCTION ON WOMEN AND HOUSEHOLDS: THE CASE OF NICARAGUA

... what aid are they giving the people? They send them to collect stones and sand, to make adobe and terraces and build houses. What kind of a favour are they doing them? (Opinion on participating in reconstruction projects post Mitch)

While concerns have been expressed in the past about women being excluded from relief and reconstruction initiatives, Mitch suggests that this lesson had been learnt and high levels of female participation were found. The nature of women's inclusion in reconstruction, and the implications of Mitch and its aftermath for women, are relatively well documented (Bradshaw 2001a, 2001b, 2002b; Cupples 2007; Delaney and Shrader 2000). Post-Mitch research also highlights that each woman will have her own subjective experience of a disaster or post-disaster period that cannot be generalised, and that the same event may be both positively and negatively understood by women over time and space (Cupples 2007). For example, one woman interviewed seemed to have ambivalent feelings around the death of her husband, since life without him was more 'peaceful', the word peaceful often being used by women to mean living without violence. One lesson to be drawn from this is the need to examine carefully the varied understandings of such events as 'disasters' (see Chapter 1).

Women were targeted by agencies and NGOs post Mitch and, when asked in an in-depth community study, over half the women felt it was women who were participating most in reconstruction (Bradshaw 2001b). However, only a quarter felt that women benefited most from the projects. This may be explained by the fact that projects were most often designed to meet women's practical needs, providing, through women, resources for the family and most notably children. Such projects may place extra time burdens on women and may reinforce existing gender roles rather than challenge them. The example of land and housing may also help explain why women felt they gained little personally.

A national level survey found a higher proportion of female than male-headed households received help with housing (CIET/CCER 1999b) and a similar proportion of female heads as male heads also received help in order to sow their land. However, within the population, women heads represent only around a third of all households. Given cultural norms, they represent an even smaller proportion of farmers. As there is no data to suggest that female heads were disproportionably affected by Mitch, the targeting of female heads seems to be related more to the agencies' priorities than actual losses. While the projects were targeted at women, they were not necessarily based on a gendered understanding of needs. For example, women received less financial aid, but more aid in the form of inputs (generally, seeds), despite the fact that female heads of household need to pay farm labourers to do certain kinds of work and have a lower level of accumulated experience. This may explain why a smaller proportion of women heads sowed in the year following Mitch and more female heads continued to live off donations compared to households headed by a man. Female heads were also the beneficiaries of housing. Yet, while benefiting in material terms, fewer female than male heads felt that their opinion had been taken into account about where to build the new housing, and even fewer about how to build new housing (Bradshaw 2001b).

Thus women were beneficiaries rather than participants in reconstruction. Whether this suggests adoption of a 'gender perspective' to reconstruction is therefore questionable. The representative from one well-known international NGO suggested that: 'we have positively discriminated towards women. Some of the resources to rehabilitate livelihoods we have given to the women'. When asked how men had reacted to this focus on women, she commented that there had not been any major problems since 'the women have their cows and the men are drinking the milk' (Bradshaw 2001a: 83). It would appear that while a large number of projects post Mitch trumpeted their gender perspective, in many cases this thinly conceals the real focus on women as efficient service providers for the family, including men (see Chapter 3).

Women's involvement in reconstruction may also have indirect, and potentially negative, outcomes. The literature suggests that, as part of coping strategies, women will enter into productive work or diversify their productive activities. The studies found that female heads did continue in income generating activities, finding what alternatives they could, often outside of the community. Post Mitch, they were both more likely to be involved in employment and reconstruction than women with male partners. Despite this increased and diversified workload, the research suggests a decline in female heads' perceptions of their own contribution to the household, with more female heads of household stating that someone else in the household, usually an adult son, was making the most important contribution after Mitch (see Bradshaw 2002b).

In terms of women with a male partner, the proportion in productive activities declined post Mitch, both in absolute numbers and relative to men's employment. This may be due to the nature of the work available since, if it was outside the community, men were disinclined to let 'their' wife work away from home and from their control. As one woman put it, 'I want to work, to have my own money, but he doesn't like the idea. He asks me why, and it's true, I don't lack anything' (Bradshaw 2001b: 45). It seems that the event was used by some men to reinforce 'traditional' women's roles, rather than to transform them. One important outcome post Mitch was that a larger proportion of households relied on a single, male, income earner. This, once again, typically reduces women's access to, and control over, household resources and increases their dependency.

This dependency on men was, and had been before Mitch, more noticeable among a particular group of women – young women (25 years old or younger) living with a male partner (see Bradshaw 2002b). That is, young women at the early stage of their 'life course'. Young women were less likely to be engaged in income generating activities both before and after the hurricane, perhaps due to having young children, and fewer participated in reconstruction. Nearly 80 per cent named the man as the person who contributed most to the household (compared to 50 per cent of older women) and this increased even more after Mitch. Moreover, in over half the households of women under 25 years old, the man bought the food, compared to only 25 per cent of households where the women was older. If a woman does not work and she does not buy the food, she does not have any access to money on a day to day basis. This seems to be the case for over half of these young women. This, coupled with the low levels of young women in productive work or participating in activities outside the home such as reconstruction, could help to explain their perception of the ability of women to survive alone, without a husband or partner. While a third of older women thought that a woman could not survive alone without a man, almost half the younger women were of this opinion. This suggests young women with male partners might be a group that should be the focus of projects addressing 'strategic gender interests' post event, yet this rarely occurs.

However, an important question raised by the in-depth community research post Mitch concerns the costs involved in participating in reconstruction. Female heads of household appear, perhaps through lack of choice, to have been engaged in both productive work and reconstruction activities post Mitch, with a cost in terms of time, increasing their work burden and elongating their working day, and an associated potential cost in terms of health and well being. In contrast, women with a male partner were less likely to return to income generating activities post Mitch. It remains unclear whether they were able to become involved in reconstruction projects because they were no longer engaged in income generating activities, or whether their inclusion in projects effectively negated their ability to undertake productive work. Their ability to lengthen their working day might be limited by the need to attend to their husband's needs, and his expectations about the home and a woman's role in the home. Those women who did substitute productive work with participation in projects, for whatever reason, may also have faced well-being costs since, while there may be a trade-off between work and participation, the two activities were not always viewed as of equal value by all involved. Men in particular often do not value women's work that does not bring an income into the home, and the study suggested that this appeared to include project work, where the benefit is 'in kind' or non-monetary. In contrast, women appear to have valued their involvement in reconstruction and the resources this brought to the home, with this appearing to translate into an improved perception of themselves as having a greater voice in the home.

The research shows that in the pre-hurricane context, for women with a male partner, the perception of the man as the main contributor to the household was strong, especially among young women. Responses about the post-Mitch situation showed changes in perceptions and more women partners stated that it was they who made the most important contribution to the household after Mitch, despite the decreasing proportion actually involved in income generating activities. This may seem strange but may be explained by the value placed by women on their involvement in reconstruction – for the resources it brings, if not to them, then to the household. However, these views may not be shared by their male partners. As one man, when asked who works hardest, notes: 'the man, because he takes responsibility for everything, for working in the fields, and he's head of the house and if there's something lacking it's the man who has to see to it. The women hardly ever think about those things, they just make tortillas and cook the beans and rice.' This, despite the fact that he also noted that 'the women get up at four in the morning and are still working at eight at night. So women do work a lot' (Bradshaw 2001b: 106). Women's unpaid or community work, then, is undervalued compared to men's 'productive' work.

Where women's male partners were also interviewed, high levels of disagreement were found on many issues. Only about half of the couples interviewed shared the same opinion around issues such as who made the most important contribution to the household, or who was the key decision-maker in the household. Post-disaster changes in perceptions of ideas around contribution may actually increase conflict between couples, as men's and women's opinions diverge (see Chapter 7). That being said, the situation is not straightforward. The research further suggests that projects with a more 'practical' needs focus may not result in conflict between men and women but may be related to violence against women, while projects with a more 'strategic' focus, that is, those that focus more on training and awareness raising, may provoke greater levels of conflict within households which does not necessarily translate into violence against women. That is, projects that focus on monetary resources alone may be more likely to result in violence within the home. Thus the nature of the project may be important in not only determining if women's gender relations are transformed or reinforced, but if they are actually worsened through violence. These issues will be explored further in the next chapter.

DRAWING THE LINKS: RECONSTRUCTION FOR TRANSFORMATION?

Post-disaster reconstruction is often thought to provide a 'window of opportunity' for transforming societies not only physically through the built environment, but also socially through changing gender roles and relations. However, examples of where this social transformation has occurred are limited. It has been suggested that reconstruction reflects the social and political ideals of a society or the values it wishes to maintain so it is perhaps not surprising that what is constructed is a re-construction of what existed beforehand. The violent destruction of buildings, land and lives does not necessarily change the way men and women view gendered roles and relations. While they may seek to construct new and better buildings, and to transform old transport systems, they may actively seek to reconstruct the social certainties of the past, including gendered roles, relations and identities.

Change may, in fact, come about in gender roles but if they are understood as a temporary response to the disaster then gender relations may remain unchanged. Even when women take on male roles, what this may demonstrate is how gendered roles shift and change, while gendered identities absorb the new roles leaving their meaning unchanged. That is, even though women are working and rebuilding and caring for home and community, and men may not have returned to their former activities as farmers and fishermen, ideas of contribution and who does most do not always change, nor always change drastically, nor always in the ways expected. These changes may also not be the same for all people.

It is important to bear in mind that societies are not homogeneous but made up of heterogeneous groups, and within groups – such as women – there are differences. The notions of reconstruction and transformation are subjective, and individual experiences of reconstruction will be subjective also. While providing new roles for some women, reconstruction may reinforce gender roles for others. Different women will experience change differently and it cannot be assumed that disasters provide a window of opportunity to all women. Even if there is an opportunity for change, and women see and take this opportunity, unless male partners support this change, or at least recognise it has occurred, seizing the opportunity may have negative rather than positive outcomes. Some change in roles may occur but while the focus of projects remains on 'reconstruction', and on practical gender needs, rather than 'transformation', and engaging with women's strategic gender interests, relations may at best remain the same and they may also deteriorate. The next chapter explores in more depth two issues that may arise post event as a consequence of reconstruction, which may have important, long-term, and negative consequences for women.

7. Case studies of secondary disasters

INTRODUCTION

This chapter will provide short case studies of some issues that may arise post event and have such negative consequences that they become 'secondary disasters'. Secondary disasters are more usually seen to be events triggered by a natural hazard that causes collateral damage, such as a fire sparked by an earthquake. Since a fire may cause more damage to properties and threaten lives more than the earthquake itself, the term 'secondary' does not refer to scale but rather sequencing. It is a damaging event triggered by the initial hazard. More recently, social research has highlighted that secondary disasters are not only physical events but can be social events also. Two such potential secondary disasters will be explored here – psychosocial impact and violence. The two are linked through the fact that they have an impact on women in particular. They raise the issue of what is the 'disaster' – the physical impact and loss of land and possessions, or a more intangible 'secondary' impact such as higher levels of violence and poor mental health?

VIOLENCE

> It has been suggested that one in three women around the world will be raped, beaten, coerced into sex or otherwise abused at some stage in her lifetime. (UNIFEM 2003)

Exact data on the prevalence and incidence of violence against women is patchy and often unreliable. This is because many women suffer in silence and do not report cases and, related to this, because legal systems often do not see such violence as a serious crime, if a crime at all. The term 'domestic violence' captures the fact that violence against women usually occurs in the domestic realm, the home. It also draws a distinction between 'violence' in general and violence against women. The latter being 'domestic' – something that is mundane, everyday, something that is a private issue, a matter for a man and 'his' wife. This is one of the reasons why many feminists and gender activists no longer use the term 'domestic violence' and instead prefer to use the terms 'Gender Based Violence' or 'Violence Against Women'.

The term, Gender Based Violence (GBV), was developed to capture a wide range of violations of women's human rights, including trafficking in women and girls, rape, sexual abuse of children, and harmful cultural practices and traditions that irreparably damage girls' and women's reproductive and sexual health. It also recognises that violence may be an explicit strategy for domination and control and violence against women, especially rape, may be used as a 'weapon of war' (see Chapter 5). The 1993 United Nations Declaration of the Elimination of Violence against Women suggests that the term Violence Against Women (VAW) means 'any act of gender-based violence that results in, or is likely to result in, physical, sexual or psychological harm or suffering to women, including threats of such acts, coercion or arbitrary deprivations of liberty, whether occurring in public or in private life'. That is, violence is not confined to a physical act but the threat of such an act, and not confined to physical pain, but also emotional harm.

How VAW is conceptualised has changed over time, not only in terms of the language used but the wider rhetoric. Perhaps most importantly, there has been recognition that women are entitled to live free from violence as a 'right'. In general terms, the 1990s witnessed a 'rise of rights' (Eyben 2003) as many organisations and international development agencies adopted some form of 'rights-based approach' to development (Molyneux and Lazar 2003; Piron 2005). While the rights-based approach has not been without its critics (see IDS 2005; Molyneux and Cornwall 2008), the potential of rights for increasing the recognition of women's demands as legitimate claims has made it particularly attractive to women's movements, and some of the most effective organising over the past twenty-five years has been around rights-related claims (Antrobus 2004a; Ruppert 2002). This being said, in recent years at a global and local level there has been an encroachment on the gains made. In particular, the lack of gendered rights, rights related to gender inequality and women's autonomy, within the Millennium Development Goals has caused concern among feminists and gender activists (WICEJ 2004). Rights-based approaches have also come under attack, with critiques from within the feminist movement (see Tsikata 2004).

It is suggested that rights are being technically packaged in ways that ignore discussions of legitimacy and, in particular, power (Pettit and Wheeler 2005) and that rights-based approaches are depoliticising (Bracke 2004). While stating a right as a right provides legitimacy, it also sidesteps discussions over that legitimacy. This is important since to uphold a woman's right to live free from violence demands a change in social norms and relations, and this implies a rebalancing of unequal power relations. If issues of power are not explicitly discussed then change will not come about. That is, while many agree with women's right to live free from violence, few discuss what this would actually mean and how it can practically be obtained. Research from Nicaragua highlights how the notion of 'rights' can mean little in reality (Bradshaw 2012, 2013). For example, when asked if a woman has the right to decide about her own body, women almost universally (96 per cent) agreed they have the 'right to decide'. However, a quarter of older rural women thought a women should have sex with her husband even if they don't want to, questioning what the 'right to decide' actually means to them. Moreover, a third of men disagreed that a woman has the right to decide over her own body. Not only does this suggest the right would be difficult to fulfil in practice but questions the legitimacy of the 'right' in the first place, as least as understood by men.

While critiques of the rights approach are valid, it does not negate advances made to promote women's rights. The fact that violence against women has become an issue of rights has meant that so too has it become a development issue, even if it is a contested one. However, it is important to be clear that violence is not a developing world nor a poverty issue, but is prevalent across all countries and all classes (Morrison, Ellsberg and Bott 2007). Violence may be understood through consideration of individual and societal root causes, such as psychological factors or patriarchal norms, and as triggered by risk factors such as male alcohol and substance abuse, unemployment or having lived with and witnessed violence as a child. One study of five Latin American and Caribbean countries found partner alcohol abuse had the strongest and most consistent effect of all factors examined on the likelihood of women experiencing violence (Flake and Forste 2006). Other studies have also found that women blame alcohol for male violence against women and tend to see this as the root cause rather than looking at what causes men to drink or what causes some to be violent when they do drink (Bradshaw 2002a; Busby 1999). As one Nicaraguan man interviewed after Hurricane Mitch notes: 'after the hurricane ... It was because I felt weak, battered, and I had a few drinks ... and the woman imagines that just by having a drink that man's a goner, he's not worth anything anymore' (Bradshaw 2001b). What triggers violence is often rooted in perceived challenges to gender norms or patriarchal power. This may stem from men feeling they are not able to fulfil their socially prescribed roles as providers. On the other hand it may be triggered by women's actions if they are seen to challenge male power. These may be as simple as not having food ready on time, failing to care 'adequately' for the children or home, questioning a man about money or girlfriends, going somewhere without his permission, or refusing him sex (Heise et al. 2002).

The debate around what causes VAW echoes the debates discussed in Chapter 3 about what explains the construction of gender identities (see O'Toole and Schiffman 1997). On the one hand, male violence can be interpreted as 'natural' and rooted in biological differences. This suggests that all men have the potential to be violent and suggests there is little ability to change the situation. The second explanation views violence as a male attribute which is learned or socialised and thus moves the focus away from the individual male to the patriarchal social structures that create and define maleness. Feminists favour this latter view since it suggests room for change. Pickup et al. (2001) refines this, and outlines three related elements that account for violence against women. First, a psychological element or an 'impaired masculinity' often thought to have been learnt through being abused or witnessing abuse when growing up. The second element recognises violence as an assertion of power and control to maintain patriarchal systems and in response to challenges to this, including women's employment. However, it should be noted that women's income generation activities can have positive as well as negative effects depending on the context. Similarly, the third element mentioned by Pickup et al., external factors such as poverty and low education levels, is not straightforward. For example, poverty in itself is not a cause of violence but rather it may aggravate or increase violence that already exists. However, evidence does exist that external factors such as political violence may mean the incidence of other forms of violence are also high (Flake and Forste 2006; Messing 1999).

It is not surprising that violence after a disaster is said to increase, given that external factors such as poverty, challenges to patriarchal power such as changing gender roles, and witnessing or living in a context of violence may all trigger violence against women. While not questioning the importance of considering the incidence of VAW in all relief and reconstruction efforts (see Phillips et al. 2010), and seeking to reduce this through mitigation projects, care does need to be exercised around how VAW is understood in the post-disaster context. Data on violence is often missing prior to an event but post-event data is even less readily available and it comes from a variety of sources and takes a variety of forms.

Early 'evidence' of violence rested on the assumptions that theoretically we might expect to see an increase in violence or that violence has become more visible (Merton 1970). However, from the start authors noted that for violence to increase there must be other factors present, that is, the disaster in itself was not enough to 'cause' violence (Barton

1970). The factors that make a person vulnerable to a natural hazard, such as poverty or positive HIV status, for example, may also make them more likely to live with violence.

Studies that have sought to collect data on violence have done so through a variety of means. For example, early studies from the US focused on community organisations, including those with 'domestic violence' programmes, and their perceptions and responses to (increases) in violence. They provided some evidence of increases in calls to helplines, reported cases including sexual assaults, and cases being taken to court or seeking injunctions (Wilson et al. 1998; Morrow 1997), increased demands on domestic violence programmes (Enarson 1999) and a general feeling among social service providers that violence had increased (Morrow and Enarson 1996). These findings were echoed by Houghton's (2009) more recent qualitative study in New Zealand and post-Katrina narratives (Brown 2012). Other qualitative work includes Fothergill's (1999) rich insight into how two women experienced and made sense of violence after the Grand Forks flood, while Jenkins' and Phillips' (2008) work highlights the difficulties faced by women living with, and who have escaped from, violence both during and after Hurricane Katrina.

Studies of violence post disaster have, then, tended to be qualitative in nature and have focused on the developed world. Disasters in the developing world have produced reports of high levels of violence but not necessarily research by which to substantiate these claims. For example, de Silva (2006: 66) suggests that during the tsunami in Sri Lanka 'many young girls were lured by men with the promise of taking them to safety and raped even on roof tops'. However, no evidence is provided to support this claim. This is not to question that such events did occur, nor the seriousness of the claims being made, but rather to highlight the need for more, and for more systematic research on this important issue. One study that sought to quantify changes in violence was the Nicaraguan Social Audit (CIET/CCER 1999a, 1999b). This national level survey of low income communities affected by Hurricane Mitch asked respondents if they felt violence against women had increased, decreased or remained the same after the hurricane. The data offered no clear answer: 21 per cent perceived an increase; 32 per cent thought it has stayed the same; and 34 per cent saw a decline. It could be read as suggesting 'a third see a decline' or as 'two thirds think it is the same or increased'. While inconclusive in terms of incidence, the value of the study lies not with the 'answers' it generated but the questions it raises.

A first question might be, 'given the reports of high levels of violence by NGOs after recent large-scale events, why are the figures from the

Nicaraguan Social Audit so low?' There are a number of inter-related responses. The answer might lie in the design of the study. This was one question on a short questionnaire and the question asked women and men if they thought physical violence against women had increased in their community. Unlike other US studies, it did not ask service providers, but the people themselves. It did not ask about their situation, but their community. It asked men and women. Considering women's responses alone increase the proportion who perceived violence to have increased to 33 per cent (with only 17 per cent of men suggesting an increase). What is important to remember, then, is who is asked, and how they are asked will influence the response.

The study may not have found a large increase since it was not measuring a change from a base line but asking people if they perceived change. This highlights a common problem – the lack of baseline data on the incidence and prevalence of violence before an event makes it difficult to measure change after it. Even more difficult to know are the processes that have led to any change. For example, a study in Nicaragua asked about perceived changes in conflict in the home and violence against women post hurricane Mitch (Bradshaw 2001a, 2001b, 2002b). While factors such as having suffered material loss or reporting emotional impact did not influence perceptions of a change in the number of arguments in the community or of incidents of violence, the study did find that those who thought there had been problems over reconstruction were more likely to think violence against women had increased and also that arguments in the home had increased. However, there was no significant relationship between the perception that arguments had increased and evidence that violence had increased. The intuitive notion that frustration with projects leads to arguments, which leads to violence is not demonstrated and the findings highlight the fact that the process by which violence is provoked is not clear-cut or straightforward.

This study supports the idea that disasters do not cause violence but, rather, may provide conditions conducive to violence. Disasters may provide triggers that, in turn, set off violence. For example, men who feel they have failed their families through not protecting them may seek solace in alcohol, and this may be a trigger for violence against a wife or child. Living conditions post event, particularly communal living in refuges and camps where women may continue with their role while that of male is subsumed by the camp, may also be important in explaining NGO and agency reports of high levels of violence. While less well documented, or perhaps less acceptable to document, incidents of violence against children at the hands of their parents, including their mothers, may also rise (Enarson 2012).

Care needs to be taken about suggesting that the 'high' levels of violence witnessed are unusual. It could be argued that in fact disasters, or their aftermath, reveal existing actual levels of violence or the potential for violence. Those who are displaced and forced to live communally may continue to carry on their private lives in public, including violence. There may be a shift in private violence being made public, which echoes the shift from private to public living. There may also be a shift from private to public violence as part of changing patterns of patriarchal control.

It is not only violence at the hands of a known male in the home that it is suggested increases after disasters, but also violence by unknowns outside the home. This may particularly be the case in large-scale camps set up for people to seek refuge. There has been documentation of abuse of women and girls in camps during conflict situations, both by men from the same and different ethnic groups. There have also been instances of protectors turning perpetrators, including UN officials (see Chapter 5). But, even outside conflict situations, there are reports of physical and sexual abuses occurring in large camps, as for example in the football stadium 'refuges' set up post Mitch in Honduras and also post Katrina in New Orleans. Again, rather than seeing the disaster as to blame, it may be better seen as providing a context conducive to violence. Women and girls are left without the usual protection of a husband, brother or father and at the same time are outside the home and the community. The usual social controls are lost and social rules no longer seen to apply.

Of course the revelation of violence in a public space also brings with it new opportunities to address that violence. As Wilson et al. (1998) noted, the way violence is addressed or even recognised post disaster may be heavily influenced by the situation pre-disaster. What is seen to be 'normal' in the home may be seen differently, both by the woman and those around her, when exercised publicly. In camps and refuges there may also be a means to address the violence quickly and effectively through camp officials and those 'policing' the camp. There may also be an opportunity to promote change, as the case of the campaign post Hurricane Mitch by the feminist organisation *Puntos de Encuentro* demonstrates, with its slogan 'Violence Against Women: A disaster men CAN prevent' (see Puntos de Encuentro website, also PAHO 2003). Rather than focusing on the illegality of violence and what a women could do if she was living with violence, the posters, billboards, calendars and other materials noted things men could do if they started to feel angry, that is, how they could prevent themselves from becoming violent.

The policing of violence has been shown to be not enough to deal with violence. While making violence against women illegal is a hugely important first step, there are questions over the extent to which achieving a legal right actually allows rights fulfilment (Bradshaw et al. 2008). While it is important for women to claim their right through using the judicial system, at the same time limitations to making a claim on the legal system exist, both in terms of the belief that the system can protect women and in terms of what this 'protection' means. Instead, for many feminists it is fundamental for a woman's realisation of her rights that she understands that violence is not acceptable or there is a change in how violence is conceptualised. This more strategic aim does need to be accompanied by attention to practical needs and in order to escape violence women need more than a law, they need to be able to live independently and, more importantly, to believe they can live independently. This suggests that if women are going to fulfil their right to live free from violence a holistic approach to addressing violence is needed with a complementary focus on economic skills training, and on associated rights such as land rights, and also emotional support through psychosocial services. It is to this latter issue of the psychosocial impact of a large-scale violent act that is addressed next.

PSYCHOSOCIAL IMPACT

Health: A state of complete physical, mental and social well-being, and not merely the absence of disease. (World Health Organization)

According to the 2001 World Health Report (WHR), neuropsychiatric disorders account for 12 per cent of the Global Burden of Disease, representing a burden greater than AIDS, TB and malaria combined and second only to infectious diseases. It has been suggested that at any time 450 million people worldwide are affected by mental, neurological or behavioural problems, and the rate is steadily rising (WHO 2006). Almost three quarters of the global burden of neuropsychiatric disorders occurs in low and middle-income countries or put simply, an estimated 80 per cent of people with mental health conditions live in low and middle-income countries (WHO 2010). Reliable figures do not exist but, in the developing world, it may be assumed that the number affected is greater than the 1 in 4 people suggested by the UK's national Psychiatric Morbidity Surveys (Meltzer et al. 1995; ONS 2000; Information Centre 2009). The lack of data, while part of the wider dearth of data for the developing world, is also related to the fact that an estimated one third of those suffering mental distress will not seek treatment. This may be due to the stigma attached to being 'mentally ill' but also due to the limited services available. Less than half of those who meet diagnostic criteria for psychological disorders are identified as such by doctors and research suggests that in developing countries between 76–85 per cent of serious cases of mental illness do not receive any treatment (WHO 2006). Serious mental disorders are not rare and in the UK, for example, it is suggested that 1 person in every 100 has a severe condition such as schizophrenia or bipolar disorder, and that every year more than 250 000 people are admitted to psychiatric hospitals. Estimates suggest almost one million people die due to suicide every year, with rates said to be increasing, and it is the third leading cause of death among young people (WHO 2001). Not only are there differences by age but also by gender: men are more prone to suicide than women. Women are more likely to be affected by anxiety and depression than men, who are more prone to suffer from substance abuse and anti-social personality disorders (see WHO nd).

Despite the prevalence of mental illness, it remains under resourced in the developed and the developing world and the WHO 'Mental Health Atlas' (2005) demonstrated that a large mental health resource gap exists, especially in the developing world countries. Since the late 1990s, mainstream development agencies have increasingly become interested in the issue and, for example, an international seminar to discuss the potential role of the World Bank concluded it should become 'more actively engaged' in the area (World Bank 2004). However, despite this, mental health is not something promoted under the Bank's lead poverty reduction strategy (Poverty Reduction Strategy Papers – PRSPs) policy and the PRSP 'Sourcebook' chapter on health only mentions mental health once, in relation to the costly nature of residential care facilities and the need to look for alternatives (Claeson et al. 2002: 221). The Bank recognises research that suggests that poor people are more likely to have symptoms of mental distress but its response tends toward an 'efficiency' approach, arguing that poor mental health can 'tip' people into poverty, highlighting the associated economic costs of mental disorders in terms of reduced productivity of the sufferer and carer(s) and the burden placed on health and social services.

Development might have been slow picking up on mental health but within disaster studies the issue has been recognised since disaster research began 50 years ago (Tierney 2000). However, as the WHO (2010) notes, despite the fact that their situations might worsen during the stress of emergencies, relief services remain inadequate at addressing the specific needs of people with mental and psychosocial disabilities.

While emergencies may exacerbate the conditions of those already suffering mental health problems, the causal link that suggests events cause mental health problems is far from proven. One thing noted by the literature is the positive effect collective action during and after a disaster can have, or the idea of the therapeutic community (see Chapter 4). This more positive understanding of the interaction between disasters and mental health, or at least a more balanced approach, is taken by what Tierney (2000) defines as 'sociologically-oriented' writers. They have tended to suggest that mental health issues that develop post event are comparatively rare and mild and also transient. Their understanding of psychological impact takes a psychosocial perspective – that is, it focuses on the broader social context and the trauma of the event itself. In contrast, she suggests that 'psychologically oriented' researchers have a tendency to characterise disasters as negative in their mental health effects, and see these as widespread, severe and with lasting consequences. Leon (2004) presents a useful summary of evidence on the extent to which disasters do bring extensive and long-lasting psychological effects. She notes there is 'strong documentation over numerous studies of the often profound and long-lasting psychological effects of disasters' and makes the important point that the effect is not just among the general public, but also disaster response personnel.

Reviewing the available data for Latin America shows a mixed picture (see Norris 2009). For example, a study by Caldera et al. (2001) in Nicaragua found 6 per cent of those studied six months after Hurricane Mitch showed symptoms of Post Traumatic Stress Disorder (PTSD), with half of these still fulfilling the criteria for a PTSD diagnosis one year after Mitch. A similar study in Tegucigalpa, Honduras three months after Hurricane Mitch found nearly double (11 per cent) the number with symptoms (Kohn et al. 2005). The variation in findings is illustrated by another study in Nicaragua focusing on young people, which found that 14–90 per cent of adolescents across the sites studied showing a range of symptoms (Goenjian et al. 2001). Very high rates of mental distress were also found one and a half years after an earthquake in Armenia in 1988 that killed 50 000 with 93.3 per cent of the elderly and 91.5 per cent of the children found to be still suffering from severe or very severe PTSD (data cited in Leon 2004). Such differences suggest caution is needed when discussing impact, and PTSD in particular, not least since, as Tierney (2000) suggests, psychologically oriented researchers may seek to 'diagnose' within existing categories and tend to look for, and find evidence of, PTSD.

Mental health disorders are not easy to diagnose, not least since many people attempt to hide their symptoms, do not seek professional help, and because symptoms may be mild, varied, and the onset delayed. For example, young people may display different symptoms to adults, and there is also variation between the very young and adolescents (Hamblen 2006). Young children for example may show increased dependency or become clingy and there may be regression in developmental actions as they return to behaviours they had previously 'grown out of'. Young adolescents tend to demonstrate minor deviant behaviour but the form this takes also depends on gender. Boys' behaviour tends to be more aggressive and anti-social, and they may take longer to recover. Girls are more verbal and show more distress. However, the long-term affect on young people is less well known. Overall, the literature suggests the majority of children and adolescents will eventually cope successfully (Benight and Bandura 2004). However, for some, there will be an increased risk of higher levels of anxiety and depression compared to children who have not experienced a disaster. Who is affected in the short and long term depends on a number of factors including personal loss, separation, family and community support, and pre-existing factors such as previous exposure to trauma, and factors related to age, race, and gender (see Osofsky et al. 2009).

Post Traumatic Stress Disorder (PTSD) is now a well-known condition and often assumed to be one that will occur after a traumatic event. However, as an edition of the PTSD Research Quarterly (2009: 1) dedicated to looking at the impact of disasters and political violence on mental health in Latin America, notes: 'cross-cultural understanding of PTSD is still in its infancy, a situation that often leads to epistemological debates that rely more heavily on accumulated wisdom than scientific evidence'. Questions about the cross-cultural validity of PTSD as a concept are considered in a study by Norris et al. (2001). The study asked 24 Mexican adults to describe, in their own words, the emotions they observed in themselves or others after disasters in their communities. Participants mentioned 14 of the 17 criterion symptoms of PTSD with little or no prompting. They also mentioned three reactions that, while linked to notions of trauma, could not be classified as specific criterion symptoms. Thus, since mental health can be experienced and understood in different ways, PTSD may not be a robust 'disease' or diagnosis, despite the scientific 'cloak'.

This is important since, if strict criteria are used to define illness, those that do not display the 'correct' symptoms may not be defined as 'ill' and thus not get the support they need. Of course, the opposite is also true: people who do not consider themselves to be ill may be told that they are. For example, history demonstrates that women have been diagnosed as 'ill' for displaying what we now see as perfectly reasonable 'symptoms' (Showalter 1985). The double standards of mental health and illness remain and there are still greater numbers of women than men in therapy, on psychiatric medication, or in mental hospitals (Ussher 1992; Chesler 1972).

Diagnosing people as 'ill' for displaying behaviour outside the 'norm' has wider implications for how they are seen and how they are treated. Such a diagnosis is not limited to women but also affects other groups such as ethnic 'minorities', and even whole regions. Bankoff (2001) notes how, although initially depicted as some sort of paradise, the tropics came to be constructed as diseased and dangerous by Western medical experts. The conceptual geography of Western medicine gradually rendered the whole area unsafe, only to make it progressively safer through offering a (Western) 'cure' for the regions' inherent dangers. As noted in Chapter 1, vulnerability to disease, much like vulnerability to disasters, can and has been used to justify Western interventions to bring about 'development'.

There is a need for care, then, when considering mental health and post-disaster mental health. One set of writers, rather than seeking a standard set of symptoms, have instead focused on understanding causes to contextualise diagnosis (Green 1982; Bolin 1988; Bolin and Bolton 1986; see Leon 2004 and Tierney 2000 for discussion). While differences exist between them, they have suggested some features of hazards that may potentially increase the probability of psychosocial problems. An event such as the collapse of the side of Volcano Casitas in Nicaragua, due to the heavy rains provoked by Hurricane Mitch, would be a good example of an event that might be expected to produce high levels of psychological impact. Within three minutes, the landslide that the collapse of the volcano wall provoked had reached and covered the two small towns at the base of the volcano, killing 2000 people. This event was terrifying, life-threatening, and it was unexpected and left no time to prepare or protect. It led to much, visible death, and it impacted the whole community. It destroyed two towns and killed all who were there at the time so reconstruction was slow and difficult. The event had all the features of a hazard with a high probability of causing psychosocial problems for those impacted. These characteristics can be summarised as related to preparedness, duration, exposure, and extent (see also Myers 1994).

Preparedness or, better put, a lack of preparedness, refers to the extent to which the event was sudden or unexpected, allowing little time to prepare. More generally, it is suggested that rapid onset events have different psychological outcomes than slow onset, technological threats, such as nuclear hazards. The latter are seen to be 'corrosive for communities' as they may engender conflict and undermine support systems. They cause longer-term anxiety as the threats associated with the hazard are ambiguous, who is exposed is unknown, and the impact of exposure is not known immediately (Tierney 2000).

It is not only the duration of the event itself that is important but also the duration of the negative affects or the speed with which people are able to return to 'normal' which also has an influence. This may be due to the occurrence of additional subsequent traumas and disruptions that require further coping (Green 1982 cited in Leon 2004) or it may be due to a lack of support, both social and governmental, making the process of reconstruction long and difficult. The Social Audit of post-Mitch Nicaragua highlighted the way that time spent in a refuge led to higher numbers of people reporting emotional effects independently of other losses (CIET/CCER 1999a, 1999b). Such further disruption, caused by the actions or inactions of responders, need to be considered as part of the event itself.

Leon (2004) suggests that the extent of exposure may be the key defining predictor of post-disaster stress and highlights the number of disaster-related deaths as important, while Bolin (cited in Tierney 2000) suggests that the amount of horror or terror people experience, and the level of feelings of imminent threat they cause, may have an important influence. A study in Tamil Nadu in India found that those who had experienced a personal injury during the tsunami were nearly three times as likely to exhibit PTSD symptoms, and those who had experienced a death in their family were more than twice as likely (Kumar et al. 2007). This supports the notion that personal exposure is important, that is, being injured. The data from Nicaragua showed that suffering material damage also resulted in higher proportions reporting emotional affect but found the single most important defining factor was bereavement. In 50 per cent of those households that had suffered loss of life, it was reported that someone had been impacted emotionally compared to 22 per cent in households with no loss of life. There was also a higher perception that those affected needed help (32 per cent reported a need for attention compared to 18 per cent where there was no loss of life) (CIET/CCER 1999a, 1999b).

The extent of the event (or exposure to it) is important not only in terms of how individuals are exposed, but also the spread of individuals exposed. Green (1982) proposed differentiating between a central as compared to a peripheral type of disaster, with the former being characterised as changing the entire physical and organizational structure of the community. This is supported by Bolin and Bolton (1986) who highlight the extent of disruption for the family, kin groups, and the community, and argues that the impact of these disruptions on social support systems are key factors in assessing long-term impact. That is, the greatest emotional impact will be registered when the resilience of a community or family is impacted, not just an individual. As noted previously, women's networks differ from, and operate differently to, men's and thus disruption to these networks and the consequences for emotional well being may also differ.

The Psychosocial Framework of the International Federation of Red Cross and Red Crescent takes a community-based approach and defines psychosocial support as 'a process of facilitating resilience within individuals, families and communities'. The focus is on facilitating community mobilisation and strengthening community relationships and networks. The Federation notes four different levels of needs and support, with level 1 being the provision of basic needs and level 4 being referral for professional psychological or psychiatric support. It stresses that outside this very specialised support for those most impacted, support should be delivered alongside other services. It summarises support as involving non-intrusive emotional support, coverage of basic needs, protection from further harm, and the organisation of social support and networks. To this end, it has produced a series of handbooks and training manuals for its staff so that they can train others, including community leaders (see IFRC 2009). As highlighted by the Federation by its Emergency Response Units, addressing psychosocial needs is based on the principle that most acute stress problems during emergencies are best managed without medication, following the principles of 'psychological first aid'.

An example of a community-focused response to the psychosocial impact of a disaster can be found post Hurricane Mitch. The initiative drew on both historical knowledge (from the revolutionary period) and international knowledge (through outside 'experts') to train a network of people in psychosocial support, who in turn shared that knowledge with others, such as teachers in communities affected by Mitch. The training workshops were led by national NGOs but sought to include state actors such as fire fighters and policemen and women in the training sessions. The initiative demonstrated the importance of collective work across organisations rather than work being centred on one organisation and it sought to establish alliances, national-local and local-local, as an integral element of the work. It is perhaps the most widely recognised achievement of civil society post Mitch (Bradshaw 2004b). Its longer-term impact was clear when people trained in Nicaragua were flown to El

Salvador after the earthquake there three years later to share their knowledge, establishing a regional chain of effect.

While the approach taken in such initiatives is at community level, it recognises that different people will react differently. It is important to remember that some people may be more pre-disposed to a negative psychological impact. If a collective response is important, then logically those with few support networks or familial support may be impacted more by the event. Individual personality traits such as resilience in the face of stress and effective coping skills also appear to be important for lessening impact.

It is suggested that more women than men will suffer psychological problems before and after events. The Nicaraguan survey showed that, overall, 24 per cent of people reported someone in their household as emotionally affected, with 74 per cent of those being women (CIET/ CCER 1999a, 1999b). Research in Palestine also points to men and women having different experiences of the same event and finding that, while men experience more traumatic events, exposure is associated with more severe psychiatric disorders among women (Punamäki et al. 2005). Why women may suffer more or more severely is less to do with them being women than to do with their position and situation in society as women. The study from Tamil Nadu (Kumar et al. 2007) showed PTSD was higher among individuals with no household incomes and those who were illiterate. Because women tend to occupy a lower socio-economic position than men they may be more susceptible to psychological problems. Emotional health is also related to physical health and, once again due to reproductive health risks and the social and economic limitations around dealing with these, women tend to be less physically well than men.

Support networks have been identified as important, and may also have a gendered aspect. It has been suggested that some cultures are better at dealing with events than others and different cultures deal with trauma differently (Wilson and Tang 2007). For example, if talking after an event is seen as important for the healing process, then those cultures where people talk to each other more may deal better with distress. While a popular stereotype is of 'gossiping' women, it is important to note that in many cultures women do not have the opportunity for such chatting having been allowed few friends through childhood or become isolated from friends on marriage (Bradshaw 2010a). Research after firestorms in the US showed that friendships could also change after an event, since those that have not lived through it are not seen as able to understand the feelings of those who have (Hoffman 1998). While this may mean a loss of friendship networks, it may also lead to new, supportive friendships being formed among survivors. However, it is also important to remember that while sharing experiences with others can decrease stress it can also normalise stress by constructing responses as being something all have to suffer and bear, leading to resignation. Relying on the support of family and friends can also have negative as well as positive consequences and, in situations where one party needs to be grateful to another, there may be a re-emergence of harmful social rules and obligations.

Thus post-event emotional feelings can differ between people and over time can change and be impacted by a number of secondary factors. The very act of surviving and how this is read by others can itself influence feelings. In cultures where survivors are seen, and see themselves, to be strong and brave and are honoured as such, there may be less emotional impact than where survival is associated with guilt. Thus feelings after an event may be ambiguous: one woman in post-Mitch Nicaragua noted that she felt peaceful, a feeling associated with the loss of her (abusive) husband during the hurricane. Once again, it is important to realise that the experience of a disaster, and indeed the extent to which an event is perceived to be, or bring, 'disaster', differs between individuals. It cannot and should not be assumed to be known before the event. While it is now assumed that there will be a negative psychosocial impact post event and that this needs to be catered for, care needs to be taken with this assumption since the evidence on which it is based, where it exists, tends to be from the West. The discussion highlights that despite the Western move toward a 'medicalisation of distress' (Summerfield 1999) it may be difficult to diagnose negative emotional impact because the 'appropriate' symptoms by which to do so may differ across cultures and by gender and generation. This being said, for those who survive and are severely emotionally impacted by the event, this impact may be greater than any economic impact. What the actual 'disaster' provoked by an event is, may not be clear at the time but, rather, will only be revealed as events unfold.

DRAWING THE LINKS: WHAT IS THE 'DISASTER'?

The case studies return us to the question raised in the first chapter – what is a 'disaster'? They highlight that disaster may be understood as the loss of possessions and livelihoods, or a more intangible loss of well being through experiencing violence or poor mental health. This calls into question the notion of these being 'secondary disasters'. They may instead suggest that they are the 'real' disaster, at least for women.

The case studies also highlight the fact that, in order to address the impact of disaster, individual responses are often not enough and a collective effort is needed to promote and establish rights, for example, or to ensure well being. This collective action may be key to achieving the transformations in gender relations so often suggested to be possible post disaster. It is collective action for change that will be considered in the next two chapters.

8. Political mobilisation for change

INTRODUCTION

As the previous chapters have shown, the impact of a disaster may be felt very much as, and by, individuals but the response usually involves collective action. Thus far this has been considered at the local or community level and in terms of practical actions for relief and reconstruction. However, collective action also occurs at the national level and actions may combine practical with more strategic or political elements. Not only do governments design and implement national reconstruction plans and lobby international governments and agencies to fund these, but other actors also work at the national and international level. Most notably civil society organisations advocate for certain ideas or perspectives to be taken into account. The importance of exogenous shocks to the political system in bringing change to it has been noted in the literature (Barrientos and Hulme 2008) and disasters are 'catalytic events' that can lead to collective action for change, with new actors becoming involved and new demands which can result in new and novel issues emerging onto the political agenda (Kreps 1998; Olson and Gawronski 2003).

This chapter uses the case study of Hurricane Mitch in Central America to explore the engagement of civil society in national level reconstruction and mitigation activities, and to consider the role of women within this. Mitch offers a good case study. The event provoked the formation of civil society coordinating bodies to respond to the crisis in each of the countries of the region so it is an example of widespread collective response. At least one of these coordinating bodies continued to function as a civil society policy think tank 15 years after the event, a longevity that is interesting to explore. The discussion of the formation and evolution of such civil society responses to events highlights some of the debates that surround organised civil society, particularly debates around the role of Non-Governmental Organisations (NGOs) in development, and also the notion of 'participatory processes' of policy design that includes non-governmental as well as governmental actors. While participation has been problematised in the development literature, now having as many critics as supporters, it is still presented as largely unproblematic within the disaster discourse, as a good thing and something to be encouraged, particularly in terms of women's participation. However, as the case study will highlight, women's participation should not be assumed to bring benefits to them and does not happen without personal cost for the women involved, a cost often not recognised or valued.

NATIONAL AND INTERNATIONAL PLANS FOR RECONSTRUCTION

Immediately after a large-scale event, particularly in the developing world, there is a heightened direct involvement by a wide range of 'outside' or international agencies and governments seeking to help in relief efforts. Often help from external governments is provided through their own personnel, using their own vehicles, and at times also involving their troops. These efforts, to the extent that they are coordinated, are coordinated through an international agency, usually the United Nations. Once the immediate crisis is over, people have been rescued, and the immediate threat has declined, the national government has the opportunity to regain some level of control. Governments, especially when an event has been nationwide, will look to develop a national plan for reconstruction that can be presented to international donors for funding. The role of international governments therefore declines or evolves, rather than disappears, since they still have an important role to play in funding reconstruction efforts. Their role, as discussed in Chapter 4, will vary according to what priority they give the country and the extent to which they are prepared to help finance reconstruction. It will also vary according to how much faith they place in the national government. As events such as the 2010 earthquake in Haiti demonstrate, at times, 'national' processes may be largely donor driven or even donor lead, rather than truly emerging from within the country. For example, Haiti's 'Action Plan' for national recovery set up a interim commission for reconstruction and stressed that the plan, despite the 'tight schedule', was Haitian since 'key sectors' of Haitian society were consulted. However, the commission that was set up was co-chaired by the Haitian prime minister along with a former president of the USA, Bill Clinton. The Action Plan notes that other than the two chairpersons, the constitution of the commission should include ten representatives from the Haitian government, plus one representative from each of the ten key donor countries. In addition there should be one person representing 'other' donors and one representative from the Caribbean Community (CARICOM). This gives the international actors a greater voice or voting rights than nationals, and in part explains why many saw the post-earthquake processes as controlled by the international community (Oxfam 2011).

While the international community may have little faith in a national government, other (non-governmental) national actors may also have concerns over a government's ability to plan. While many of these may centre on fears of corruption or embezzlement, they may also stem from differences of opinion around what reconstruction should look like, what should be the priority, and who should take the lead. For example, governments often emphasise reconstruction for economic growth, and place re-establishing infrastructure for trade and commerce at its centre, rather than reconstructing communities and people. This is not surprising since large-scale infrastructure, such as roads and bridges, is something that governments have to take responsibility for. Moreover, the dominant neo-liberal development paradigm dictates that priority should be given to economic growth initiatives (see Chapter 2). For example, the Nicara-guan government's initial proposal for reconstruction post-Mitch was entitled 'Of Potholes and Crossroads' – highlighting its focus on rebuild-ing the physical infrastructure of the country. The fact it was also written in English (rather than the native language, Spanish) highlights the fact that its target audience was international not national actors. Only after receiving criticism, from both international and national actors, was it drastically revised and re-titled 'From Reconstruction to Transformation' and translated into Spanish for circulation within the country.

The rebuilding of infrastructure is, of course, important and, in particular, structural mitigation infrastructure, such as levees, needs repairs and improvements to keep the population safe in the future. Building back structural mitigation mechanisms raises questions around what level of structure is needed to keep the population safe. Should a government just 'build back', or build back better, or build back 'the best'? That is, should they plan for the worst-case scenario? This issue was brought to the fore by Hurricane Katrina. Many had predicted such a catastrophe could occur since the levees that were breached were only built to withstand a category 3 storm, not the category 5 that Katrina reached at her peak. While known to be inadequate, it had been accepted as sufficient up to this point, that is, the risk had been regarded as acceptable given the low likelihood of a breach and despite the potential high losses (see also Chapter 1). This in part can be explained by the fact that other risks seemed higher or more of a priority, such as the risk posed by 'terrorism' and the 'war on terror' and this external threat took resource precedence over the internal threat of storm surges (Ross 2012). After Katrina, it was no longer acceptable to build the levees back only to the same level, and post Katrina a $15 billion scheme to improve the system was instigated. However, a report from the National Academy of Engineering suggests that the levees remain inadequate. The problem Katrina highlights is that governments need to balance the cost of providing protection now against the willingness of the population to pay for an event that may never occur, or at least not in their lifetime. This is an issue brought to the fore by climate change (see Chapter 9): the risks that need mitigating against now cannot be known since they are future risks. Climate change also presents a dilemma since if it is 'known' that there may be a sea level rise building defences against the current worst possible scenario is inadequate. Instead, future risk needs to be taken into account – a risk that cannot be known with any certainty and may not materialise.

The alternative is to seek to protect 'at risk' residents by relocating them to 'safer' areas. Relocation was the preferred action in many countries hit by the Indian Ocean tsunamis, accompanied by new 'zoning' regulations to stop the building of properties close to the shore line (see Chapter 6). The policy was justified as a means to protect the population but the extent to which such zoning offers protection is itself contested (Baird 2006). The plans met with great resistance because of the implications for people's livelihoods. The 'buffer' zones saw low-income families forced away from their homes and livelihoods, while large hotel chains were allowed to repair their properties and continue marketing themselves as offering 'beach front' accommodation. This was justified by the fact they could build to the required tsunami 'proof' standards. In Sri Lanka, the National Tourism Board noted: 'In a cruel twist of fate, nature has presented Sri Lanka with an unique opportunity, and out of this great tragedy will come a world class tourism destination' (cited in Tourism Concern 2005). The buffer zones therefore may be seen as introduced not to ensure protection, but to ensure profits.

What these examples highlight is that government plans for rebuilding post event do not necessarily ensure or indeed seek to build back safer communities and livelihoods. Such governmental plans are not without opposition as the president of Sri Lanka found out as he presented the proposed reconstruction plans which promoted the interests of the international tourism industry, noting 'the vociferous minority cannot be allowed to hinder the forward march of a nation towards peace and economic prosperity'. Yet national governments do increasingly have to take into account the views of the 'vociferous minority' who seek to represent the interests of those affected the most – not least since these are often the people least able to get their voices heard. These non-government or civil actors lobby to influence government plans for reconstruction, finding voice through the 'participatory' processes increasingly insisted upon by international donor governments and agencies as a condition of funding. As noted in Chapter 5, conditions are increasingly being applied even to humanitarian relief, and post-disaster reconstruction can be used by donors to ensure that the demands of civil society are included in discussions over what reconstruction should look like, presenting this participation as good for the wider aims of democracy and good governance.

Civil society organisations are not just important actors in delivering relief and reconstruction but also in influencing what reconstruction looks like. As Miller and Rivera (2007) note, while communities do not have the ability to decide what is destroyed during an event they do have the ability to decide what is reconstructed. That reconstruction then symbolises the values a society seeks to highlight and the social and political ideals a society values (Foote 1997; Baker 2003). Thus civil actors will seek to ensure that the vision presented in the national plans for reconstruction reflect their vision for the future as well as that of the government. Increasingly, donors also seek to ensure that the views of both governmental and non-governmental actors are reflected in plans for reconstruction. This inclusion of 'civil society' in the formulation of policy processes reflects the growing importance of this sector. The following section will introduce the notion of civil society and NGOs before presenting a case study from Nicaragua to explore the role they can and do play in reconstruction.

CIVIL SOCIETY IN POST-DISASTER RECONSTRUCTION

It has been suggested that there are five main arenas within the social space of a modern consolidated democracy: the state apparatus; the judicial system; economic society; political society; and civil society (Linz and Stepan 1996). Civil society as a 'sphere of social reproduction' enjoys a long history of discussion by thinkers such as Hegel, Marx and Gramsci. Yet a wide range of different definitions and interpretations of what civil society is, or is composed of, exist (see McIlwaine 1998a, 1998b). Civil society can include manifold social movements, such as women's groups, neighbourhood associations, religious groupings, and intellectual organisations, and civil associations from all social strata, such as trade unions, entrepreneurial groups, journalists, or lawyers (Linz and Stepan 1996: 7). While it generally refers to any organisation that mediates between the individual and the state, based on a right to associate (Fundación Arias 1998), an alternative way of thinking about civil society is as the 'space between'. Civil society links the individual and the state via organisations or organised action. Thus, it is the role played, or space occupied, by campaign and protest groups. It can be an informal rather than formal grouping, for example, anti-war marches that bring together a large and diverse grouping of people linked by a common cause, to stop war, using the streets as a site of protest. It can also be a more formal or organised grouping where people 'belong' or are members of a movement such as the Stop the War Coalition.

Social movements have a long history, with the first being the Trade Union movement focused on class-based actions. Over time, the influence of Trade Unions has (been) lessened, particularly with the rise of neo-liberal thinking and its focus on individualism. In many parts of the developing world, the Trade Union movement does not have a strong tradition and, instead, class-based movements took a more radical approach by taking up arms to overthrow the ruling classes. Not all armed actions resulted in more egalitarian governments, however, and, for example, during the 1970s, Latin America was characterised by military dictatorships. In this instance the key social movement was focused on demanding (re-)democratisation. Social movements of the 1970s became defined as 'new social movements' since their focus was on 'new' issues such as democracy. They were also seen to be new in terms of how they protested, adopting a diverse range of strategies from the Chipko 'tree huggers', to the 'Mothers of the Disappeared' who used their motherhood as a form of public protest, to the women of Chile who made *arpillera* (small quilts made using appliqué) which depicted the repression they faced under the Pinochet dictatorship. The third new element concerned who took part and women in particular were seen to be key actors in new social movements (see Radcliffe and Westwood 1993). While credited with helping bring change, the fourth element of new social movements is that because they are issue-based they also tend to be short-lived. Newer social movements articulate themselves around social contradictions such as gender, lifestyles, racial inequality, and war. Many question the globalisation process and its expressions of 'western modernity'. These organisations tend to politicise previously non-politicised spaces and connect the local with the global by linking their activities to locally-based grass-roots organisations and national and international NGOs (MacDonald 1994, 1997). To promote their interests, they often have the capacity for mass mobilisation and use this it as an element of pressure to defend or change existing society. This also includes the use of the internet and may include virtual protests, often through a mass logging on to sites designed to crash them. This was a strategy adopted in 1999 as part of the anti-WTO protests and more recently, in 2012, it has been used in the battle over the introduction of USA anti-piracy laws seeking to legislate against the 'illegal' sharing of films, music and other media via the internet.

The actions of many social movements lead to measures by governments to curb their activities. Foley and Edwards (1996: 142) have captured the governmental 'backlash' that may occur as movements grow strong as the 'paradox of civil society'. The positive democratic effects on governability that may arise from civil societies' role as a pressure group are contrasted with a potentially conflictive situation that can arise when a strong politically independent civil society makes excessive demands of the government that ultimately may not be consistent with democracy and good governance. This backlash in part explains why some elements of some movements choose to formalise their existence by setting up NGOs. The legal recognition afforded to NGOs gives them some level of protection against hostile national governments, while also facilitating support, particularly financial support, from international governments and organisations.

Non-Governmental Organisations

The rise of developmental NGOs is a phenomenon across the globe and has been much written about (see Lewis and Kanji 2009). NGOs proliferated under Structural Adjustment in the 1980s, which saw the application of neo-liberal policies in the Third World (see Chapter 2). Within the 'debt crisis', Third World governments were constructed as corrupt, and non-governmental organisations offered a (supposedly) non-partisan alternative. Adjustment policies that saw the state 'rolled' back and saw cut backs in welfare spending, left a 'service gap'. NGOs stepped in to supply goods and services to the poor that the state could not, or would not, supply. This is at the heart of one of the many debates around NGOs, in that while providing goods and services to the poor may help them in the short term, in the longer term this provision may merely allow the state to shirk its responsibility. Since the poor are receiving the resources they do not look to hold the state accountable. This means that the existence of welfare-focused NGOs may actually stop a movement demanding state welfare provision from emerging, which explains why many regard NGOs as de-politicising and harming social movements.

However, not all NGOs are welfare-focused and Korten (1990) proposes that there have been four generations of NGOs. The first generation focused on relief and welfare, or the direct delivery of services to meet immediate deficiency. This remains relevant in times of crisis and the delivery of emergency or humanitarian relief. The second generation focused more on building local self-reliance, or the development of the capacities of people to better meet their own needs. Evolving from this are what have been identified as a third generation of NGOs that have the development of sustainable development systems as their aim. This evolution may mean NGO actions focus more on the policy formulation process of governments and multilateral organisations than on delivering 'practical' or material goods and services. A fourth generation may also be identified in Korten's work, that of political advocacy and campaigning in order to support people's movements and promote a broader social vision. Networking and research are increasingly important in contemporary NGOs (Vakil 1997), although NGOs have been criticised for failing to capitalise on their knowledge of grass roots realities in their dialogue with government and donor agencies (Clark 1992).

This knowledge of 'grass roots realities' is what makes many donors favour NGOs over governments. In practical terms, NGOs are often the favoured service provider and channel for donors' monies since they are generally seen to be more efficient at delivering goods and services to the poor. NGOs are defined by their 'not for profit' status, suggesting that they will be able to provide goods and services more cheaply than private firms. They are also favoured because of the way they work – closer to the 'grass roots' and thus with a better understanding of the needs and priorities of potential beneficiaries. Finally, they are favoured because of who works for them. It is suggested that those that work for NGOs, compared to those who work in government or private firms, will not only work for less but will work harder for less. In return for their altruism, rather than a monetary reward, NGO workers get a 'warm glow' (Andreoni 1990; Scott and Hopkins 1999).

This view constructs NGOs as benevolent organisations working hard to promote the best interests of the poor. This is a view that is contested. It has been suggested that there has been an 'NGO'isation' of social movements, particularly the women's movement and this is seen to be de-politicising (Alvarez 1999). This understanding of NGOs suggests that they do not support social movements or help the voices of the movements be heard, but rather present themselves, or allow themselves to be perceived by others to be 'the' voice of the movement. As receivers of funds from donors, they are seen as eroding the power of progressive political formations at local and national level, which reinforces neo-liberal policies of state withdrawal and privatisation (Toye 1987). They are then seen to be part of a process of privatisation of both development and democracy (Petras 1997).

Despite widespread debate about the utility and desirability of NGOs in the development and feminist literature, they are often presented as the 'solution' to post-disaster reconstruction and treated as unproblematic entities. The following case study of post-Mitch reconstruction seeks to critically examine the interaction of international, governmental and non-governmental actors in the post-disaster context to problematise the role of NGOs.

Civil Society and National Processes of Reconstructions: Post-Mitch Case Study

After Hurricane Mitch, one hope was for a transformation not only of the material conditions under which the majority of the population lived, but the context in which these conditions were being produced and repro-duced. The idea that out of the devastation a transformation could take place appears to have been accepted by the governments of the region. This is suggested by slogans such as 'The government invites you to reconstruct and transform Nicaragua together'. Hopes were high that a joint process of reconstruction could occur, in which civil actors would work with national and international governments toward a common goal. National level coordination of civil society actors emerged in all countries in the aftermath of the hurricane, with two of the strongest being in the countries worst hit – Espacio Interforos in Honduras and the Civil Coordinator for Emergency and Reconstruction (CCER) in Nicara-gua (see Bradshaw, Linneker and Zúniga 2002; Bradshaw 2002). Each of the five national level coordinating bodies for civil society looked to influence the plans for reconstruction of their respective governments.

The organisational structures of national and regional civil society and NGO coordination will vary depending on the countries concerned, and their historical, cultural, political and economic development with regard to internal and external power relations (Hengstenberg et al. 1999). The CCER in Nicaragua, for example, was able to bring together 21 existing networks, which in turn represented the involvement of more than 350 civil organisations. Given that political advocacy and campaigning was the main focus of the majority of the participant networks and an important element of the work of many of their member organisations, it is perhaps not surprising that the CCER's initial objectives included:

- To actively work together to respond to the needs of the affected population
- To gather and disseminate pertinent information on the reconstruction efforts
- To influence national and international reconstruction and transformation plans.

That is, the 'practical' element – to provide relief aid – quickly gave way to a more strategic aim as the CCER sought not only to influence the national plans for reconstruction but also to formulate their own. The CCER demonstrates the different generations of NGOs as proposed by Korten, and illustrates the fact it is not necessarily a progression but that all can co-exist within one organisation.

The post-disaster umbrella organisations sought to influence national and international processes and to counteract the focus on economic growth and infrastructure of the governmental proposals for reconstruction. Recognised as the voice of civil society they were given further legitimacy by the international community who invited them for the first time to participate in the Consultative Group meeting to discuss regional reconstruction plans that resulted in the 'Stockholm Declaration' of 1999. Such umbrella organisations are useful for international actors post disaster as they provide a reference point through which to gauge 'civil society' opinion without having to set up a full participatory process, which costs both time and money. Thus they are 'participatory' but at the same time shut down wider participation since the extent to which such organisations do and can reflect the opinion of 'civil society' is open to question. Also open to question is the extent to which they and their views are recognised by national actors, especially governments. As Foley and Edwards' (1996) paradox of civil society thesis suggests, the demands of civil society, and the ability of the coalitions to present these demands effectively, may be greater than the governments' willingness or ability to respond to them. This appears to have been the case in both Nicaragua and Honduras as government-civil society relations deteriorated and the promises contained in the Stockholm Declaration failed to be fulfilled (Bradshaw, Linneker and Zúniga 2002).

A year later, at the meeting to evaluate progress towards the Declaration's aims, the policy landscape had changed and, instead of a review of reconstruction, the international and governmental focus was on the World Bank's Poverty Reduction Strategy Paper (PRSP) process. Civil society was once again left out of the meeting, suggesting a shift back in terms of territory gained at the international as well as the national level. Thus, only one year after Stockholm, the policy agenda had moved forward, and while ideas of reconstruction were still evident it was not the priority – reconstruction being replaced by wider 'development' aims. The policy arena demonstrates the continued separation of development and disasters, and that the discrete stages of the disaster cycle do persist. Both the CCER and Interforos similarly shifted emphasis from reconstruction to development and sought to influence the emerging PRSP process with some level of success (Bradshaw and Linneker 2003) – thus suggesting a lasting legacy of reconstruction to be a strengthening of civil society.

However, the seeming strengthening of civil society through post-disaster processes may also be not as clear-cut as it seems, as the unity suggested by collective action may conceal divisions within the coordinated groups and within civil society, in particular along gender lines. One of the divisions within the women's movements post Mitch was around whether to participate in the civil society initiatives and official or governmental initiatives, as both were seen to bring potential problems. This will be explored further below, but first the notion of participation will be explored and the debates within the development literature summarised.

GENDERED PARTICIPATION POST DISASTER

The notion of participation and participatory development, while not a new phenomenon, rose to prominence amongst development agencies in the late 1980s and early1990s. Its roots can be traced back to the work of Chambers and originally arose from a methodological innovation that suggested that experts should listen to, and actively seek out, local knowledge. This led to innovations in data collection techniques based on participation of the poor themselves, and methods such as Participatory Rural Appraisal (PRA) and the more radical Participatory Action Research that builds on the critical pedagogy put forward by Paulo Freire. Like many concepts that begin life as radical 'alternatives' the concept of participation has evolved over the decades and is now very much within the dominant development discourse. In particular it is linked to promoting democracy and also notions of 'good governance'.

Participation is promoted as a mechanism for change, as a means to build consensus and as a step toward action. Not only is the outcome or product of participation seen to be important, but also the process itself is seen to have intrinsic value as an individual's participation is linked to ideas of collective and individual 'empowerment'. Participation and, particularly and explicitly, participation of the poorest and most vulnerable participants, is often promoted as a human right. However, an argument more favoured by organisations such as the World Bank when promoting participatory processes is that involvement of the main stakeholders increases ownership, allows better use of resources and enables the mobilisation of local resources, that is, it makes projects more cost-efficient.

By the mid-90s, among development academics and practitioners there were as many critics as promoters of participation (see Cooke and Kothari 2002; Hickey and Mohan 2004). The same level of deconstruction of participation and participatory processes does not seem to have occurred in the disaster discourse. Instead, participation is usually presented as something to strive for, and the focus continues to be on fighting exclusion, rather than problematising inclusion. The issues that have been raised by participatory development practices are useful lessons to be learned for disaster response at all levels.

Critics argue that participatory processes, even those initiated from the 'bottom up' are not necessarily either inclusive or egalitarian and frequently exclude or marginalise the very poor, women and other disadvantaged groups. Rather than empowering, participation can be seen to reinforce power relations and the position of those with a voice or in power, since those with power will be most able to participate and have the time and skills necessary to do so effectively. It has also been suggested that the rhetoric of participation has been used to mask processes in which participation is extremely superficial or unequal or manipulated to support the ends of one powerful group. There are practical and theoretical limitations to group networks and sizes and their abilities to perform. Research suggests those with minority views will be swayed towards the majority perspective (Olson 1971, 1982). Thus, rather than promoting social change, participation may build consent not consensus, and processes tend to uphold the status quo rather than bring radical change.

In gender terms, it has been suggested that women's participation will 'engender' processes to formulate policies and projects (see Chapter 3). Alongside the arguments above, critics also note that this supposes that women will prioritise their gender above all other characteristics during a participatory discussion. This may not be the case and, for example, a woman may promote her ethnic group rather than her gender if this is her key self-identity. Engendering participatory processes is not just about ensuring women can speak, nor that their voices are heard, but that gender issues are raised and taken into account, by men and women.

For some, what is needed is 'real' or better participation, but for others participation in itself is the issue (Cooke and Kothari 2002; Hickey and Mohan 2004; IDPM 2003). That is, even the best planned participatory practice will not change the fact that what people are often being asked to do is to make bounded choices. For example, participatory budgets don't seek to set the size of the budget, merely how it should be divided up, asking the people themselves to decide on who wins and who loses out within this. Post-disaster participatory needs assessments work on the same principles – asking those who have lost possessions and loved ones to rank losses and decide who is most in need. This raises moral and ethical issues that are rarely discussed or acknowledged.

More fundamentally, questions are raised about what participation means for those seeking to use it from 'within' to bring about change. The World Bank's PRSP initiative is a good example of why some people suggest the need to problematise the current focus on participatory processes. Unlike the Structural Adjustment Programmes that preceded them, the conditionalities attached to PRSPs are said to be process rather than policy focused (Booth 2003). That is, governments must present a plan for a participatory design process which includes civil society actors in order to receive World Bank or IMF backing. This presents a dilemma for civil society – to participate or not? Can official 'participatory' processes by their very nature and design be expected to bring change, or should they be seen as always and inherently perpetuating the existing model of 'development'? That is, by 'participating', even to voice dissent, do participants do little more than legitimise what they themselves may see to be illegitimate processes and actors? Is active non-participation the real political action in this context? Such questions have plagued civil society actors faced with the chance to 'participate' in governmental and World Bank backed processes. The decision can be divisive and effectively weaken civil society rather than strengthen it.

The relevance of these issues in the post-disaster context will be illustrated through consideration of how women engaged, or did not, with post-Mitch participatory processes and its consequences, drawing on empirical studies undertaken over a number of years working in and with civil society organisations (see Bradshaw and Linneker 2003; Bradshaw 2004a).

Gender and Women's Movements: Post-Mitch Case Study

Women's groups and women leaders were among the first to respond individually and collectively after Hurricane Mitch. At a local level, actions very quickly moved from a personal response to a collective practical response, and then to a political role, which sought to influence the civil society response at the local level as well as that of the government (Walker 2000). Local level activities mirrored what was occurring at the national level, and women's groups and movements which sought to influence the government's plans for reconstruction first had to find a voice within the civil society response.

Although after Hurricane Mitch both Interforos in Honduras and the CCER in Nicaragua brought together some of the most important civil society actors and organisations, many women and elements of the women's movements felt themselves to be largely excluded from the outset. Others chose to exclude themselves (see Bradshaw and Linneker 2003 for full discussion). In Honduras, although the women's movements had organised to respond to the disaster, they were not 'invited' to participate in the production of the 'civil society' proposal for reconstruction, which was formulated by Interforos. A draft proposal was produced by a small group of people within Interforos and then presented to wider organised civil society for consultation. Some women did meet to discuss the proposal as part of the consultation process but found themselves with one day to try to 'engender' the document. Thus the proposal has some gender content but the process by which it was produced did not. Women leaders in Honduras suggested gender relations to be a problem in Interforos and some went so far as to suggest that rather than offering solidarity and a shared agenda, the coalition was a new battleground in the struggle against discrimination and sexist attitudes (Bradshaw and Linneker 2003). This highlights that it should not be assumed that men within civil society organisations are automatically or necessarily more open to gender than are those working within government or international agencies.

In contrast to Honduras, feminist activists in Nicaragua had been involved in the CCER from the beginning and the first spokesperson of the CCER was a woman. The presence of women and women's groups in the CCER may help to explain why from the outset attempts were made to 'engender' the process by which the CCER's proposal for reconstruction would be produced – the aim was to engender the process not just the product. To this end, one of the first commissions established in the new organisation, and one with independent funding, was the gender commission. However, from the start some important individuals and elements of the women's movement chose not to participate. The reasons for this are documented elsewhere (Bradshaw and Linneker 2003) and represent existing divisions in the movement around a variety of issues, including the issue of participating in 'mixed' gender spaces. Past experiences, where the women who participated felt that their voices had not been heard, meant they were reluctant to engage with the CCER from the outset. Their fears proved to have some basis because, although the CCER's proposal for reconstruction ultimately had a clear gender perspective (see CCER 1999), achieving this was not straightforward. The aim was to engender the design process through a member of the gender commission participating in every other commission involved in the proposal design process. This proved unsuccessful and in the end representatives of the gender commission of the CCER had to hold a one-day meeting of women's groups and movements to make suggestions on how to improve the draft document once it was written. In comparison to Interforos, representatives from the women's movement were then able to work as part of the final editing team to ensure that all the suggestions were fully incorporated into the final document. While many point to the gendered nature of the proposal as a success for the women's movement, and it does demonstrate an openness to gender issues, for those women inside and outside the CCER the fact the process was not fully gendered meant there was a cost to be paid for this success.

Those who have studied the Nicaraguan women's movement over many years agree that, in contrast to the consolidation of civil society prior to Mitch, during the post-Mitch period the women's movements became divided (Babb 2001; Clulow 2002). It would be too simplistic to place the blame on the CCER; rather, the CCER brought some ongoing issues to a head, particularly differences in opinion around how best women's interests can be served – through engagement in mixed spaces or through separate women only actions and agendas. However, while the situation in Nicaragua could be said to be divisive, the post-Mitch period in Honduras can be defined as one of rupture and fragmentation of the women's movement (Bradshaw 2004a). The suggestion once again is not that the hurricane, or indeed Interforos, caused this rupture but that events following the disaster highlighted and amplified inequalities within the women's movement. In Honduras, as elsewhere in the region, recent decades have seen the proliferation of NGOs, often established by actors in existing social movements or informal grassroots organisations, including women's movements. This became an issue in Honduras at that particular time mainly because of the nature of the reconstruction process and the role of international actors in it. Honduras saw an influx of new international donor organisations after the hurricane, many of them committed to including gender issues in any projects they undertook. These organisations needed to find an efficient means to enter into dialogue with the women of the country, since the 'participation' of women has become part of, and a strategy for, gender mainstreaming which is now standard institutional practice for most international agencies (see Chapter 3; Cornwall 2001; McGee 2002). The 'tyranny of the urgent' that tends to prevail after a disaster meant that talking to the 'representatives' of the wider women's movement was the simplest and quickest way to make contact with women. At the same time, financing NGOs to implement projects is more straightforward than financing the actors and activities of social and women's movements. This led to accusations that some women and organisations had presented themselves as the 'voice of the movement' and had channelled more than their share of reconstruction funds through their own NGOs. As one woman suggested, 'some compañeras, some NGOs, have traded on the famous gender perspective' (Bradshaw and Linneker 2003: 16). This fuelled divisions within the movement around the perceived negative impact of the so-called 'NGO'isation' of women's movements (Alvarez 1999). This is a debate which has received much attention within development circles but has yet to be fully explored within the post-disaster context, despite the fact that the post-disaster period may both reveal and exacerbate the relative power of NGOs compared to wider social movements.

Another, less well-documented explanation of the rather fraught nature of relations within civil society during this time may lie with the simple fact that all women activists, whatever route they took or role they played, found their workloads increased dramatically post Mitch. This is something that has been increasingly documented post disaster (see David and Enarson 2012). Not only did workloads increase, but also many NGOs post disaster had to change the focus of their work or added new activities such as housing projects to respond to the immediate needs of the people. This not only meant working in a new area but also often with new partner organisations, and for some this meant working closely for the first time with men. This, of course, brought its own problems. There were positives, however, as organisations worked together to share skills and knowledge including, for example, the sharing of house building skills by women carpenters and construction workers. Another achievement was the establishment of a network to provide psychosocial care post Mitch, which successfully provided care on the ground and had a key role in trying to influence the post-disaster policy process as well as popular perceptions of mental health (see Chapter 7).

However, the sudden and relatively large expansion of funding and programmes post Mitch for some organisations not only put a burden on the organisational capacity in the short run, with individuals bearing the cost of higher work loads, but also led to problems of sustainability in the longer term. The focus was on the practical but for many women's organisations more strategic elements were often also included, for example, house building was as much about a process of building 'healthy communities' as providing bricks and mortar. However, this more holistic, participatory and long-term approach, which was aimed at reducing the vulnerability of people and communities, did not always fit well with donor expectations and time lines. Money to continue with the work that had started immediately after the event was not always forthcoming. This added yet another burden as women leaders attempted to bridge the gap between people's expectations and funding realities. This was something that became increasingly difficult in the years following Mitch as donor priorities changed, moving funding away from Latin America and towards Africa, and away from women's empowerment and toward more general poverty programmes as dictated by the Millennium Development Goals (MDGs).

Women were among the first to respond post Mitch. Women and women's movements assumed the responsibility for reconstruction and took on the commitment to rebuilding homes and lives, of caring for those affected, both physically and mentally. In short, took on the gender stereotypical 'caring' roles that many individually and collectively had been working to challenge. A number of women, reflecting on the processes post-Mitch, noted how their learnt 'feminist' responses appear to have been overruled by socialised gendered roles immediately after the event (Bradshaw 2004b). These stereotypical caring roles were further reinforced by the reconstruction process, not least because the responsibility for engendering reconstruction was not only assumed by women, but may have been assumed to be the responsibility of women. Donors and international agencies seeking to ensure a 'gender perspective' in their work sought out women's groups and organisations and they became the favoured means of delivering both development and 'gender' objectives. Much like individual women, women's groups and gendered NGOs were targeted on efficiency and equality grounds, and while the wider collective benefits, to family, community and society, are clear, the benefits for the women themselves are less clear. The costs to women and women's groups, as the example above demonstrates, can be high. Rather than the 'participation' of women in reconstruction, which would suggest they somehow gain from their involvement, what occurred may be better seen to be a 'feminisation of disaster response', a phenomenon also apparent in post-tsunami Sri Lanka (Overton 2007). That is, women are the key deliverers of reconstruction rather than the beneficiaries, a phenomenon noted and much debated within development and which will be further discussed in the next chapter.

DRAWING THE LINKS: PARTICIPATION, FRAGMENTATION AND FEMINISATION

Post disaster the current development discourse means that the international community actively seeks the participation of civil society actors in reconstruction. Disasters may thus provide a 'window of opportunity', even if short-lived, for strengthening non-governmental actors and allowing their voices to be heard. However, the international community's enthusiasm for civil society participation is not necessarily matched by national governments', and the extent to which civil actors are able to engage actively in anything more than delivering reconstruction for international donors 'on the ground' is open to question. The 'paradox of civil society' may mean that, as internal and international efforts strengthen non-governmental actions, these actions may threaten weak governments and result in a backlash against them. Collective actions to respond to the immediate effects of a disaster may see a coordination of civil actors emerge that may become consolidated and formalised over time. As the policy context shifts from reconstruction to development, they seek to continue as a voice within the new policy landscape. Such coordinating bodies, while a positive presence, are not without problems, however, and they raise issues about inclusion and exclusion when they present themselves, or are perceived to be, the 'voice' of civil society. Among the voices they potentially exclude or silence may be those of women and the women's movement.

While international actors seek to ensure a 'gender perspective' within reconstruction, often the focus is on the product – that the plan is gendered or women are included in the project. The process by which this engendering occurs is less often evaluated. However, the process of engendering national and local plans for reconstruction is not easy or straightforward. It cannot be assumed that men within civil society organisations are any more open to gender than governmental or international actors, and those women seeking to engender processes of reconstruction may face a difficult task. Recognising this from the beginning, some women and women's groups may decide to remain outside collective processes, and the perceived strengthening of civil society may conceal a weakening of women's movements. It is not to suggest that civil society coordinating bodies cause this weakening, but that it is a catalyst for fragmentation along existing fault lines. One such fault line is the presence of NGOs and their relative power compared to wider civil actors, which constructs them as the voice of civil society listened to by international donors and financed by them.

Whatever the positioning of women and women's groups as inside or outside governmental and collective reconstruction processes, women and women's groups do respond to disasters. This response may mirror stereotypical caring roles and women may assume the responsibility for ensuring reconstruction occurs. Moreover, it may be assumed by the international community that they will assume this responsibility and rather than participation, a 'feminisation' of disaster response may be evident.

9. Disaster Risk Reduction

INTRODUCTION

The opening chapters of this book explored the discourses of disasters and development. They considered what makes a hazard a disaster, exploring notions of vulnerability and risk. Subsequent chapters have looked at the relief and reconstruction phases. This chapter will return to the discourses of disasters and development but this time the focus will be on the policy rather than the academic discourse. The chapter will focus on the 'last' stage of the disaster cycle, which may also be read as the 'first' stage – preparation. It will explore the evolution in the disaster discourse to the present focus on Disaster Risk Reduction (DRR). Despite the regularity with which they occur, disasters continue to be conceptualised as extraordinary events that break the established processes of 'development'. However, more recently, there has been growing interest in 'disaster proofing' development. The notion of risk that has emerged as central to the disaster discourse has also become more central to the World Bank discourse around social protection and poverty alleviation. This chapter will focus on the global agreement that frames DRR – the Hyogo Framework for Action (HFA). It will explore how the HFA relates to other global initiatives such as those addressing climate change as well as the global development framework – the Millennium Development Goals (MDGs). At the same time as there has been a move to disaster proof development there has been a move to 'engender' disasters. Drawing on experience of engendering development, this chapter will consider the extent to which processes of feminisation of disaster response and risk reduction have occurred and what they mean for the women involved.

THE EVOLUTION IN CONCEPTUALISING DISASTER RISK REDUCTION

Once reconstruction is 'over' the disaster cycle (see Box I.1 on page x) would suggest thoughts turn to preparing for the next event and since natural hazards cannot be prevented, disaster management programmes seek to implement measures to reduce or mitigate the social and economic impacts of an event. Mitigation focuses on proactive measures taken to lessen the impact disasters have on people and property before an event occurs. Disaster mitigation measures may be structural, such as building levees or dykes, or non-structural such as land use zoning. The issue for successful mitigation is identifying hazard risks and then taking action to address and minimise them. Actions for mitigation need to be taken well ahead of any event and are focused on reducing impact in the long term.

Preparedness also includes activities that should be carried out prior to notice of an approaching hazard being received. Preparedness is not about reacting to notification of an event but preparing for that notification ahead of time and being able to react to early warnings more quickly and effectively. Early warning is key to responding effectively to an event but it only works when people are prepared and ready to respond. Early warning systems are best understood as the set of capacities needed to generate and disseminate timely and meaningful warning information to enable individuals, communities and organisations threatened by a hazard to prepare and to act appropriately, and in sufficient time, to reduce the possibility of harm or loss. They can have a technical focus or be more people centred. Even when 'technical' in their focus, this technology can be as simple as a bicycle and a hand bell. What is important is that there is someone there to issue the warning, they do so in a timely manner and, most importantly, that the warning is understood and heeded, and that people act and are prepared to act quickly. Preparation activities that allow a rapid response can be quite simple actions that occur at different levels. For example, within the household a key preparedness measure would be having an emergency bag prepared and always ready. This may be particularly important for some groups of people who have particular health needs, for example, or needs specific to age or disability (see Davis and Rouba 2012; Zotti et al. 2012). At the community level, it could be establishing which buildings will be used as refuges while, at a national level, activities such as having local evacuation plans in place are included in the idea of preparedness.

More recently, the concept of Disaster Risk Reduction (DRR) has emerged which encompasses ideas of mitigation and preparedness but places these within a context of sustainability and vulnerability. An accepted definition of DRR is: 'the conceptual framework of elements considered with the possibilities to minimize vulnerabilities and disaster risks throughout a society, to avoid (prevention) or to limit (mitigation and preparedness) the adverse impacts of hazards, within the broad context of sustainable development' (ISDR 2004: 2). While there are similarities, the United Nations International Strategy for Disaster Reduction (ISDR 2004: 13) offers a comparison of DRR with earlier conceptual frameworks (based on Jeggle 2001) noting differences in a number of elements. These differences mirror the evolution in thinking around disasters highlighted in Chapter 1, as emphasis has shifted from a primary focus on the hazard in earlier frameworks, to an emphasis on vulnerability and risk within DRR. A change in the nature of operations is implied by this move to a DRR approach with, for example, a shift from a single authority to multiple authorities, actors and interests being involved. Time horizons are also different since disasters are now seen not as urgent events to respond to in the short term, but rather as events that raise issues to be dealt with in the medium and long term. This shift in time span is something that mirrors changing ideas around humanitarianism (see Chapter 5). The rationale for response has also shifted from being a matter of public security and safety to one of public interest, investment and safety. The final difference is around information use and management, with DRR using accumulated and historical data to prepare for and mitigate the effects of events.

The disaster risk reduction framework is composed of many elements and includes (ISDR 2004: 1)

- Risk awareness and assessment including hazard analysis and vulnerability/ capacity analysis
- Knowledge development including education, training, research and information
- Early warning systems including forecasting, dissemination of warnings, preparedness measures and reaction capacities
- Public commitment and institutional frameworks, including organisational, policy, legislation and community action
- Application of measures including environmental management, land use and urban planning, protection of critical facilities, application of science and technology, partnership and networking, and financial instruments.

It is acknowledged that risk assessment is the first stage of DRR. As demonstrated in Chapter 1, risk is subjective and gendered, and any assessment needs to take into account local understandings and the prioritising of risk by both men and women, and also, given the thesis that young adults appear to have lower perceptions of risk than older people, be differentiated by age also. Despite the rhetoric, it is often assumed that risks are 'known' and it has been suggested that there remains a need for scientists to collaborate more closely with local knowledge networks and take into account people's risk perceptions (O'Brien et al. 2008: 21). An assumption by risk experts may be that disaster risk is gender neutral and this can mean that interventions will be inappropriate or ineffective and may actually create or exacerbate gender inequalities and vulnerabilities. Risk assessment continues to stem from expert knowledge: local knowledge tends to be used only in an assessment of (people's) vulnerabilities and capacities. The Capacity and Vulnerability Analysis (CVA) matrix is a well-established tool for using local knowledge to establish the situation on the ground (see Anderson and Woodrow 1998). It is easily adapted to provide a gendered analysis but its utility is lessened if a gendered understandings of risk is not established first.

The ISDR publication 'Making Disaster Risk Reduction Gender-Sensitive' highlights why all elements of DRR need to be considered through a gender lens if it is to be effective and it provides practical examples of how this might be approached (UNISDR 2009b). It notes, for example, that research suggests that women are more likely to receive and act upon early warnings (Fordham 2001; Enarson 2006). When warning systems do not take into account gendered differences, the consequences can be great as the 1991 Bangladesh Cyclone demonstrated. Early warning information about the cyclone and the floods was transmitted by men to men in public spaces, rarely reaching women directly and in part explaining why five times more women than men died (Skutsch 2004). In comparison Buvinić (1999) suggests that part of the reason why La Masica in Honduras reported no deaths after hurricane Mitch lay with the fact women had been educated in, and were in charge of, the early warning system.

The focus on risk and vulnerability within DRR means the framework offers opportunities not only to 'engender' processes but also offers possibilities for incorporating a development perspective into disaster risk reduction activities and vice versa. However, the extent to which DRR has entered the development discourse 'on the ground' is still limited. While a number of bilateral donors have specific financing for DRR, it is often tied to response and early recovery programmes, rather than programmed as part of 'regular' development and it is often funded from humanitarian budgets and coordinated from humanitarian aid departments (Mitchell and van Aalst 2008a). Many donors continue to conceptualise disasters as 'natural' rather than social events and focus on outcomes rather than causes, thus limiting their disaster-oriented work to relief and reconstruction activities. At the local level, development-focused DRR initiatives may struggle to find funding because their projects are seen as being too disaster focused when donor priorities lie with 'development' or, conversely, for not being sufficiently disaster focused in terms of how donors define 'disaster' work.

At the international level, there has been a much greater drive to integrate disasters and development through both disaster initiatives and development initiatives. The global disaster framework, as set by the Hyogo Framework for Action, and the global development framework, defined by the Millennium Development Goals (MDGs), will be discussed before the prospects for 'disaster proofing' development are considered. However, first an issue that links them both needs to be considered – climate change.

CLIMATE CHANGE ADAPTATION AND DISASTER RISK REDUCTION

> There is significant overlap between the practice and theory of disaster risk reduction and climate change adaptation. However, there is limited coherence and convergence in institutions, organisations and policy frameworks. Both struggle to be incorporated into regular development planning and this aspiration is slowed down by duplicated activities, ineffective use of resources and confusing policies. (Mitchell and van Aalst 2008b: 1)

While climate change is a contested notion, there is a general consensus that change is expected to be the 'norm rather than the exception' when it comes to extreme events such as floods, cyclones and wildfires (O'Brien et al. 2008). This has suggested the need for populations to adapt to new climates, and 'adaptation' is the term used to describe the steps taken to cope with changed climatic conditions (ISDR 2009) or to moderate harm and exploit any opportunities to benefit from climate changes. One possible harm that will need moderating in the future will be the effects of natural hazards, since climate change is said to increase the frequency and intensity of the natural hazards that provoke large-scale disasters. ISDR (2009) suggests climate change will affect the risk of disasters in two ways. First, through the likely increase in weather and climate hazards. The likelihood of increased weather extremes in the future suggests that the number and scale of weather-related disasters will also increase. Secondly, through increases in the vulnerability of communities to natural hazards, particularly through 'ecosystem degradation, reductions in water and food availability, and changes to livelihoods'. This has led to the suggestion that 'the possible effects of climate change cannot be understood independently of larger social and economic and cultural changes' (O'Brien et al. 2008: 15).

The overlap between Climate Change Adaptation (CCA) and Disaster Risk Reduction (DRR) is clear since both aim to reduce the impacts of shocks by 'anticipating risks and addressing vulnerabilities' (Mitchell and van Aalst 2008). It should be noted, however, that for some vulnerabilities the risk reducing potential of adaptation is either very limited or very costly. In other words, there are absolute limits faced by many ecosystems (Schneider et al. cited in O'Brien et al. 2008). The World Resources Institute (WRI) suggests that adaptation will involve a 'continuum of responses' to climate change, with 'pure' development activities at one end and very explicit adaptation measures at the other (McGray 2007). It suggests four types of Climate Change Adaptation

1. Addressing the drivers of vulnerability – factors making people vulnerable to harm
2. Building response capacity – laying the foundation for more targeted actions
3. Managing climate risk – reducing the effects of climate change on resources and livelihoods
4. Confronting climate change – highly specialised activities, such as relocating communities in response to sea level rise.

While DRR measures typically fall under categories 2 and 3, they could fit into every category (Tearfund 2008). The evolution in the disaster discourse suggests greater convergence is possible with, for example, the shift from disaster management to disaster risk management allowing a more anticipatory and forward-looking approach (Thomalla et al. 2006). This is important, since a difference between the CCA and DDR approaches has been that DRR focuses on existing climate variations. However, as Tanner (2007) suggests, an improved ability to cope with existing situations may provide a good basis for adapting to future changes. While this may be the case, caution is needed because DRR measures, such as sea defences, put in place to mitigate current levels of hazard, may give people a false sense of security and lead to risks being taken rather than avoided in a belief that they are 'safe' (Tearfund 2008). This suggests that DRR must be based not only on past and current experiences but also look to future risks and address the consequences of climate change. Despite the obvious overlaps, there has, however, been limited convergence of the DRR and CCA agendas (Tearfund 2008).

The teams working on DRR and CCA issues at an international and national level often work within different areas of government or different agencies within governments and international organisations, under different bosses and have different funding streams. They also respond to different policy instruments with the DRR agenda being framed by the HFA (see below) while the CCA agenda is within the main international forum for formulating climate change policy – the United Nations Framework Convention on Climate Change (UNFCCC). The Convention (United Nations 1992) mentions the need for 'special attention for developing countries prone to natural disasters', but makes no further reference to hazard or disaster risk. Its focus on long-term climatic changes rather than extremes and shocks associated with current climate variability makes it difficult to integrate DRR into the Convention. In contrast the HFA explicitly recognises the need to anticipate changing risks that may come about through global climate change. However, the UNFCCC is the stronger and more binding convention. Moreover, the lack of commitment to DRR within the UNFCCC may not be an accident as it has been suggested that some key donor governments (and major polluters) are opposed to further integrating DRR and the language of humanitarian assistance into UNFCCC text because this might create 'complex and potentially expensive overlaps associated with commitments to finance disaster relief' (Mitchell and van Aalst 2008a: 11). That is, funding decisions and notions of responsibility may be key to understanding why there has not been further convergence of the climate change and disaster risk agendas. If this is the case, then it may also suggest little prospect for greater integration in at least the short term.

A final commonality that they do share is that those working in both CCA and DRR suffer similarly from a 'lack of political influence and human capacity' necessary to get adaptation and risk reduction onto the mainstream development agenda (Mitchell and van Aalst 2008a: 6). The extent to which this has occurred and what has limited this in terms of DRR will now be considered.

DISASTERS AND THE DEVELOPMENT AGENDA

There have been some moves to explicitly connect disaster and development, not least World Bank initiatives to engage with post-disaster reconstruction on a local level and also its involvement at the international level through the Global Facility for Disaster Reduction and Recovery (GFDRR) launched in 2006 in conjunction with the UN's International Strategy for Disaster Reduction (ISDR) to finance initiatives aimed at reducing vulnerability to natural hazards. However, the development and the disaster policy frameworks remain largely separate. Despite recognition of the problems this raises, moves to better integrate the two have not met with much success, not least because, as the following discussion suggests, there are politics and (unequal) power relations involved which hamper such attempts.

The Hyogo Framework for Action

The Hyogo Framework for Action 2005–2015: Building the Resilience of Nations and Communities to Disasters (hence forth HFA) is the international framework for disaster risk reduction, which was endorsed by 168 national governments at the second World Conference on Disaster Reduction in 2005. The HFA lays out five priorities for action

- making disaster risk a national and local priority;
- improving risk information and early warning;
- building a culture of safety and resilience;
- reducing the risks in key sectors;
- strengthen preparedness for an effective response at all levels.

These are designed to meet its overall aim to bring about a 'substantial reduction of disaster losses, in lives & in the social, economic and environmental assets of communities and countries'. While representing a move forward in a number of ways, the HFA has limited possibilities for achieving its goals, not least because it does not contain a financial mechanism and is not legally binding. The opening section (preamble) states 'the Conference provided a unique opportunity to promote a strategic and systematic approach to reducing vulnerabilities and risks to hazards'. It underscored the need for, and identified ways of, building the resilience of nations and communities to disasters. However, a footnote defines both vulnerability and the more straightforward notion of hazard, and in conceptual terms the HFA is limited, given that key notions such as vulnerability and risk are not explored within the document and their complexity not recognised. The notion of risk is used extensively throughout but it is never actually defined in the main body of the document and, more importantly, its subjectivity is not recognised and discussed. Thus, while the rhetoric of the document fits with the vulnerability discourse, what is actually understood by terms such as 'vulnerability' is open to interpretation. Overall, the content of the document displays a continuing hazard and management focus, although there are social and vulnerability elements included, most obviously the priority to 'reduce the underlying risk factors'.

Blaikie et al.'s (1994) model (see Chapter 1) would suggest that actions to reduce underlying risk require quite far-reaching changes that address issues of inequality and power. However, many of the actions, even under the 'social and economic development practices' section focus on protecting 'critical public facilities' and physical infrastructure. There is also a focus on finding 'alternative and innovative' financial instruments for addressing disaster risk, suggesting a (further) move toward a privatization of disaster response. There are some elements of a more people-centred approach. For example, it notes the need to 'promote diversified income options for populations in high-risk areas to reduce their vulnerability to hazards, and ensure that their income and assets are not undermined by development policy and processes that increase their vulnerability to disasters'. However, how this will be done, who will do it and, perhaps most importantly, how it will be financed is not discussed. Perhaps, this is not surprising, given that addressing underlying risk demands the most far-reaching changes and it is this aspect of the HFA that has been least implemented to date. How advancement will be measured is also an important omission and the HFA does not include timed and measurable indicators of progress.

In gender terms, the HFA has been seen as a step forward and an important stage in the advances that have progressively been made since 2001, given that it contains the 'most explicit reference to gender of any other international policy frameworks for DRR' (see UNISDR 2009b). Presumably this reference to gender is the statement in the 'Priorities for Action 2005–2015 – General Considerations' section that notes a 'gender perspective should be integrated into all disaster risk management policies, plans and decision-making processes, including those related to risk assessment, early warning, information management, and education and training'. However, gender is not a focus of the document and in the remainder of it the term is only used twice in a substantive way, with women used once. The fact the HFA fails to explicitly integrate gender into the priorities and actions laid out says much about the (limited) possibilities for such integration to occur in practice.

At the 2009 International Conference on Gender and Disaster Risk Reduction, participants recognised that gender 'remains a marginalized issue in the current national and international negotiations around DRR and adaptation and that gender considerations have been hardly applied as a fundamental principle in policy and framework development' (cited in UNISDR 2009: 7). A survey in 2010 by ISDR highlighted the continued marginality of gender in DRR. A review of over 14 000 diverse pieces of material lead to their classification into themes and issues followed by a survey of 1856 DRR professionals to ascertain broad acceptance of these. It also asked them to indicate if these themes and issues were areas of specialism and which areas needed more expertise (UNISDR 2011). Reviewing the results, the highest number of respondents stated 'disaster risk management' was their area of 'expertise' (61 per cent) and this also scored highly as an area needing strengthening (36 per cent). Newer areas that are key to disaster 'risk reduction' (as opposed to risk management) scored lower on both expertise and as areas needing strengthening. For example, 42 per cent of respondents said they had expertise in risk identification and only 28 per cent thought it was an area that needed strengthening, while climate change scored lower still on expertise (20 per cent) but was more readily identified as an area that needed greater expertise (35 per cent). However, the theme that scored lowest on both expertise and recognition of the need to strengthen knowledge in this area was 'gender' with only 13 per cent suggesting they had expertise in the area and only 13 per cent suggesting it was an area that they need to strengthen. This suggests that the key focus continues to be disaster risk management rather than risk reduction, and that despite the apparent advances, there is still a long way to go to convince DRR professionals of the importance of adopting a gender perspective.

While the HFA is not aligned to any of the key gendered conventions and international agreements it does attempt to align with the key conventions in the related fields of Climate Change Adaptation and development. In terms of CCA, it notes the need to 'promote the integration of risk reduction associated with existing climate variability and future climate change into strategies for the reduction of disaster risk and adaptation to climate change'. In terms of development, the need to link the HFA with the MDGs is acknowledged. One of its three strategic goals is 'to effectively integrate, in a coherent manner, disaster risk considerations into sustainable development policies, planning, programming, and financing at all levels of government'. More explicit alignment with the MDGs is apparent in recent documentation that notes that the aim of the HFA is to reverse the trend in disaster losses by 2015. Reading like a MDG and with the same time frame, the HFA appears to be aligned to the MDGs, yet a closer examination highlights that this is not a straightforward relationship, and that it may be one-sided.

Disaster Proofing the Millennium Development Goals

The global development context is presently dominated by the MDGs. All the states that made up the United Nations at the time of the Millennium Summit held in New York in 2000, agreed a Millennium Declaration. This and the UN conferences of the 1990s, such as Cairo and Beijing promoting women's rights, and Rio recognising the environment as a key development issue, provided the basis for the formulation of the 8 Millennium Development Goals with their related targets and indicators. The majority of the world's governments have committed to help achieve these by 2015. It is to be noted that the work of formulating the goals was a 'collaborative' effort – collaboration including the involvement of the World Bank and the International Monetary Fund in their formulation. This new 'consensus' between these institutions is seen by some to be better read as 'cooption' of the United Nation's agenda by the two financial institutions, making the MDGs another type of 'conditionality' (Barton 2004). The narrow nature of the MDGs is the second commonly held critique of the goals. The goals do widen the notion of 'development' from the narrow economic growth focus of the World Bank and the IMF, with the key aim being to cut in half, by 2015, the numbers living in extreme poverty and hunger. The 8 goals include indicators for improved access to education, health, infant and maternal mortality, and epidemics including HIV/AIDS, gender, the environment and North-South relations. However, they also represent a narrowing of the agendas that emerged from the conferences of the 1990s with some central agreements being notable by their absence. Notable absentees include women's reproductive and sexual health and rights and gender-based violence; sexualities, differing abilities, ethnicity and race; and disasters, conflict and war.

There is a gender-focused goal, and MDG3 states the aim to 'promote gender equality and empower women'. However, examination of the related targets and indicators highlights that equality and empowerment is measured in terms of education, seats in parliament and women's 'non-agricultural' employment. This focus on education, employment and formal politics suggests a clear 'liberal feminist' or Women in Development approach, which has been highly critiqued (see Chapter 3). The other goal that is specifically about women is MDG5, which aims to improve maternal health. This is focused on providing reproductive health services to mothers, not on ensuring women's reproductive and sexual rights. In gender terms, activists and analysts debated the utility of engaging with the MDGs from the beginning (see WICEJ 2004 for discussion) and it has been suggested that MDG is better understood as a

'Most Distracting Gimmick' rather than a goal for women (Antrobus 2004b). Many of the concerns rest on what is seen to have been a politicisation of the process and the involvement of fundamentalist groups – both religious (of all denominations) and economic – in ensuring the 'deliberate exclusion' of women's sexual and reproductive rights from the millennium development agenda (ibid.). Even the Task Force set up to review how to operationalise MDG3 expressed serious concerns and stressed the need to include issues such as gendered rights if the goal were to succeed. Similar discussions do not seem to have occurred in the same way among those working within the 'disasters' context, despite its absence from the Goals. Instead discussion has focused on why DRR is important for achieving the MDGs, rather than why the MDGs should have a DRR goal.

The initial UN document on which the MDGs are based, the Millennium Declaration, did recognise the risks to development of disasters and resolved to intensify collective efforts to reduce the number and effects of natural and man-made disasters. However, in the move from the Declaration to the Development Goals this resolution was lost. The absence of specific mention of disasters within the MDGs is important given that the major agencies (such as the UN), major institutions (such as DFID in the UK), and International NGOs (such as Oxfam), are committed to the MDGs and funding is geared toward achieving these goals. What does not fit within the MDG framework struggles to achieve funding. A narrower approach to channelling funding accompanies this new narrower funding focus. The so-called 'sectoral approach' sees organisations fund MDG themes or sectors, such as the health sector or education, rather than specific projects, and make monies available to governments to use alongside their own budgetary resources. The negative consequences for funding of themes that do not fit within the MDGs or which have a more holistic approach, such as risk reduction work, is clear. The lack of financial commitment to the HFA further exacerbates the situation.

The HFA notes the need for the MDGs to incorporate a disaster response but makes no real demands or headway in achieving this. It suggests disaster risk reduction is an important element for the achievement of internationally agreed development goals 'including those contained in the Millennium Declaration'. Calling on the Declaration is presumably done to suggest that a disaster response is implicit or underpins the Millennium Development process despite its absence from the Goals. The Bureau for Crisis Prevention and Recovery of the United Nations Development Programme (2004: 15) recognises that 'at first glance, it may appear that the MDGs do not relate specifically to conflict, crisis or natural disasters'. It then seeks to demonstrate the ways in which MDGs are implicitly related to disaster-related initiatives and disaster-related initiatives could be informed by the Goals. While it concludes that meeting the MDGs will not be possible while disaster risk management is 'left outside' development, once again the report does not represent a demand to include disaster reduction as a Goal for the millennium. It highlights, instead, opportunities that exist within the current MDG framework for including risk and mitigation initiatives. Interestingly, the goal which the report suggests offers the 'most far-reaching' opportunities for disaster risk reduction – MDG8 Developing a Global Partnership for Development – is the goal that is perhaps the least developed and most criticised of all the MDGs. The focus on MDG8 is interesting as it implies implicit acceptance of the political nature of disasters, and the need for global 'partnership' or responsibility in tackling them. However, it is these issues of responsibility, and the high costs of assuming responsibility for disasters, that may keep it from the mainstream agendas such as the MDGs and the UNFCCC.

More generally, the discourse around the need to include disasters within development initiatives draws on the links between disasters and poverty and how disasters can undermine advances in poverty reduction. That is the central argument of recent calls to 'disaster proof' development. There are two perspectives through which the disaster-development relationship can be understood. In the first, poverty reduction is seen as a means to reduce disaster risk. In this context, 'disaster proofing' would understand risk reduction as an essential building block that forms the foundation of all development plans and policies (Duryog Nivaran 2009). Conversely, disasters may be seen to hinder the achievement of development goals and it is this that is key to understanding the new focus on 'disaster proofing' development (Bradshaw 2011). This is no more evident than in the 2010 United Nation's International Strategy for Disaster Reduction (ISDR) document entitled, 'Disaster Risk Reduction: an instrument for achieving the MDGs'.

The Global Facility for Disaster Reduction and Recovery (GFDRR), a partnership between the ISDR and the World Bank, suggests there is 'ample evidence' that poverty is the most important trigger for turning hazards into disasters. It suggests poverty-related policy objectives cannot be met if disaster risks are not taken into account and justifies its aim of mainstreaming disaster resilience into policy initiatives to safeguard 'development investments'. Thus, the threat posed by disasters is related to the risk of economic loss, and the protection that is needed is a product of any economic growth gains. While it could be argued that this focus is in line with the remit of the World Bank as a 'development' organisation, such an argument does not recognise that disasters are part of development and vulnerability arises from a lack of development or problematic 'development' processes (see Chapter 1). In line with the World Bank's discourse, in its call to 'disaster proof' development, DFID (2004) notes that poorer people tend to be more susceptible to hazards and that disasters can induce poverty, making the poor destitute. It does not confine itself to a homogeneous notion of 'the poor' but refines its analysis to highlight how female household heads, being more asset poor, may be more impacted by natural hazards. It justifies a focus on disasters by noting how they can 'wipe out any gains that may have been made through poverty reduction programmes or pro-poor economic growth' (DFID 2004: 3). The argument for 'disaster-proofing' then is very much an efficiency rather than a normative or moral discourse.

Both the development and the disaster risk reduction discourses highlight economic growth as the key policy issue but also suggest that they aim to 'protect' the poor. They justify policies using efficiency arguments but also suggest that there are equality gains to be made through their implementation, in particular in terms of gender equality. Gender has emerged as an important element of the development, and more recently, the disaster policy discourse. It is an interesting issue to consider because it more than any other issue highlights the double efficiency and equality role of such policy initiatives. It also highlights the assumptions being made about the nature of risk and vulnerability within development and, increasingly, disasters policy initiatives – and the consequences of these for effectively delivering on policy promises to 'protect' the poor.

FEMINISATION OF DEVELOPMENT AND DISASTER DISCOURSE

A recent United Nation's initiative suggested that 'women always tend to suffer most from the impact of disasters' (UN/ADPC 2010: 8). DFID (2004: 3) seemingly go one step further in singling out female household heads, suggesting that 'female-headed households in developing countries are amongst those most asset-poor and have been found to be among those most affected by natural disasters'. As they do not cite any study to back up this claim about impact it appears to be based on the assumption that asset poverty is directly linked to vulnerability to disasters. DFID are not alone in drawing this link between poverty and vulnerability, or in assuming that women, because of their poverty, will be more vulnerable to natural hazards. There are three related assumptions: that the poor are more at risk from disaster; that women are more poor; and that female heads are the poorest of the poor. They are based on popular notions of gendered poverty contained in the 'feminisation of poverty' thesis (see Chant 2008a).

Feminisation of Poverty, or Feminisation of Poverty Alleviation?

The DFID argument suggests that women suffer more from disasters because they are poorer. However, it is not possible to say with certainty who will be the most affected by disasters, given that the impact of any event will be time, place and person specific or depend on a mix of location, event and vulnerability. While poverty is a key component of vulnerability, it is not the only, nor necessarily the main component, in terms of predicting impact. A study of 141 countries found that more women than men die from natural hazards and this is linked most strongly to women's unequal position in society. Put another way, where the status of women is low more women than men die or they die at a younger age (Neumayer and Plümper 2007 cited in UNISDR 2009b: 35). As the study notes, inequality does not only stem from, nor can it be measured by, income poverty. Using poverty as a proxy for vulnerability ignores factors such as social norms and relations that inform individual status and individual response. Ideas around relative poverty are themselves contested, particularly the notion of feminised poverty. What has been stressed is that, instead of constructing women as poorest, there is a need to focus on how women and men, and various groups of women, experience poverty differently (see Jackson 1996, 1998). This includes women's differing experiences of poverty within households, where women with a male partner suffer a lack of control over available household funds, while female heads suffer from a lack of access to funds. Women's poverty, then, is not a 'given' nor is it a 'known' as it may differ between women (see Chapter 2).

The link between gender and poverty has been much contested in recent years. The notion of a 'feminisation of poverty' acquired something of its current status as a global 'orthodoxy' in 1995 when the eradication of the 'persistent and increasing burden of poverty on women' was adopted within the Beijing Platform for Action (Chant 2008a). The feminisation of poverty thesis has over time come to be equated with the idea that more women are poor and more women are among the poor, that this is a rising trend, and that it is related to a feminisation of household headship. Underpinning this is the notion of women heads as being the poorest of the poor. However, while these ideas appear to have become received wisdom there is still no conclusive research to support the feminisation of poverty thesis, and research fails to confirm any consistent linkage between the 'feminisation of poverty' and the 'feminisation' of household headship (Chant 2008b). Jackson (1996) called for a move to 'rescue' gender from this 'poverty trap', noting that equating gender and poverty may run the risk that policies to address poverty are assumed to automatically address gender inequality, or are implemented in the name of women and gender equality. This inclusion of women to address poverty rather than because of their own experience of inequality, may help to explain why the UN Economic Commission for Latin America and the Caribbean (ECLAC 2004) found that the percentage of women participating in poverty reduction pro-grammes in the region was actually much higher than the percentage of women identified as poor. This high 'participation' of women in poverty reduction programmes has led some to suggest that, rather than the feminisation of poverty, we should talk of the 'feminisation of poverty alleviation' (Chant 2008a): women are being constructed not as the most poor, but as the most efficient means by which to reduce the number of the poor. Conditional Cash Transfer (CCT) programmes, pioneered in Mexico and Brazil, are a good example of this trend. Perhaps best known, not least since the World Bank has used it as a model for programmes across the globe, is Mexico's Progresa (later renamed Oportunidades) programme (Molyneux 2006, 2007, 2009).

CCT programmes aim to alleviate short-term poverty through cash transfers to poor households and to reduce longer-term poverty through making these transfers conditional on household investment in the human capital of their children. Backed by World Bank research that highlights the efficiency gains from channelling resources through women, it is women who receive the transfers on the condition that health, education and nutrition targets have been met. Women beneficiaries must also attend training sessions and in some cases undertake community works. In the Progresa programme, families also receive extra monetary incentives to send girls to school and keep them there. However, not all programmes have included this element, the Nicaraguan programme being a case in point (Bradshaw and Víquez 2008). The authors of CCT programmes often claim more than material improvement from the programmes and point to wider empowerment aims, generally the improvement in the situation and position of women and girls. Others highlight that far from being 'empowering', the programmes seek to define the identity of women as being focused on mothering as well as what it means to be a 'good' mother (Bradshaw 2008).

While those who promote CCTs claim great success for the pro-grammes across the globe, doubts have been raised over the key elements of the initiatives, not least the need for conditionalities (Hooper 2006). There are also doubts over their general applicability – the suggestion being the policies work best in middle-income rather than poor countries (Rawlings 2004) – and their long-term effectiveness. The key aim of the programmes is not poverty reduction *per se*, but to change the behaviour of the poor to reduce their own poverty in the future, through punitive conditionalities that remove funding if the poor do not comply. The fact that women have been targeted as the 'beneficiaries' of cash transfers with responsibility for ensuring the related conditions and behaviour changes are met has led some to suggest that women are at the service of the 'new' poverty agenda rather than served by it (Molyneux 2006). That is, we have moved from an era of the 'feminisation of poverty' to one of the 'feminisation of poverty alleviation', with a resultant 'feminisation of responsibility and obligation' where women are assuming greater liability for dealing with poverty and have progressively less choice other than to do so (Chant 2006, 2008a). While women are expected to take on new roles, these are conceptualised as part of their existing gendered roles as mothers and carers and thus reinforce gendered divisions of labour and do little to change the situation and position of women (Molyneux 2006, 2007).

It has been suggested that in the past decade social protection policies such as CCTs have assumed a growing role in the World Bank's response to both rapid and slow onset disasters, particularly though cash transfers and public works programmes (Heltberg 2007). CCTs have been presented as having the potential to enhance households' *ex-ante* risk management strategies (Vakis 2006). This makes them potentially important for understanding disaster response, while the wider issues CCTs raise about processes of 'feminisation' within development are interesting, and ones that might usefully be used to explore ongoing processes to 'engender' disasters (see Bradshaw 2009, 2010b).

The Feminisation of Disasters

From Hurricane Mitch onwards, studies suggest evidence for a move toward an engendering of disaster response and they demonstrate how women have become key 'beneficiaries' of reconstruction, actively sought out by NGOs and other agencies to be central to the organised response (see Chapter 6). That women should benefit from relief and reconstruction is not being questioned here. Nor is the fact that women are being targeted as beneficiaries being questioned. What is being questioned is why women are being targeted. This is important for understanding what drives this apparent engendering of disasters:

whether it is equality or efficiency concerns, since, if it is the latter rather than the former, women may be seen to be at the service of the disaster agenda as well as the development agenda. As the disaster cycle, unlike processes of development, is made up of apparently clear and discrete stages, it is also important to ask – what is feminised?

Over time women have been increasingly constructed as a vulnerable group in the face of natural hazards. However, while this has led to the recognition that women have specific gender needs, it has not resulted in disasters being understood as gendered experiences. Much like the feminisation of poverty, the thesis has meant that all women are constructed as vulnerable, rather than understanding the different experiences of women and men based on gender, class, age, ethnicity and other factors. The construction of women's vulnerability has also not been 'proved' in that it is not based on any objective feminised impact since, as discussed in Chapter 4, conclusive data still does not exist to support claims that women more than men suffer loss of life and limb and, particularly in Latin America, the opposite might be true given men's socially prescribed riskier behaviour in the face of danger. While there may be a feminised impact in terms of loss of material goods, again it is questionable as to the extent that this can be asserted with any certainty. Gender disaggregated data still tend to differentiate not between men and women within households but instead record household loss, and thus reflect only differences between male and female-headed households. Again, while female heads may suffer greater losses we do not have the studies to evidence such as assertion. What may actually influence this feminised notion of risk is not so much the actual situation but perceptions of the relative situation of female heads of household and, in particular, their assumed greater vulnerability. Thus a focus on women might tell us not so much about actual loss but rather how loss is understood and, as suggested in Chapter 1, disasters should be understood in relation to such responses (Dynes 1998).

Women's assumed vulnerability and their related assumed higher losses, appears important in understanding an apparent feminisation of reconstruction. Hurricane Mitch demonstrates that women were key 'beneficiaries' of reconstruction and women, individually and collectively, were sought out by international NGOs and other donors. The key question is – Why? It may be due to a gender perspective which seeks to use the hypothesised 'window of opportunity' to address gender inequalities through projects that challenge gender stereotypical roles and aim to address women's strategic interests as well as practical needs. However, again, there is little evidence of such holistic projects and even less documenting their success (see Chapter 6).

However, the focus on women post disaster may not be so much driven by concerns around gender inequality but rather by gendered roles and relations. That is, as with the CCT programmes, projects target resources at women because they see women as the best means to ensure a fair distribution of those resources within households. It is interesting then that Vakis (2006) suggests CCTs as a key option for disaster response. He uses, as an example, the Nicaraguan CCT, the Red de Protección Social (RPS) and suggests a CCT programme could enhance a household's capacity for income diversification through *ex-ante* risk management strategies, as well as reduce the need for adverse coping mechanisms *ex-post*, such as children dropping out of school. The key aim is to reduce 'household' risk. Reducing this collective risk may put women at economic risk in the short term, with the time spent on the programme having an impact on women's ability to undertake productive work. In the longer term it may see an expansion of women's caring role to include providing economic resources for children, with or without a programme in place, in the future. While the programme is in place, women must ensure that the conditionalities are adhered too and there may be a pressure to conform to the notion of the 'good mother' being promoted by the programme. CCTs are institutionalised coping strategies and much like the coping strategies adopted by households in times of crisis there may be benefits to the household but with a high cost for women (Bradshaw 2011).

In the past decade, social protection has assumed a growing role in the World Bank's response to both rapid and slow onset disasters, particularly though cash transfers and public works programmes (Heltberg 2007). The use of CCT type programmes post disaster suggests that criticisms that have been levelled at them and similar programmes within the development literature may also be applicable post disaster. Thus, the feminisation of reconstruction might be best understood not as a desire to engender disaster response, but as an element of wider feminisation processes within development. This occurs not only among individual women, but is also apparent within women's groups and movements as, despite all that is known about the social construction of roles and responsibilities and the need to challenge these, many women's groups take on the role of carer post disaster, reinforcing the notion of a feminised responsibility to care (Bradshaw 2004b).

However, while these feminised roles of responding to an event and caring for those who survive are clear immediately after the event, the evidence that they are sustained over the longer term as a 'feminisation of mitigation' is less clear, not least because very little post-post disaster research exists, and even less charting how women's organised activities change over time. Interviews with leaders of women groups undertaken by the author 10 years after Hurricane Mitch in Nicaragua showed that while a practical involvement in mitigation may have continued, more strategic engagement in DRR had lessened or ceased. Women do continue to mobilise at the grass roots level to help protect their communities, families and goods. The third role within women's 'triple burden' has long been shown to be community management. Increasingly, this may come to include disaster risk management activities and early warning exercises, as long as these are culturally acceptable and can fit within existing gendered identities, for example to care for children. Fordham's (2009b) study in Central America highlights that the women's committees set up to explicitly to consider risk and emergency responses quickly disintegrated. Women did continue to organise to reduce disaster risk, but this organisation was not explicitly around 'disasters' but rather related to issues such as health. This was perhaps because this fitted better with culturally prescribed roles as carer (of health) rather than protector (from disasters). At the more 'strategic' level of advocating for mitigation and adaptation to address structural causes of vulnerability, women seem less visible. This may have a number of explanations.

In contrast to reconstruction, within the mitigation discourse there continues to be a focus on notions of 'managing' risk. This suggests there are competing disaster discourses – the discourse of reconstruction which is social science based, focused on vulnerability and holistic in its approach, and the discourse of mitigation which, despite the advances made in the rhetoric, maintains a hazard focus, is oriented toward managing risk and is dominated by a 'masculine culture' (Fordham 2009b). This may mean that after the reconstruction period (male) 'experts' once again come to the fore, displacing those with (only) on-the-ground experience and introducing a more technical language and an associated exclusionary approach. The mitigation discourse and culture, then, may have little place for gender other than recognising that a feminised vulnerability may exist but seeing the solution in managing risk. Risk is conceptualised as generic, not gendered. The key is seen to be improving risk management in general, and this may come through including women in the process. Engendering disaster risk reduction, as with development, does not seek to change how risk is constructed, only how it is managed through an efficient targeting of resources – at women.

Not only may women be displaced from the disaster arena after reconstruction 'ends', but women's groups may withdraw from the field because it does not fit well with a more holistic feminist approach. This decision may be reinforced by their experiences of reconstruction and the high costs that women responders pay individually and institutionally (see Chapter 8). This is further compounded by the fact that funding for women's groups has declined in recent years, as has funding for projects not directly linked to the MDGs. This situation has been made worse both by the 'credit crunch' of 2008 and the feeling that there has been a backlash against women's hard won rights linked to the rise of religious and economic fundamentalisms. This may have led to a re-focusing of activities and the re-establishment of priorities for groups and movements based on those gender issues now on the margins of development – gender based violence and sexual rights. If they are only on the margins of development agendas, these issues are very clearly missing entirely from the disasters discourse. As a result, women's groups at a local level may continue with mitigation-related measures as a practical goal but women's movements may, quite rationally, see the price of engaging with disaster-related work as too high and not worthwhile as a strategic gendered goal.

DRAWING THE LINKS: GLOBALISATION OR FEMINISATION OF RESPONSIBILITY?

Despite the fact that it is now largely accepted that climate change will bring a greater number of more damaging 'disasters' and the recognition that disasters 'set back' development, there is little convergence of disaster risk reduction and climate change adaptation activities. The influence of either on the development discourse is even less evident. Climate change has been used to contextualise risk in the development discourse, and rather than informing how risk is conceptualised, disasters are constructed as a development risk. There is a lack of importance given to disasters as events in themselves and, instead, they are concep-tualised as harming economic development gains and it is these gains that need 'protecting'. Thus, reducing the impact of disasters is seen as a means to an end, rather than a goal in itself. Ultimately disaster-proofing development does not seek to give disaster risk reduction a higher profile as a goal in itself, but rather seeks to protect development gains. At the heart of this reluctance to incorporate disasters into the climate change and development agendas may be a reluctance to assume responsibility. The inclusion of a disaster-related goal into the MDGs for example, could prove very costly if it meant a genuine effort were made by the international community to reduce underlying risk factors. While respon-sibility has not been assumed at the international or macro level, it has been apportioned at the micro level and women have been placed at the service of the disaster as well as the development agenda.

Despite the fact that advances have been made both in terms of integrating the disaster and the development agendas, and in terms of integrating gender within this, there is still no coherent gender-disasters-development policy discourse. However, there are patterns in common, and parallels with the development agenda are apparent in terms of a seeming process of 'feminisation of responsibility', which extends this responsibility to cover not only social protection through poverty reduction, but protecting the family from disaster losses. This feminisation of relief and reconstruction, while related to some understanding of a gendered risk, may be better understood as being driven by efficiency rather then equality. The processes may be better understood as being part of a wider feminisation process within development than an engendering of disasters.

While the exclusion of women and gender from the disaster risk reduction discourse can be problematised, women's inclusion in relief and reconstruction also needs to be treated with care, given that women may be included not as a means to improve their position and situation, but rather that of others, including children and the wider community in general. Processes of feminisation see women's roles and responsibilities being ever more expanded, but any personal benefits they bring for women will remain elusive while efficiency, not equality, remains the key driver behind 'engendering' development and disasters.

Conclusion – Drawing the links: gender, disasters and development

This book has sought to draw links between the development and the disaster discourse and practice and explore what this means for 'engendering' disasters. While, in conceptual and theoretical terms, the development discourse appears to be more advanced than that of disasters, concepts quite new to development, such as vulnerability and risk, have a long tradition of discussion among disaster specialists. While the official development discourse, such as that presented by the World Bank, has more recently begun to treat the notion of risk as a central concern, it has not drawn on this disaster-related literature to inform its conceptualisation. Rather than help conceptualise the development discourse around risk, disasters are instead conceptualised as risk. The heightened awareness of the risk disasters pose to development arises from concerns over extreme weather hazards, said to be on the increase as a result of climate change. It also arises from an acceptance that disasters can 'set back' development, in particular pushing people back into poverty or leaving the poor destitute. With the creation of the HFA, the global disaster framework has recognised this link, and the formation of the Global Facility for Disaster Reduction and Recovery (GFDRR) suggests recognition by key development actors such as the World Bank also. However, despite calls to 'disaster proof' development and the increasing commonalities of the development and disaster lexicons, ultimately, the two continue to be distinct policy and funding areas. The Millennium Development Goals highlight this separation. They also highlight how the relationship that does exist is constructed, in that disaster risk reduction is presented as necessary for achieving the Goals rather than as a goal in itself.

The construction of disasters within the development discourse is as a risk to development, and the justification for taking this risk into account is on efficiency not responsibility grounds, the argument being an economic not a moral one. This has similarities to how gender has been integrated into development: as an efficiency rather than an equality concern. In turn, gender is being integrated into disasters, seemingly borrowing from this same efficiency rhetoric. More recently, the notion of protection has been noticeable, if implicit, within both discourses. The disaster discourse, like that of development, constructs women as both needing protection and as protectors. The need for protection arises from their assumed vulnerability to economic and natural hazards, which in turn arises from their smaller asset base. Acceptance of this might suggest building up women's assets – addressing practical needs – or addressing the unequal gender relations that are at the root of this – a more strategic approach. In reality, neither is generally taken. Instead, the focus is on 'protecting' women and their children once they are affected by an event. In the disaster context, this need for protection also extends at times to an explicit recognition of women needing protection from men. This is problematic in two ways. First, in times of disaster it constructs men as moving from 'lurking in the shadows' (Cornwall 1998) to taking a central and aggressive, if not violent, role. This, of course, does not characterise all men or all women's experiences of disasters and, while not calling here for a focus on masculinities, the demonisation of men, and particularly the racialised demonisation of men, seen post Katrina and after the earthquake in Haiti needs to be addressed and redressed. Second, while violence against women is assumed to be an issue post disaster it, like the event itself, is constructed as 'extra-ordinary', as arising from the circumstances and not something which is a lived reality for many, many women across the globe as they go about their day to day 'normal' lives. While welcoming the ability to raise the issue of violence against women that disasters bring, it is important to make sure that this violence is not constructed as an abnormal, extra-ordinary reaction to the situation – violence should not be considered 'normal' or acceptable but nor can it be considered to be something that is not the norm for many women. The need then is to address violence as both a development and a disaster issue. The protection discourse within development does not stretch to providing protection for women living with violence in 'normal' times. Within the development discourse, the protection agenda has been more focused on women's poverty but, while framed as protecting women, it is women's role in protecting or caring for others, particularly children, that is actually evident.

In development terms, women's poverty is assumed in the feminisation of poverty thesis. While this appears to make women and their situation visible, it may have the opposite outcome in that it has become received wisdom that women are in all circumstances poor. As such there is little attempt to take forward thinking around how different women live and understand their relative poverty. In particular, how poverty is constructed within households is ignored and, in this context, the household is a site that remains a policy taboo. Policies aim to address the behaviour of households, of individuals within households, and how people should live within them. Policies even seek to regulate who can live together. But, policies do not aim to address or redress inequalities within gendered household functioning. What they do is tackle the outcome of inequality through targeting women with resources, effectively circumventing the real issue – unequal gender relations. Increasingly, policies in both the development and disaster contexts target women as 'beneficiaries', assuming women will use the resources provided more 'efficiently' and fairly than men. How this occurs – household functioning – is not considered, nor are the profound changes a policy can have on how households function, nor their possible impact in making household relations 'dysfunctional'. Dysfunctional households, when considered, are considered to be those which are outside the norm, in particular, female-headed households. If women are constructed as poor, then female heads, despite the empirical evidence problematising this assumption, have been constructed as the poorest of the poor. This allows policy makers to circumvent the real issue – gender relations between women and male partners – and instead focus on 'abnormal' gender roles, that is, female headship. This contrasts with the implicit recognition that all is not well in male-headed households, which sees women, rather than male heads, targeted as 'beneficiaries' of resources.

This feminisation of resource allocation has been problematised by gender academics as putting women at the service of the poverty or policy agenda (Molyneux 2006) and, as such, representing a feminisation of obligation, leaving women with the responsibility for ensuring that poverty alleviation and other policy obligations are achieved (Chant 2008a). The discussion throughout this book suggests this feminisation process is now also being witnessed within disaster discourse and practice.

Due to their poverty, women, like the developing world, are constructed as 'at risk' within the disaster discourse. Given current conceptualisations of vulnerability, it is easy to see why the developing world is seen to be prone to disasters. Modernisation theory would suggest this vulnerability arises from a lack of 'development' and propose the solution to be further Western interventions to change the internal structures and people that produce this vulnerability. In contrast, Dependency theory would suggest this vulnerability stems neither from internal 'backwardness' nor the poverty of the Third World nations, but rather from the global inequalities of trade and aid perpetuated by 'development'. While a 'risk society' (Beck 1998) is seen by some to be the product of a striving for modernisation or 'development', this is not recognised within the dominant development and disaster discourse. It is disaster not development that is constructed as the 'risk' and, despite the rhetoric, the natural hazard remains the problem to be tackled, not the continued reconstruction of vulnerability that the development process produces. What is the real risk is a key issue that needs to be addressed since, at present, the Western construction of risk may differ from the Southern lived reality.

Risk is a subjective notion, as is the notion of disaster, and while Western experts may suggest a place is too risky to live in, those who have no alternative but to live there may differ in their understandings of the location, seeing it instead as simply 'home' with all the social and emotional attachment that brings. Those that remain in locations deemed risky are constructed as placing themselves at risk and become undeserving victims for whom outside authorities have little responsibility. This notion of individuals having a role to play in constructing their own risk occurs when natural hazards continue to be constructed as such – as 'natural' – and there is a continued idea that disasters are in some way an act of God. As such, the notion of a responsibility to respond, to protect and to mitigate impact remains a thorny issue.

The immediate response to disasters in the developing world tends to be dominated by international relief aid framed within the humanitarian discourse. This, then, is aid given as a moral, not a legal, responsibility and, as such, cannot be expected to be given. The discussion of 'new humanitarianism' highlights the increased acceptance that far from neutral, any aid is driven as much by politics as it is by morals. Other elements of the new humanitarianism that emerged from acceptance of the problematic international response to conflict situations since the Cold War, may be welcome in the post-disaster context – the new understanding that relief aid should support or at least not undermine longer-term development goals, for example. However, such a linking of relief to development in real terms can result in aid conditionalities, something that has been critiqued within development policy at the macro level with Structural Adjustment Programmes (SAPs) and, more recently, with the micro-level conditionalities of CCTs.

A further shift in how humanitarianism is understood focuses on the people impacted by events, and the rise of the notion of the undeserving victim, something even more evident post 9/11. Even in conflict situations, who is the aggressor and who is the victim cannot always be known at the time. In disaster situations, it might be suggested that all are 'deserving' victims, yet as Katrina demonstrates, this is not always seen to be the case, as black men in particular became constructed as 'aggressor' rather than victim. Women have tended to be classed as 'deserving' of aid and seen as non-combatants in conflict and as helpless victims in disasters, constructing the need to protect them. While bringing aid to women, this is not always a helpful construction. Universalism would suggest women should be beneficiaries for their 'sameness' not their difference (Ticktin 2011). Yet women do experience events differently, from men and from other women. Women both experience loss differently and their losses are different. Women are victims of violence, including sexual violence, martial and marital rape, in conflict and disaster. Responses need to take this into account and also move past current attempts to bring perpetrators to 'justice' and rather seek longer-term social justice for women.

As the chapters have shown, in current post-disaster response efforts, women are at once made highly visible and simultaneously rendered invisible. During, and immediately after events, individual women are active, yet their actions may be constructed as helpers rather than rescuers. The media circus that often follows large-scale events portrays women as helpless victims and primarily as mothers, setting up a contradiction as women are simultaneously portrayed as needing protection and as providing protection. This is also the case when national and international aid arrives and women become constructed as beneficiaries due to their gendered identities as mothers. In relief camps and refuges, their private role ironically becomes the more public and 'productive' of roles, while men's role as protector and provider is taken over by international aid givers. Patriarchal dominance does not decline but diversifies from the private to the public, demanding a further construction of women as grateful recipients of aid and protection. This also suggests why the seeming shift in roles, from the male head as the public figure to this role having a feminine face, does not translate into a shift in gender relations. Women's new role seemingly takes the place of the male head but it demands non-masculine characteristics if it is to be fulfilled effectively. Any change in role may also be transitory and understood as such. However, such 'transitory' changes may extend past relief and into the reconstruction period, and relief interventions may actively seek to promote changes in gender roles or to build on existing ones.

While the 'window of opportunity' analogy is often used to define the reconstruction phase, very few studies demonstrate any longer-term changes in gender relations as emerging post disaster. This may be due to the projects instigated, which create new roles for women but pay little attention to gender relations, focusing instead on ensuring women are able to fulfil 'their' practical needs. This focus ensures that the family needs are met, rather than questioning why women have the responsibility to fulfil those needs. Even when women's participation brings material goods into the home, these may be little valued by men, influencing how women's contribution to the household is understood. Productive, income generating work may continue to be most valued and women's community work, like their reproductive work, will not give them a greater voice in the home. It may instead lead to an increased real or perceived economic dependency in the longer term. Women's involvement in reconstruction may be seen as part of 'women's work' or another gendered role but one that does not confer voice or status. It merely adds a new responsibility for women, related to reconstruction and risk reduction. Parallels can be drawn with work that suggests that policy initiatives that focus on women providing poverty alleviation may not improve the situation or position of women because gender identities absorb these new roles, leaving their gendered meaning largely unchanged. The longer-term impact on women of a natural hazard may not be the hazard itself but what follows, and the disaster may be as much the post-disaster initiatives to engender the response to disasters as the gendered impact of the event itself.

It is not only individual women that may feel the impact of post-disaster interventions but women's groups and organisations also. Women leaders have noted that their learnt feminist analysis often goes out of the window during an event and a socialised gender role, to protect and care, kicks in. This is then utilised by donors, international NGOs and governments, through targeting women's groups, and especially NGOs with resources as effective providers on a collective stage. While NGOs are often also invited to help design reconstruction initiatives in the name of participation and participatory development, questions have been raised over the extent to which this actually has the opposite effect, as NGOs become the voice of civil society, negating the need to talk to people on the ground. The functioning of civil society organisations, just like households, can be defined as displaying cooperative conflict with different actors having different positions of power and voice. Disasters can strengthen 'the voice' of civil society but some voices may be muted or silenced within this collective strengthening. Women's voices in particular may not be heard, and women may instead seek 'women only' spaces. Even within women only spaces and movements, disasters can reveal existing fault lines and fracture them further, leading to a simultaneous strengthening of some groups and a fragmentation of the wider movement.

Yet there persists the notion of a window of opportunity existing after an event. It has been noted that reconstruction reflects the social and political ideals of a society or the values it wishes to maintain (Baker 2003). As such, it is perhaps not surprising that what, at times, is desired is the reconstruction of what existed beforehand: the familiar and the known. Men and women may actively seek to re-construct the social certainties of the past, including gendered roles, relations and identities. As feminists and gender activists, we all want a window of opportunity to exist for what we see to be the positive changes to occur, and we want to build something good from the suffering, loss and destruction that has occurred. Yet, while we should keep hold of this desire, there is a need to question what others desire when they seek to open this window. While 'engendering' development and disasters may seem a worthy aim that we should all support, the 'feminisation' agenda suggests a darker side to these initiatives and a need to proceed cautiously.

The message of this book is that we all need to be gender reflective practitioners, academics, thinkers and, above all, scholars. We need to learn from development, not in terms of 'how to', but in terms of the lessons that can be learned from development practice to avoid the negatives and build on the positives. In particular, it is important to understand that the participation of women is not, in itself, automatically or necessarily a good thing for them. Rather, participation should be a choice and should bring benefits to those who participate – practical and strategic. When participation becomes an obligation it should be questioned. The fact that women may not want to participate should be examined and understood in relation to their perception of priorities and risks. Risk from natural hazards is real, but understandings of this are subjective and we need to understand that women, and men, understand, and address the risks they face differently. Disaster risk, then, is not about the natural hazards that are faced. Risk arises from poverty and violence and, most importantly, from inequality. Women are not vulnerable because they are women but because of the gendered inequalities that are associated with being a woman, and these are diverse in nature. Disasters, then, are experienced as gendered events and the notion of what is a 'disaster' is gendered. Without care, the disaster for women may be as much the post-disaster interventions as the event itself.

What feminist critiques of development have taught us is that the 'why' matters and engendering for efficiency rather than equality reasons brings mixed results for women. As processes to engender disasters are still at an early stage there is potential to focus more on equality, something that concepts central to the disaster discourse, such as vulnerability and risk, suggest as being key. At the very least, where efficiency is the aim, the fact that women are good at delivering policy initiatives should be valued as a skill. Instead of merely shifting responsibility to them, women should be recognised and rewarded for being the best able to take on this responsibility. If not, women's inclusion in processes of development and in disasters is as problematic as their exclusion.

In disaster terms, the micro-level responsibility for disaster response seems to have been placed at the door of women yet this feminised response has not been matched by acceptance of a globalised responsibility. Until such a time, engendering disasters should proceed with caution.

Bibliography

Action Aid (2006), 'Tsunami response: A human rights assessment', Action Aid International, London, January 2006.

Afshar, H. and C. Dennis (1992), *Women and Adjustment Policies in the Third World*, London: Macmillan.

Agarwal, B. (1997), 'Bargaining and gender relations: Within and beyond the household', *Feminist Economics*, **3** (1), 1–51.

Agarwal B. (2003), 'Gender and land rights revisited: Exploring new perspectives via the state, family and markets', in R. Shahra (ed.), *Agrarian Change, Gender and Land Rights*, Oxford: UNRISD/ Blackwell, pp. 184–224.

Allen, T. and A. Thomas (eds.) (2000), *Poverty and Development into the 21st Century*, Oxford: Oxford University Press.

Almond, G.A. and S. Verba (1963), *The Civic Culture: Political Attitudes and Democracy in Five Nations*, Newbury Park: Sage.

Alvarez, S.E. (1999), 'Advocating feminism: The Latin American feminist NGO "boom"', *International Feminist Journal of Politics*, **1** (2), 181–209.

Anderson, C. (2009), 'Organising for risk reduction: The Honolulu call for action', in E. Enarson and D. Chakrabarti (eds.), *Women, Gender and Disaster: Global Issues and Initiatives*, India: Sage, pp. 40–56.

Anderson, M. (1999), *Do No Harm: How Aid Can Support Peace – or War*, Boulder, CO: Lynne Rienner Publishers.

Anderson, M. (2011), *Disaster Writing: The Cultural Politics of Catastrophe in Latin America*, Charlottesville, VA: University of Virginia Press.

Anderson, M. and P. Woodrow (1998), *Rising from the Ashes: Developing Strategies in Times of Disaster*, Boulder, CO: Westview Press.

Andreoni, J. (1989) 'Giving with impure altruism: Applications to charity and Ricardian equivalence', *Journal of Political Economy*, **97** (6), 1447–1458.

Andreoni, J. (1990), 'Impure altruism and donations to public goods: A theory of warm-glow giving', *Economic Journal*, **100** (401), 464–477.

Antrobus, P. (2004a), *The Global Women's Movement: Origins, Issues and Strategies*, London: Zed Books.

Antrobus, P. (2004b), 'MDGs – The most distracting gimmick', in WICEJ (ed.) (2004), *Seeking Accountability on Women's Human*

Rights: Women Debate the Millennium Development Goals, Women's International Coalition for Economic Justice, 14–16, available at http://www.banulacht.ie/onlinedocs/WICEJ_Seeking_Accountability_on_ Womens_Human_Rights_UN_MDGs_(2004).pdf (accessed 14 August 2012).

Ariyabandu, M. (2006), 'Gender issues in recovery from the December 2004 Indian Ocean tsunami: The case of Sri Lanka', *Earthquake Spectra*, **22** (S3), S759–S775.

Ariyabandu, M. (2009), 'Sex, gender and gender relations in disasters', in E. Enarson and D.Chakrabarti (eds.), *Women, Gender and Disaster: Global Issues and Initiatives*, Sage: India, pp. 5–17.

Babb, F. (2001), *After Revolution: Mapping Gender and Cultural Politics in Neo Liberal Nicaragua*, Austin, TX: University of Texas Press.

Baird, A.H. (2006), 'Tsunamis: Myth of green belts', SAMUDRA Report, No. 44, July 2006, available at http://eprints.jcu.edu.au/18132/ 1/Barid_2009_myth_of_green_belts.pdf (accessed 14 August 2012).

Baker, J.K. (2003), *Landscapes: Nature, Culture and the Production of Space*, Pittsburgh, PA: University of Pittsburgh Press.

Ball, J. and R. Xan (2011), 'Somalia famine appeal raises far less than previous disasters', the *Guardian*, Monday 8 August 2011, available at http://www.guardian.co.uk/world/2011/aug/08/somalia-famine-appeal-raises-less.

Bandarage, A. (1984), 'Women in development: Liberalism, Marxism and Marxist Feminism', *Development and Change*, **15**, 495–515.

Bankoff, G. (2001), 'Rendering the world unsafe: "Vulnerability" as Western Discourse', *Disasters*, **25** (1), 19–35.

Bankoff, G. (2003a), *Cultures of Disaster: Society and Natural Hazard in the Philippines*, London: Routledge Curzon Press.

Bankoff, G. (2003b), 'Vulnerability as a measure of change in society', *International Journal of Mass Emergencies and Disasters*, **21** (2), 5–30.

Bankoff, G. (2004), 'The historical geography of disaster: "vulnerability" and "local knowledge" in Western Discourse', in G. Bankoff, G. Frerks and T. Hilhorst (eds.), *Mapping Vulnerability: Disasters, Development and People*, London: Earthscan, pp. 25–36.

Baran, P.A. (1957), *The Political Economy of Growth*, New York: Monthly Review Press.

Barnshaw, J. and J. Trainor (2007), 'Race, class, and capital amidst the Hurricane Katrina diaspora', in D. Brunsma, D. Overfelt and J.S. Picou (eds.), *The Sociology of Katrina: Perspectives on a Modern Catastrophe*, Maryland: Rowman and Littlefield, pp. 91–106.

Barrientos, A. and D. Hulme (2008), 'Social protection for the poor and poorest: An introduction', in A. Barrientos and D. Hulme (eds.), *Social*

Protection for the Poor and the Poorest: Concepts, Policies, Politics, Houndsmills: Palgrave MacMillan, pp. 1–26.

Barrios, R. (2009), 'Tin roofs, cinder blocks, and the Salvatrucha Gang: The semiotic-material production of crisis in post-hurricane Mitch reconstruction', in M. Ensor (ed.), *The Legacy of Hurricane Mitch: Lessons from Post-Disaster Reconstruction in Honduras*, Arizona: University of Arizona Press, pp. 156–183.

Barton, A.H. (1970), *Communities in Disaster: A Sociological Analysis of Collective Stress Situations*, New York: Doubleday.

Barton, C. (2004), 'Women's movements and gender perspectives on the Millennium Development Goals', in UNDP (ed.), *Civil Society Perspectives on the Millennium Development Goals*, New York: UNDP pp 1–27, available at http://www.undp.org/content/undp/en/home/librarypage/mdg/civil-society-perspectives-on-the-mdgs1.html (accessed 14 August 2012).

Beck, U. (1998), *Risk Society: Towards a New Modernity*, London: Sage.

Becker, G.S. (1981), *A Treatise on the Family*, enlarged edition 1991, Cambridge, MA: Harvard University Press.

Beechey, V. (1979), 'On Patriarchy', *Feminist Review*, **3**, 66–82.

Bello, W. (2006), 'The rise of the relief-and-reconstruction complex', *Journal of International Affairs*, **59** (2), 281–296.

Beneria, L. and S. Feldman (eds.) (1992), *Unequal Burden: Economic Crisis, Persistent Poverty and Women's Work*, Boulder, CO: Westview Press.

Benight, C.C. and A. Bandura (2004), 'Social cognitive theory of posttraumatic recovery: The role of perceived self-efficacy', *Behaviour Research and Therapy*, **42**, 1129–1148.

Bennett, R. and M. Daniel (2002), 'Media reporting of Third World disasters: The journalist's perspective', *Disaster Prevention and Management*, **11** (1), 33–42.

Bennett, R. and R. Kottasz (2000), 'Emergency fund-raising for disaster relief', *Disaster Prevention and Management*, **9** (5), 352–360.

Bernstein, P.L. (1996), *Against the Gods – The Remarkable Story of Risk*, New York: John Wiley.

Blaikie, P. and T. Cannon, I. Davis, B. Wisner (1994), *At Risk: Natural Hazards, People's Vulnerability, and Disasters*, (also published in 2003), London, New York: Routledge.

Blumberg, R.L. (ed.) (1991), *Gender, Family and Economy: The Triple Overlap*, London and New Delhi: Sage.

Bolin R. (1988), 'Response to natural disasters', in M. Lysted (ed.), *Mental Health Response to Mass Emergencies*, New York: Brunner/Mazel, pp. 22–51.

Bolin, R. and P. Bolton (1986), 'Race, religion, and ethnicity in disaster recovery', Program on Environment and Behavior, Monograph #42, Boulder, CO: University of Colorado.

Bonin, H. and A. Constant, K. Tatsiramos, K.F. Zimmermann (2010), 'Native-migrant differences in risk attitudes', *Applied Economics Letters*, **16** (15), 1581–1586.

Booth, D. (2003), 'PRSPs – Introduction and overview', *Development Policy Review*, **21** (2), 131–159.

Boserup, E. (1970), *Woman's Role in Economic Development*, New York: St Martin's.

Botzen, W.J.W. and J.C.J.H. Aerts, J.C.J.M. Van de Bergh (2009), 'Dependence of flood risk perceptions on socioeconomic and objective risk factors', *Water Resources Research*, **45**, 1–15.

Bouta, T. and G.E. Frerks, I. Bannon (2005), *Gender, Conflict and Development*, Washington, DC: World Bank.

Bouwer, L. (2011), 'Have disaster losses increased due to anthropogenic climate change?', *Bulletin of the American Meteorological Society*, **92** (1), 39–46.

Bowden, G. (2011), 'Disasters as system accidents: A socio-ecological framework', in R. Dowty and L. Allen (eds.), *Dynamics of Disaster: Lessons on Risk, Response and Recovery*, London and Washington, DC: Earthscan, pp. 47–60.

Bracke, S. (2004), 'Different worlds possible: Feminist yearnings for shared futures', in J. Kerr, E. Sprenger and A. Symington (eds.), *The Future of Women's Rights: Global Visions and Strategies*, London and New York: Zed Books, pp. 97–115.

Bradshaw, S. (2001a), 'Reconstructing roles and relations: Women's participation in reconstruction in post-Mitch Nicaragua', *Gender and Development*, **9** (3), 79–87.

Bradshaw, S. (2001b), *Dangerous Liaisons: Women, Men and Hurricane Mitch / Relaciones Peligrosas: Mujeres, Hombres y el Mitch*, Managua, Nicaragua: Puntos de Encuentro.

Bradshaw, S. (2002a), *Gendered Poverties and Power Relations: Looking Inside Communities and Households / La pobreza no es la Misma ni es Igual: Relaciones de Poder Dentro y Fuera del Hogar*, Managau, Nicaragua: Puntos de Encuentro.

Bradshaw, S. (2002b), 'Exploring the gender dimensions of reconstruction processes post-hurricane Mitch', *Journal of International Development*, **14**, 871–879.

Bradshaw, S. (2004a), 'Socio-economic impacts of natural disasters: A gender analysis', United Nations Economic Commission for Latin America and the Caribbean (ECLAC) Serie Manuales 32, available at http://www.eclac.org/publicaciones/xml/3/15433/lcl2128i.pdf (accessed 14 August 2012).

Bradshaw, S. (2004b), 'On the margins and the mainstream: Engendering the disasters agenda', paper presented at Gender Equality and Disaster Risk Reduction Workshop, Honolulu, Hawaii, 10–12 August, 2004, available at http://gdnonline.org/resources/bradshaw-margins-and-main stream.pdf (accessed 14 August 2012).

Bradshaw, S. (2008), 'From structural adjustment to social adjustment: A gendered analysis of conditional cash transfer programmes in Mexico and Nicaragua', *Global Social Policy*, **8** (1), 188–207.

Bradshaw, S. (2009), 'Engendering disasters: Feminisation of response or a feminisation of responsibility?', *Regional Development Dialogue*, **30** (1), 123–131.

Bradshaw, S. (2010a), *Decisiones Económicas e Intimas de las Mujeres*, Nicaragua: Puntos de Encuentro, available at http://sidoc.puntos.org.ni/isis_sidoc/documentos/13137/13137_00.pdf (accessed 14 August 2012).

Bradshaw, S. (2010b), 'Feminisation or de-feminisation? Gendered experiences of poverty post-disaster', in S. Chant (ed.), *International Handbook on Gender and Poverty*, Cheltenham and Northampton, MA: Edward Elgar, pp. 627–632.

Bradshaw, S. (2011), 'Disaster-proofing development and engendering disasters: Exploring understandings of risk, responsibility and social protection in the development and disaster contexts', paper presented at a workshop, Gender and Social Policy in Latin America: Current Research Directions, 10 May 2011, University of London.

Bradshaw, S. (2012), 'Does women's work, work for women? The influence of work on economic and intimate decision making in low income Nicaraguan households', paper presented at the International Association for Feminist Economics (IAFFE) Annual Conference, 27–29 June, 2012, Barcelona, Spain.

Bradshaw, S. (2013), 'Women's decision-making in rural and urban households in Nicaragua: The influence of income and ideology', *Environment and Urbanization*, **25** (1).

Bradshaw, S. and A. Arenas (2004), 'Análisis de género en la evaluación de los efectos socioeconómicos de los desastres naturales', Comisión Económica para América Latina y el Caribe (CEPAL), *Serie Manuales* 33, available at http://www.aprchile.cl/pdfs/genero_desatres_cepal.pdf (accessed 14 August 2012).

Bradshaw, S. and B. Linneker (2003), 'Challenging women's poverty: perspectives on gender and poverty reduction strategies from Nicaragua and Honduras', *CIIR-ICD Briefing*, London: CIIR-ICD, available at http://www.progressio.org.uk/sites/default/files/ Challenging-womens-poverty.pdf (accessed 14 August 2012).

Bradshaw, S. and A. Quirós Víquez (2008), 'Women beneficiaries or women bearing the cost? A gendered analysis of the Red de Protección Social in Nicaragua', *Development and Change*, **39** (5), 823–844.

Bradshaw S. and B. Linneker, R.E. Zúniga (2002), 'Social roles and spatial relations of NGOs and Civil Society: Participation and effectiveness post Hurricane Mitch', in C. McIlwaine and K. Willis K (eds.), *Challenges and Change in Middle America: Perspectives on Development in Mexico, Central America and the Caribbean*, Harlow: Prentice Hall/Pearson, pp. 243–269.

Bradshaw, S. and V. Castillo, A. Criquillion, G. Wilson (2008), 'Women mobilising to defend abortion rights in Nicaragua: Is therapeutic abortion the wrong right to promote?', in M. Mukhopadhya (ed.), *Gender, Rights and Development*, Gender, Society and Development Series, Amsterdam: Royal Tropical Institute, pp. 57–68.

Bretton Woods Project, http://www.brettonwoodsproject.org/ (accessed 14 August 2012).

Brown, B.L. (2012), 'Battered women's shelters in New Orleans: Recovery and tranformation', in E. David and E. Enarson (eds.), *The Women of Katrina: How Gender, Race and Class Matter in an American Disaster*, Nashville, TN: Vanderbilt University Press, pp. 17–189.

Brown, E.P. (1991), 'Sex and starvation: famine in three Chadian societies', in R.E Downs, D.O Kerner and S.P Reyna (eds.), *The Political Economy of African Famine*, Philadelphia, PA: Gordon and Breach Science Publishers.

Brown, P. and J. Minty (2006), 'Media coverage and charitable giving after the 2004 tsunami', *William Davidson Institute Working Paper*, Number 855, available at http://www.wdi.umich.edu/files/Publications/ WorkingPapers/wp855.pdf (accessed 14 August 2012).

Bruce, J. (1989), 'Homes divided', *World Development*, **17** (7), 979–991.

Brunsma, D. and D. Overfelt, J.S. Picou (eds.) (2007), *The Sociology of Katrina: Perspectives on a Modern Catastrophe*, Maryland: Rowman and Littlefield.

Bureau for Crisis Prevention and Recovery (2004), 'Reducing disaster risk: A challenge for development', United Nations Development Programme, available at http://www.unisdr.org/2005/mdgs-drr/ undp.htm (accessed 14 August 2012).

Burgess, R. (1978), 'Petty commodity housing or dweller control? A critique of John Turner's views on housing policy', *World Development*, **6** (9–10), 1105–1133.

Burgess, R. (1982), 'Self-help housing advocacy: A curious form of radicalism. A critique of the work of John F.C. Turner', in P. Ward (ed.), *Self-help Housing: A Critique*, Mansell: Alexandrine Press Book, pp. 56–98.

Burn, D.H. (1999), 'Perceptions of flood risk: A case study of the Red River flood of 1997', *Water Resources Research*, **35** (11), 3451–3458.

Busby, C. (1999), 'Agency, power and personhood: Discourses of gender and violence in a fishing community in South India', *Critique of Anthropology*, **19** (3), 227–248.

Buvinić, M. (1999), 'Hurricane Mitch: Women's needs and contributions', Inter-American Development Bank, Sustainable Development Department, *Technical Papers Series*, available at http://idbdocs.iadb.org/wsdocs/getdocument.aspx?docnum=816307 (accessed 14 August 2012).

Byrne, B. and S. Baden (1995), 'Gender, emergencies and humanitarian assistance', *BRIDGE Report*, No. 35, Sussex: IDS available at http://www.bridge.ids.ac.uk/reports/re33c.pdf (accessed 14 August 2012).

CAF (2007), Charities Aid Foundation: UK Giving 2007, available at, http://www.cafonline.org/pdf/2007%20UK%20Giving%20Report.pdf (accessed 14 August 2012).

Caldera, T. and L. Palma, U. Penayo, G. Kullgren (2001), 'Psychological impact of hurricane Mitch in Nicaragua in a one-year perspective', *Social Psychiatry and Psychiatric Epidemiology*, **36**, 108–114.

Cannon, T. (1994), 'Vulnerability analysis and the explanation of "natural" disasters', in A. Varley (ed.), *Disasters, Development and Environment*, Chichester; New York; Brisbane; Toronto and Singapore: John Wiley, pp. 13–29.

Card, C. (1991), 'Rape as a terrorist institution', in R.G. Frey and C.W. Morris (eds.), *Violence, Terrorism, and Justice*, New York: Cambridge University Press, 296–319.

Card, C. (1996), 'Rape as a weapon of war', *Hypatia*, Special Issue: Women and Violence, **11** (4), 5–18.

Card, C. (2002), *The Atrocity Paradigm*, Oxford: Oxford University Press.

Cardona, O.D. (2004), 'The need for rethinking the concepts of vulnerability and risk from a holistic perspcetive: A necessary review and criticism for effective risk management', in G. Bankoff, G. Frerks and T. Hilhorst (eds.), *Mapping Vulnerability: Disasters, Development and People*, London: Earthscan, pp. 37–51.

Cardona, O.D. and M.K. van Aalst, J. Birkmann, M. Fordham, G. McGregor, R. Perez, R.S. Pulwarty, E.L.F. Schipper, B.T. Sinh (2012), 'Determinants of risk: Exposure and vulnerability', in *Managing the Risks of Extreme Events and Disasters to Advance Climate Change*

Adaptation, Cambridge, UK, and New York: Cambridge University Press, pp. 65–108, available at https://www.ipcc-wg1.unibe.ch/srex/downloads/SREX-Chap2_FINAL.pdf (accessed 14 August 2012).

Cardoso, F.H. and E. Faletto (1979), *Dependency and Development in Latin America*, Berkeley, CA: University of California Press.

CARMA (2006), *The CARMA Report on Western Media Coverage of Humanitarian Disasters*, CARMA International, available at http://www.imaging-famine.org/images/pdfs/carma_%20report.pdf (accessed 14 August 2012).

Castells, M. (1983), *The City and the Grassroots: A Cross-cultural Theory of Urban Social Movements*, Berkeley, CA: University of California Press.

CCER (1999), *Proposal for the Reconstruction and Transformation of Nicaragua: Converting the Tragedy of Mitch into an Opportunity for the Sustainable Human Development of Nicaragua*, Managua, Nicaragua: Civil Coordinator for Emergency and Reconstruction/Carqui Press.

CEPAL (2003), *Handbook for Estimating the Socio-economic and Environmental Effects of Disasters*, Mexico: Comisión Económica para América Latina y el Caribe, available at http://www.preventionweb.net/english/professional/publications/v.php?id=1099 (accessed 14 August 2012).

Chambers, R. (1995) 'Poverty and livelihoods: Whose reality counts?', *IDS Discussion Paper* 347, Brighton: IDS.

Chambers, R. (1997), *Whose Reality Counts? Putting the First Last*, London: Intermediate Technology Publications.

Chambers, R. and G. Conway, (1992), 'Sustainable rural livelihoods: Practical concepts for the 21st century', *IDS Discussion Paper* 296, Brighton: IDS.

Chandler, D. (2001), 'The road to military humanitarianism', *Human Rights Quarterly*, **23** (3), 678–700.

Chandler, J. and T.M. Griffin, N. Sorensen (2008), 'In the "I" of the storm: Shared initials increase disaster donations', *Judgment and Decision Making*, **3** (5), 404–410.

Chant, S. (2000), 'From "woman-blind" to "man-kind": Should men have more space in gender and development?', *IDS Bulletin*, **31** (2), 7–17.

Chant, S. (2003), *Female Household Headship and the Feminisation of Poverty: Facts, Fictions and Forward Strategies*, London School of Economics and Political Science, London: Gender Institute, available at http://eprints.lse.ac.uk/574/ (accessed 14 August 2012).

Chant, S. (2006), 'Re-thinking the "feminization of poverty" in relation to aggregate gender indices', *Journal of Human Development*, **7** (2), 201–220.

Chant, S. (2008a), 'The "feminisation of poverty" and the "feminisation" of anti-poverty programmes: Room for revision?', *Journal of Development Studies*, **44** (2), 165–197.

Chant, S. (2008b), 'Dangerous equations? How female-headed households became the poorest of the poor: causes, consequences and cautions', in J. Momsen (ed.), *Gender and Development: Critical Concepts in Development Studies*, London: Routledge.

Chant, S. and M. Gutmann (2000), *Mainstreaming Men into Gender and Development: Debates, Reflections and Experiences*, Oxford: Oxfam Publishing.

Chant, S. and C. McIlwaine (2009), *Geographies of Development in the 21st Century: An Introduction to the Global South*, Cheltenham and Northampton, MA: Edward Elgar.

Chesler, P. (1972), *Women and Madness*, New York: Palgrave Macmillan.

CIET-CCER (1999a), *Social Audit for the Emergency and Reconstruction: Phase 1 – April 1999*, Managua, Nicaragua: Civil Coordinator for Emergency and Reconstruction /CIETinternational /Carqui Press.

CIET-CCER (1999b), *Auditoría Social para la Emergencia y la Reconstrucción – Fase 2 – Noviembre*, Managua, Nicaragua: Civil Coordinator for Emergency and Reconstruction/CIETinternational/Carqui Press.

Claeson, M. and C.G. Griffin, T. Johnston, M. McLachlan, A. Soucat, A. Wagstaff, A. Yazbeck (2002), 'Health, nutrition, and population', in J. Klugman (ed.), *A Sourcebook for Poverty Reduction Strategies*, Washington, DC: World Bank.

Clark, J. (1992), 'Policy influence, lobbying and advocacy', in M. Edwards and D. Hulme (eds.), *Making a Difference: NGOs and Development in a Changing World*, London: Earthscan.

Clarke, M. and S. Murray (2010), 'The voices of international NGO staff', in M. Clarke, I. Fanany, and S. Kenny (eds.), *Post-Disaster Reconstruction: Lessons from Aceh*, London: Earthscan, pp. 155–185.

Clulow, M. (2002), *The Central American Women's Movement and Public Policy: Analysis by Five Feminist Organizations*, Building Women's Citizenship and Governance, European Commission and the UK Lottery Fund.

Coates, T. (2010), *'The Conscious Community: Belonging, identities and networks in local communities' response to flooding'*, Unpublished PhD thesis, Middlesex University, available at http://eprints.mdx.ac.uk/6592/ (accessed 14 August 2012).

Cockburn, C. (2001), 'The gendered dynamics of armed conflict and political violence', in C. Moser and C. Clark (eds.), *Victims, Perpetrators or Actors? Gender, Armed Conflict and Political Violence*, London: Zed Books.

Collier, P. (1998), 'Social capital and poverty, social capital initiative', *Working Paper*, No. 4, Washington, DC: World Bank.

Conway, D. (1982), 'Self-Help Housing, the commodity nature of housing and amelioration of the housing deficit: Continuing the Turner-Burgess Debate', *Antipode*, **14** (2), 40–46.

Cooke, B. and U. Kothari (eds.) (2002), *Participation: The New Tyranny?*, London: Zed Books.

Corbridge, S. (1993), *Debt and Development*, Oxford: Blackwell.

Cornhiel, S. and Z. Garcia Frias (2005), 'Gender and land rights: Findings and lessons from country studies', in *Gender and Land Compendium of Country Studies*, Rome: Food and Agriculture Organization of the United Nations.

Cornia, G. and R. Jolly, F. Stewart (eds.) (1987), *Adjustment with a Human Face*, Oxford: Clarendon Press.

Cornwall, A. (1998), 'Gender, participation and the politics of difference', in I. Guijt and M.K. Shah (eds.), *The Myth of Community: Gender Issues in Participatory Development*, London: Intermediate Technology Publications, pp. 46–57.

Cornwall, A. (2001), 'Making a difference? Getting serious about gender and participatory development', *IDS Discussion Paper*, No. 378, Brighton: IDS.

Cornwall, A. (2002), 'Making a difference? Gender and participatory development' in S. Razavi (ed.), *Shifting burdens: Gender and Agrarian Change under Neoliberalism*, Bloomfield, CT: UNRISD/ Kumarian Press, pp. 197–232.

Crush, J. (ed.) (1995), *Power of Development*, London: Routledge.

Cupples, J. (2007), 'Gender and Hurricane Mitch: Reconstructing subjectivities after disaster', *Disasters: The Journal of Disaster Studies, Policy and Management*, **31** (2), 155–175.

Curtis, D. (2001), 'Politics and humanitarian aid: Debates, dilemmas and dissension', *HPG Report* 10, London: ODI, available at http://www.odi.org.uk/resources/docs/295.pdf (accessed 14 August 2012).

Cutter, S.L. (2001), 'The changing nature of risks and hazards', in S. Cutter (ed.), *American Hazardscapes: The Regionalization of Hazards and Disasters*, Washington, DC: Joseph Henry Press, pp. 1–12.

Darcy, J. (2004), 'Locating responsibility: The Sphere Humanitarian Charter and its rationale', *Disasters*, **28** (2), 112–123.

Das, V. and A. Kleinman (2000), *Violence and Subjectivity*, Berkeley, CA: University of California Press.

Dasgupta, P. and I. Seregeldin (1999), *Social Capital: A Multifaceted Perspective*, Washington, DC: World Bank.

da Silva, J. (2010), *Lessons from Aceh: Key Considerations in Post-Disaster Reconstruction*, report for the Disasters Emergency Committee/Arup, Warwickshire: Practical Action Publishing.

David, E. and E. Enarson (eds.) (2012), *The Women of Katrina: How Gender, Race and Class Matter in an American Disaster*, Nashville, TN: Vanderbilt University Press.

Davies, S. (1993), 'Are coping strategies a cop out?', *IDS Bulletin*, **24** (4), 60–72.

Davis, E. and K. Rouba (2012), 'Out of sight, out of mind: Women's abilities and disabilities in crisis', in E. David and E. Enarson (eds.), *The Women of Katrina: How Gender, Race and Class Matter in an American Disaster*, Nashville, TN: Vanderbilt University Press, pp. 76–89.

de Brouwer, A. (2007), 'Sexual violence against women during the genocide in Rwanda and its aftermath', Solace Ministries International Conference, 30 April–4 May 2007, Einigen, Switzerland.

de Silva, S. (2006), 'The trauma of tsunami-affected women in Sri Lanka', in M. Domroes (ed.), *After the Tsunami: Relief and Rehabilitation in Sri Lanka*, New Delhi: Mosaic Books, pp. 61–70.

de Waal, A. (1989), *Famines that Kill: Darfur, Sudan, 1984–85*, Oxford: Clarendon Press.

Dean, M. (1999), *Governmentality: Power and Rule in Modern Society*, London: Sage.

Deere, C.D. and M. León (1982), *Women in Andean Agriculture: Peasant Production and Rural Wage Employment in Colombia and Peru*, Ginebra: International Labour Office.

Deere, C.D. and M. León (2001), *Empowering Women: Land and Property Rights in Latin America*, Pittsburgh, PA: University of Pittsburgh Press.

Deininger, K. and P. Olinto (2000), *Asset Distribution, Inequality and Growth*, Washington, DC: World Bank.

Delaney, P. and E. Shrader (2000), 'Gender and post-disaster reconstruction: The case of hurricane Mitch in Honduras and Nicaragua', Decision review draft presented to the World Bank, January 2000.

Derrida, J. (1976), *Of Grammatology* (trans. Gayatri Spivak), Baltimore, MD: Johns Hopkins University Press.

Derrida, J. (1978), *Writing and Difference* (trans. Alan Bass), Chicago: University of Chicago Press.

Desai, V. and R. Potter (eds.) (2008), *The Companion to Development Studies*, London: Arnold.

DFID (2004), 'Adaptation to climate change: Making development disaster-proof', *DFID Key Sheet* 06.

Dietz, T. and P. Druijven, D. Foeken (1992), 'Coping mechanisms and livelihood strategies – A summary of concepts', in T. Dietz and L. de Haan (eds.), *Coping with Semiaridity: How the Rural Poor Survive in Dry Season Environments*, Amsterdam: University of Amsterdam, pp. 37–43.

Dijkhorst, H. and S. Vonhof (2005), *Gender and Humanitarian Aid a Literature Review of Policy and Practice*, Wageningen Disaster Studies: Wageningen University.

Dollar, D. and R. Gatti (1999), 'Gender inequality, income, and growth: Are good times good for women?', *Gender and Development Working Papers*, No. 1, World Bank, May 1999.

Dollar, D. and A. Kraay (2000), *Growth is Good for the Poor*, World Bank Development Research Group, available at http://siteresources.worldbank.org/DEC/Resources/22015_Growth_is_Good_for_Poor.pdf (accessed 14 August 2012).

Dombrowsky, W. (1998), 'Again and again: Is a disaster what we call a "disaster"?', in E.L. Quarantelli (ed.), *What is a Disaster?: Perspectives on the Question*, London and New York: Routledge, pp. 13–24.

Domroes, M. (2006), 'The Tsunami catastrophe in Sri Lanka – Its dimension, relief and rehabilitation', in M. Domroes (ed.), *After the Tsunami: Relief and Rehabilitation in Sri Lanka*, New Delhi: Mosaic Books, pp. 1–33.

D'Ooge, C. (2008), 'Queer Katrina: Gender and sexual orientation matters in the aftermath of the disaster', in B. Willinger (ed.), *Katrina and the Women of New Orleans: Executive Report and Findings*, New Orleans: Newcomb College, Tulane University.

Dos Santos, T. (1970), 'The Structure of dependence', *The American Economic Review*, **60** (2), 231–236.

Douglas, M. (1992), *Risk and Blame: Essays in Cultural Theory*, London: Routledge.

Drabek, T. (1996), *The Social Dimensions of Disaster* (FEMA Emergency Management Higher Education Project College Course Instructor Guide), Emmitsburg, MD: Emergency Management Institute.

Drabek, T. (1997), *Multi Hazard Identification and Risk Assessment*, Washington, DC: FEMA.

Dumroes, M. (2006), 'The tsunami catastrophe in Sri Lanka: Its dimensions, relief and rehabilitation', in M. Dumroes (ed.), *After the Tsunami: Relief and Rehabilitation in Sri Lanka*, New Dehli: Mosaic Books, pp. 1–33.

Duncan, B. (2004), 'A theory of impact philosophy', *Journal of Public Economics,* **88**, 2159–2180.

Duryog Nivaran, (2009), 'Disaster risk and poverty in South Asia, A contribution to the 2009 ISDR Global Assessment Report on Disaster

Risk Reduction', available at http://www.duryognivaran.org/ (accessed 14 August 2012).

Dwyer, D. and J. Bruce (eds.) (1988), *A Home Divided: Women and Income in the Third World*, Stanford, CA: Stanford University Press.

Dyer, C. (2002), 'Punctuated entropy as culture induced change: The case of the Exxon Valdez oil spill', in S. Hoffman and A. Oliver-Smith (eds.), *Catastrophe & Culture: The Anthropology of Disaster*, New Mexico: School of American Research Press, pp. 159–186.

Dynes, R. (1998), 'Coming to terms with community disaster', in E.L. Quarantelli (ed.), *What is a Disaster? Perspectives on the Question*, London and New York: Routledge, pp. 109–126.

Dynes, R. and H. Rodríguez (2007), 'Finding and framing Katrina: The social construction of disaster', in D. Brunsma, D. Overfelt, and J.S. Picou (eds.), *The Sociology of Katrina: Perspectives on a Modern Catastrophe*, Maryland: Rowman and Littlefield, pp. 23–34.

Eade, D. and S. Williams (1995), *The Oxfam Handbook of Development and Relief*, 3 vols, Oxford: Oxfam UK and Ireland.

ECA (2000), 'Independent evaluation of expenditure of DEC Central American Hurricane appeal funds', San Jose, Costa Rica, available at http://www.alnap.org/pool/files/erd-2873-full.pdf (accessed 14 August 2012).

ECLAC (2004) 'Roads towards gender equity in Latin America and the Caribbean', paper prepared for the 9th Regional Conference on Women in Latin America and the Caribbean, Mexico City, Mexico, 10–12 June 2004, published by the United Nations Economic Commission for Latin America and the Caribbean.

El Bushra, J. (2000), 'Rethinking gender and development practice for the twenty-first century', *Gender and Development*, **8** (1), 55–62.

Elson, D. (1989), 'The impact of structural adjustment on women: Concepts and issues', in O. Bade (ed.), *The IMF, The World Bank and The African Debt. Vol. 2*, London: Zed Books.

Elson, D. (1991), 'Male bias in macro-economics: The case of Structural Adjustment', in D. Elson (ed.), *Male Bias in the Development Process*, Manchester: Manchester University Press, pp. 164–90.

Enarson, E. (1999), 'Violence against women in disasters: A study of domestic violence programs in the US and Canada', *Violence Against Women*, **5** (7), 742–768.

Enarson, E. (2000), 'Gender issues in natural disasters: Talking points and research needs', ILO In Focus Programme on Crisis Response and Reconstruction Workshop, May 3–5, 2000, Geneva, Switzerland.

Enarson, E. (2004). 'Gender matters: Talking points on gender equality and disaster risk reduction', available at http://gdnonline.org/resources/gendermatters-talkingpoints-ee04.doc (accessed 14 August 2012).

Enarson, E. (2006), 'SWS Fact Sheet: Women and disaster', available at http://www.socwomen.org/web/images/stories/resources/fact_sheets/fact_10-2006-disaster.pdf (accessed 14 August 2012).

Enarson, E. (2009), 'Gender', in B. Phillips, D. Thomas, A. Fothergill and L. Blinn-Pike (eds.), *Social Vulnerability to Disasters*, Boca Raton, FL: CRC Press, pp. 123–154.

Enarson, E. (2012), 'Women and girls last? Averting the second post-Katrina disaster', in E. David and E. Enarson (eds.), *The Women of Katrina: How Gender, Race and Class Matter in an American Disaster*, Nashville, TN: Vanderbilt University Press, pp. 10–14.

Enarson, E. and D. Chakrabarti (eds.) (2009), *Women, Gender and Disaster: Global Issues and Initiatives*, India: Sage.

Enarson, E. and L. Meyreles (2004), 'International perspectives on gender and disaster: Differences and possibilities', *International Journal of Sociology and Social Policy*, **24** (10), 49–93.

Enarson, E. and B. Morrow (eds.) (1998), *The Gendered Terrain of Disasters*, Westport, CT and London: Praeger.

Ensor, M.O. (ed.) (2009), *The Legacy of Hurricane Mitch: Lessons from Post-Disaster Reconstruction in Honduras*, Tuscon, AZ: University of Arizona Press.

Eriksson, J. (1996), 'The international response to conflict and genocide: Lessons from the Rwanda experience – Synthesis report', Copenhagen: Steering Committee Joint Evaluation of Emergency Assistance to Rwanda, available at http://www.oecd.org/derec/50189495.pdf (accessed 14 August 2012).

Escobar, A. (1995), *Encountering Development: The Making and Unmaking of the Third World*, Princeton, NJ: Princeton University Press.

Escobar, A. and S. Alvarez (eds.) (1992), *The Making of Social Movements in Latin America: Identity, Strategy, and Democracy*, Boulder, CO: Westview Press.

Eyben, R. (2003), 'The rise of rights: Rights-based approaches to international development', *IDS Policy Briefing*, **17**, Brighton: Institute of Development Studies.

Fadlalla, A.H. (2007), 'The neo-liberalization of compassion: Darfur and the mediation of American faith, fear and terror', in J. L. Collins, M. di Leonardo and B. Williams (eds.), *New Landscapes of Inequality: Neo-liberalism and the Erosion of Democracy in America*, Santa Fe, New Mexico: School for Advanced Research Press.

Fanany, I. (2010), 'Toward a model of constructive interaction between aid donors and recipients in a disaster context: The case of Lampuuk', in M. Clarke and I. Fanany (eds.), *Post-Disaster Reconstruction*, London: Earthscan, pp. 235–249.

FAO (2002), 'Gender and access to land', *FAO Land Tenure Studies* 4, Rome: Food and Agriculture Organisation of the United Nations.

FAO (2006), *Land Tenure Alternative Conflict Management, FAO Land Tenure Manuals 2*, Rome: Food and Agriculture Organization of the United Nations.

Fenney, S. and M. Clarke (2007), 'What determines Australia's response to emergencies and natural disasters?', *Australian Economic Review*, **40** (1), 24–36.

Fisher, S. (2009), 'Sri Lankan women's organisations responding to post-tsunami violence', in E. Enarson and D. Chakrabarti (eds.), *Women, Gender and Disaster: Global Issues and Initiatives*, India: Sage, pp. 233–249.

Fitzpatrick, D. (2007), 'Access to housing for renters and squatters in tsunami affected Aceh', Asia Research Institute, *Aceh Working Paper*, No. 2, Indonesia, Faculty of Law, National University of Singapore, available at http://www.ari.nus.edu.sg/docs/downloads/aceh-wp/aceh wps07_002.pdf (accessed 14 August 2012).

Fitzpatrick, D. (2008), 'Addressing land issues after natural disasters: Case study Aceh, Indonesia', available at http://www.aceh-eye.org/ data_files/english_format/acheh_disaster/acheh-eye_disaster_reports/ tsunami_special_reports_occ/tsunami_special_reports_occ_2008_00_ 00.pdf (accessed 14 August 2012).

Flake, D.F. and R. Forste (2006), 'Fighting families: Family characteristics associated with domestic violence in five Latin American countries', *Journal of Family Violence*, **21** (1), 19–29.

Flint, C.G. and A.E. Luloff (2005), 'Natural resource-based communities, risk and disaster: An intersection of theories', *Society and Natural Resources*, **18**, 399–412.

Flint, M. and H. Goyder (2006), *Funding the Tsunami Response*, London: Tsunami Evaluation Coalition.

Folbre, N. (1994), *Who Pays for the Kids? Gender and the Structures of Constraint*, London and New York: Routledge.

Foley, M. and R. Edwards (1996), 'The paradox of civil society', *Journal of Democracy*, **7** (3), 35–52.

Foote, K.E. (1997), *Shadowed Ground*, Austin, TX: University of Texas Press.

Fordham, M. (1998), 'Making women visible in disasters: Problematising the private domain', *Journal of Disaster Studies, Policy and Management*, **22** (2), 126–43.

Fordham, M. (2001), 'Challenging boundaries: A gender perspective on early warning in disaster and environmental management', United Nations Division for the Advancement of Women (DAW), International Strategy for Disaster Reduction (ISDR), Expert Group Meeting on

Environmental Management and the Mitigation of Natural Disasters: A Gender Perspective, Ankara, 6–9 November, 2001.

Fordham, M. (2009a), 'Editorial introduction', *Regional Development Dialogue*, **30** (1), iii–xii.

Fordham, M. (2009b), 'We can make things better for each other: Women and girls organise to reduce disasters in Central America', in E. Enarson and D. Chakrabarti (eds.), *Women, Gender and Disaster: Global Issues and Initiatives*, India: Sage, pp. 175–188.

Fothergill, A. (1999), 'An exploratory study of woman battering in the Grand Forks flood disaster: Implications for community responses and policies', *International Journal of Mass Emergencies and Disasters*, **17** (1), 79–98.

Fothergill, A. and L. Peek (2008), 'Children's displacement in Louisiana after Katrina', in L. Peek and L. Weber (eds.), *Displaced: Voices from the Katrina Diaspora*, New York: Columbia University Press.

Foucault, M. (1976), *Power/Knowledge*, New York: Pantheon.

Foucault, M. (1980), *The History of Sexuality Vol. I: An Introduction*, New York: Vintage.

Fox, F. (2001), 'New Humanitarianism: Does it provide a moral banner for the 21st century', *Disasters*, **25** (4), 275–289.

Frailing, K. and D. Wood Harper (2007), 'Crime and hurricanes in New Orleans', in D. Brunsma, D. Overfelt and J.S. Picou (eds.), *The Sociology of Katrina: Perspectives on a Modern Catastrophe*, Maryland: Rowman and Littlefield, pp. 51–70.

Frank, A.G. (1967), *Capitalism and Underdevelopment in Latin America*, New York: Monthly Review Press.

Fraser, N. and L. Nicholson (1990), 'Social criticism without philosophy: An encounter between feminism and post-modernism', in L. Nicholson (ed.), *Feminism/Post-modernism*, New York: Routledge, pp. 19–38.

Friedmann, J. (1966), *Regional Development Policy: A Case Study of Venezuela*, Cambridge, MA: MIT Press.

Fritz, C.E. (1961), 'Disasters', in R.K. Merton and R.A. Nisbet (eds.), *Contemporary Social Problems*, New York: Harcourt, pp. 651–694.

Fundación Arias (1998), 'Marco Juridico que Regula a las Organizaciones Sin Fines de Lucro en Centroamerica', *Serie: El Derecho y la Sociedad Civil*, No. 3, Fundación Arias para la Paz y el Progreso Humano, San José, Costa Rica.

Gault, B. and H. Hartmann, A. Jones-DeWeever, M. Werschkul, E. Williams (2005), *The Women of New Orleans and the Gulf Coast: Multiple Disadvantages and Key Assets for Recovery. Part I. Poverty, Race, Gender and Class*, Washington, DC: IWPR.

Gender and Disaster Network (GDN) (2006), *Gender and Disasters Sourcebook,* available at http://www.gdnonline.org/sourcebook/ (accessed 14 August 2012).

Gilbert, C. (1995), 'Studying Disaster: A Review of the Main Conceptual Tools', *International Journal of Mass Emergencies and Disasters,* **13** (3), 231–240.

Glaesser, D. (2006), *Crisis Management in the Tourism Industry,* second edition, Oxford and Waltham, MA: Butterworth-Heinemann.

Glazer, A. and K.A. Konrad (1996), 'A signaling explanation for charity', *American Economic Review,* **84** (4), 1019–1028.

Goenjian, A.K. and L. Molina, A.M. Steinberg, L.A Fairbanks, M.L Alvarez, H.A Goenjian (2001), 'Posttraumatic stress and depressive reactions among Nicaraguan adolescents after Hurricane Mitch', *American Journal of Psychiatry,* **158**, 788–794.

Gomáriz Moraga, E. (1999), 'Género y desastres: Introducción conceptual y análisis de situación', paper prepared for the IDB technical meeting on the effects of Hurricane Mitch on women and their participation in the reconstruction of Central America.

González de la Rocha, M. (2001), 'From the resources of poverty to the poverty of resources? The erosion of a survival model', *Latin American Perspectives,* **28**, 72–100.

Green, B.L. (1982), 'Assessing levels of psychological impairment following disaster. Consideration of actual and methodological dimensions', *The Journal of Nervous and Mental Disease,* **170** (9), 544–552.

Greenaway, S. (1999), 'Post-modern conflict and humanitarian action: Questioning the paradigm', *The Journal of Humanitarian Assistance,* available at http://www.jha.ac/articles/a053.htm (accessed 14 August 2012).

GTZ (1999), 'Gender responsive land tenure development. Sector-Project land tenure in development cooperation', GTZ, December, 1999.

Haddad, L. (2007), 'Comment on "The role of Social Risk Management in development: A World Bank view"', *IDS Bulletin,* **38** (3), 14–16.

Hamblen, J. (2006), 'PTSD in children and adolescents: A National Center for PTSD fact sheet', available at http://wps.ablongman.com/ab_myhelpinglab_resources_1/59/15297/3916266.cw/content/index.html (accessed 14 August 2012).

Haney, T. and J. Elliott, E. Fussell (2007), 'Families and hurricane response: Evacuation, separation and emotional toll of Hurricane Katrina', in D. Brunsma, D. Overfelt and J.S. Picou (eds.), *The Sociology of Katrina: Perspectives on a Modern Catastrophe,* Maryland: Rowman and Littlefield, pp. 71–90.

Harriss, J. and P. Renzio (1997), '"Missing link" or analytically missing: The concept of social capital', *Journal of International Development*, **9** (7), 919–937.

Hartmann, B. (1987), *Reproductive Rights and Wrongs: The Global Politics of Population Control and Contraceptive Choice*, New York: Harper and Row.

Hartmann, H. (1981), 'The unhappy marriage of Marxism and Feminism: Towards a more progressive union', in L. Sargent (ed.), *Women and Revolution: A Discussion of the Unhappy Marriage of Marxism and Feminism*, Boston, MA: South End Press, pp. 1–41.

Hartsock, N. (1990), 'Foucault on power: A theory for women?', in L. Nicholson (ed.), *Feminism/Post-modernism*, London: Routledge, pp. 157–75.

Heise, L. and M. Ellsberg, M. Gottmoeller (2002), 'A global overview of gender-based violence', *International Journal of Gynaecology and Obstetrics*, **78** Suppl. 1, S5–S14.

Heltberg, R. (2007), 'Helping South Asia cope better with natural disasters: The role of social protection', *Development Policy Review*, **25** (6), 681–698.

Henderson, J.C. (2006), *Managing Tourism Crises: Causes, Consequences and Management*, Oxford and Waltham, MA: Butterworth-Heinemann.

Hendrickson, D. (1998), 'Humanitarian action in protracted crises: the new relief "agenda" and its limits', *Relief and Rehabilitation Network*, Paper No. 25, London: Overseas Development Institute.

Hengstenberg, P. and K. Kohut, G. Maihol (1999), *Sociedad Civil en América Latina: Representación de Intereses y Gobernabilidad*, Asociación Alemana de Inverstigación sobre América Latina (ADLAF), Friedrich Ebert Stiftung-FES, Editorial Nueva Sociedad, 1999.

Henrici, J.M. and A. Suppan Helmuth, A. Carlberg (2012), 'Double displaced: Women, public housing, and spatial access after Katrina', in E. David and E. Enarson (eds.), *The Women of Katrina: How Gender, Race and Class Matter in an American Disaster*, Nashville, TN: Vanderbilt University Press, pp. 142–154.

Hewitt, K. (1983), *Interpretations of Calamity from the Viewpoint of Human Ecology*, London: Allen & Unwin.

Hewitt, K. (1995), 'Sustainable disasters? Perspectives and powers in the discourse of calamity', in J. Crush (ed.), *Power of Development*, London: Routledge, pp. 115–128.

Hewitt, K. (1998), 'Excluded perspectives in the social construction of disaster', in E.L. Quarantelli (ed.), *What is a disaster? Perspectives on the Question*, London and New York: Routledge, pp. 71–88.

Hickey, S. and G. Mohan (eds.) (2004), *Participation: From Tyranny to Transformation?*, London and New York: Zed Books.

Hilhorst, D. (2003), *The Real World of NGOs: Discourses, Diversity and Development*, London: Zed Books.

Hilhorst, D. (2007), 'Saving lives or saving societies? Realities of relief and reconstruction', inaugural lecture, Wageningen University, available at http://www.disasterstudies.wur.nl/NR/rdonlyres/E08690FD-1923-4358-B3B4-FBA2F7734B91/42913/Savinglivesorsavingsocieties.pdf (accessed 14 August 2012).

Hindin, M.J. and S. Kishor, D.L. Ansara (2008), *Intimate Partner Violence among Couples in 10 DHS Countries: Predictors and Health Outcomes*, Calverton, MD: Macro International Inc. and USAID.

Hirschman, A.O. (1958), *The Strategy of Economic Development*, New Haven: Yale University Press.

Hoffman, S. (1998), 'Eve and Adam among the embers: Gender patterns after the Oakland Berkeley Firestorm', in E. Enarson and B. Morrow (eds.), *The Gendered Terrain of Disasters*, Westport, CT and London: Praeger, 55–62.

Hoffman, S. (2002), 'The monster and the mother: The symbolism of disaster', in S. Hoffman and A. Oliver-Smith (eds.), *Catastrophe & Culture: The Anthropology of Disaster*, New Mexico: School of American Research Press, pp. 113–142.

Hoffman, S. and A. Oliver-Smith (eds.) (2002), *Catastrophe & Culture: The Anthropology of Disaster*, New Mexico: School of American Research Press.

Holzmann, R. and S. Jørgensen (2000), 'Social Risk Management: A new conceptual framework for social protection and beyond', *Social Protection Discussion Paper Series 0006*, Social Protection Unit, Human Development Network, World Bank, February 2000.

Holzmann, R. and V. Kozel (2007), 'The role of Social Risk Management in development: A World Bank view', *IDS Bulletin*, **38** (3), 8–13.

hooks, b. (1988), *Talking back: Thinking feminist, thinking black*, Toronto, Canada: Between the Lines.

hooks, b. (1991), *Yearning: race, gender, and cultural politics*, Boston, MA: South End Press.

Hooper, E. (2006), 'Social protection and human security', paper presented at the 3rd International Congress of Human Resource Development, Islamabad, November 2006.

Horlick-Jones, T. and G. Peters (1991), 'Measuring disaster trends Part One: Some observations on the Bradford Fatality Scale', *Disaster Management*, **3** (3), 144–148.

Hoselitz, B.F. (1952), *The Progress of Underdeveloped Areas*, Chicago, IL: University of Chicago Press.

Houghton, R. (2009), '"Everything became a struggle, absolute struggle": Post-flood increases in domestic violence in New Zealand', in E. Enarson and D. Chakrabarti (eds.), *Women, Gender and Disaster: Global issues and initiatives*, India: Sage, pp. 9–111.

House of Commons Select Committee on International Development, 7th Report (HC Paper (2009–10) 404), *Draft International Development (Official Development Assistance Target) Bill*, available at http://www.publications.parliament.uk/pa/cm200910/cmselect/cmintdev/404/404.pdf (accessed 14 August 2012).

Hulme, D. (2000), 'Protecting and strengthening social capital in order to produce desirable development outcomes', *SD SCOPE Paper*, No. 4, London: UK-DFID.

Hume, M. (1997), *Whose War is it Anyway? The Dangers of the Journalism of Attachment*, InformInc (Living Marxism) Ltd.

Hyndman, J. and M. de Alwis (2003), 'Beyond gender: Towards a feminist analysis of humanitarianism and development in Sri Lanka', *Women's Studies Quarterly*, **31** (3–4), 212–226.

Hyogo Framework for Action (2005), 'Building the resilience of nations and communities to disasters', available at http://www.unisdr.org/we/coordinate/hfa (accesssed 14 August 2012).

IASC (2007), 'Guidelines on mental health and psychosocial support in emergency settings', available at http://www.who.int/mental_health/emergencies/guidelines_iasc_mental_health_psychosocial_june_2007.pdf (accessed 14 August 2012).

IDPM (2003), 'Participation: From tyranny to transformation?', Conference proceedings, available at http://www.sed.manchester.ac.uk/idpm/research/events/participation03/index.htm.

IDS (2005), 'Developing rights', *IDS Bulletin* Special Edition, **36** (1), Institute Of Development Studies, January 2005.

IFRC (2006), *World Disasters Report – Focus on Neglected Crisis*, International Federation of Red Cross and Red Crescent Societies, Geneva: ATAR Roto Press.

IFRC (2009), 'Psychosocial interventions: A handbook', International Federation of Red Cross and Red Crescent Societies Reference Centre for Psychosocial Support, Denmark, available at http://mhpss.net/wp-content/uploads/group-documents/22/1328075906-PsychosocialinterventionsAhandbookLowRes.pdf (accessed 14 August 2012).

IILS (1996), *Social Exclusion and Anti-poverty Strategies*, International Institute for Labour Studies, United Nations Development Programme, Geneva, Switzerland.

Illich, I. (1973), *Deschooling Society*, Harmondsworth: Penguin.

Information Centre (2009), 'Adult psychiatric morbidity in England: Results of a household survey', available at http://www.ic.nhs.uk/pubs/psychiatricmorbidity07 (accessed 14 August 2012).

International Journal of Mass Emergencies and Disasters (1999), **17** (1) (Special edition on gender and emergencies).

IRP (2009), 'Gender issues in recovery. Executive briefs for recovery: Extracts from key documents series', compiled by International Recovery Platform.

ISDR (2004), 'Living with risk: A global review of disaster reduction initiatives', Volume I, New York and Geneva: United Nations, available at http://www.unisdr.org/files/657_lwr1.pdf (accessed 14 August 2012).

ISDR (2009), 'Adaptation to climate change by reducing disaster risks: Country practices and lessons', Briefing Note 2, New York: UNISDR, available at http://www.unisdr.org/files/11775_UNISDR BriefingAdaptationtoClimateCh.pdf (accessed 14 August 2012).

Jackson, C. (1996), 'Rescuing gender from the poverty trap', *World Development*, **24** (3), 489–504.

Jackson, C. (1998), 'Rescuing gender from the poverty trap', in R. Pearson and C. Jackson (eds.), *Feminist Visions of Development: Gender Analysis and Policy*, London: Routledge, pp. 39–64.

Jaquette, J. (1982), 'Women and modernisation theory', *World Politics*, **1**, 267–284.

Jeggle, T. (2001), 'The evolution of disaster reduction as an international strategy: Policy implications for the future', in U. Rosenthal, R.A. Boin and L.K. Comfort (eds.), *Managing Crises: Threats, Dilemmas, Opportunities*, Illinois: Charles C Thomas Publishers.

Jenkins, P. and B. Phillips (2008), 'Battered women, catastrophe, and the context of safety after Hurricane Katrina', *Feminist Formations*, **20** (3), 49–68.

Kabeer, N. (1994), *Reversed Realities: Gender Hierarchies in Development Thought*, London: Verso.

Kaldor, M. (2006), 'New and old wars: Organised violence in a global era', Talk for the RSA, 23 October, available at http://www.thersa.org/__data/assets/pdf_file/0014/806/New-and-Old-Wars-kaldor_231006.pdf (accessed 14 August 2012).

Kanbur, R. (2002), 'Education, empowerment and gender inequalities' paper prepared for the Annual Bank Conference on Development Economics, Washington, DC, 29–30 April, 2002, available at http://siteresources.worldbank.org/DEC/Resources/84797-1251813753820/6415739-1251814045642/Kanbur.pdf (accessed 14 August 2012).

Kaniasty, K and F. Norris (2004), 'Social support in the aftermath of disasters, catastrophes, and acts of terrorism: Altruistic, overwhelmed, uncertain, antagonistic, and patriotic communities', in R.J. Ursano, A.E. Norwood and C.S. Fullerton (eds.), *Bioterrorism: Psychological and Public Health Interventions*, Cambridge: Cambridge University Press, pp. 200–231.

Katz, E. and J.S. Chamorro (2002), 'Gender, land rights and the household economy in rural Nicaragua and Honduras', paper prepared for USAID/ BASIS CRSP.

Kenny, S. (2010), 'Reconstruction through participatory practice?', in M. Clarke, I. Fanany and S. Kenny (eds.), *Post-disaster Reconstruction: Lessons from Ache*, London: Earthscan, pp. 79–104.

Kent, R.C. (2004), 'The United Nations' humanitarian pillar: Re-focussing the UN's disaster and emergency role and responsibilities', *Disasters*, **28** (2), 216–233.

Killick, T. (2002), 'Responding to inequality', Inequality Briefing Paper 3, London: Overseas Development Institute, March 2002, available at http://www.odi.org.uk/PPPG/publications/briefings/inequality_briefings/03.html (accessed 14 August 2012).

Kishor, S. and K. Johnson (2004), *Profiling Domestic Violence: A Multi-Country Study*, Calverton, MD: ORC Macro.

Klasen, S. (1999), 'Does gender inequality reduce growth and development? Evidence from cross-country regressions', World Bank, *Gender and Development Working Papers*, No. 7, November 1999, available at http://siteresources.worldbank.org/INTGENDER/Resources/wp7.pdf (accessed 14 August 2012).

Kleinman, A. and J. Kleinman (1997), 'The appeal of experience; The dismay of images: Cultural appropriations of suffering in our times', in A. Kleinman, V. Das and M. Lock (eds.), *Social Suffering*, Berkeley, CA: University of California Press, pp. 1–24.

Knack, S. (1999), 'Social capital, growth and poverty: A survey of cross-country evidence', Social Capital Initiative, *Working Paper*, No. 7, World Bank, May 1999.

Kohn, R. and I. Levav, I. Donaire Garcia, M.E. Machuca, R. Tamashiro, (2005), 'Prevalence, risk factors and aging vulnerability for psychopathology following a natural disaster in a developing country', *International Journal of Geriatric Psychiatry*, **20**, 835–841.

Korten, D. (1990), *Getting to the 21st Century: Voluntary Action and the Global Agenda*, West Hartford: Kumarian Press.

Krafess, J. (2005), 'The Influence of Muslim religion in humanitarian aid', *International Review of the Red Cross*, **87** (858), 327–341.

Kreps, G.A. (1998), 'Disaster as systematic event and social catalyst', in E.L. Quarantelli (ed.), *What is a Disaster? Perspectives on the Question*, London and New York: Routledge, pp. 25–50.

Kroll-Smith, S. and V. Gunter (1998), 'Legislators, interpreters and disasters: The importance of how as well as what is a disaster', in E.L. Quarantelli (ed), *What is a Disaster? Perspectives on the Question*, London and New York: Routledge, pp. 161–178.

Kumar, M.S. and M.V. Murhekar, Y. Hutin, T. Subramanian, V. Ramachandran, M.D. Gupte (2007), 'Prevalence of Posttraumatic Stress Disorder in a coastal fishing village in Tamil Nadu, India, after the December 2004 Tsunami', *American Journal of Public Health*, **97** (1), 99–101.

Lacan, J. (1977), *Écrits: A Selection* (trans. by Alan Sheridan and revised version, 2002, trans. by Bruce Fink), New York: W.W. Norton & Co.

Leader, N. (2000), *The Politics of Principle: The Principles of Humanitarian Action in Practice*, HPG Report, No. 2, March, London: Overseas Development Institute.

Leon, G. (2004), 'Overview of the psychosocial impact of disasters', *Prehospital and Disaster Medicine*, **19** (1), 4–9.

Le Pape, M. and P. Salignon (eds.) (2003), *Civilians Under Fire: Humanitarian Practices in the Congo Republic 1998–2000*, Brussels: Médecins Sans Frontières.

Lewis, D. and N. Kanji, (2009), *Non-Governmental Organizations and Development*, New York: Routledge.

Lindell, M.K. and R.W. Perry (2004), *Communicating Environmental Risk in Multiethnic Communities*, Thousand Oaks, CA: Sage.

Linz, J. and A. Stepan (1996), *Problems of Democratic Transition and Consolidation*, Baltimore, MD: Johns Hopkins University Press.

Lipton, M. and M. Revallion (1995), 'Poverty and Policy', in J. Behrman and T.N. Srinivasan (eds.), *The Handbook of Development Economics*, Vol. III, Amsterdam: North Holland, pp. 2551–2657.

Liverman, D.M. (1990), 'Vulnerability to global environmental change', in K. Dow, R. E. Kasperson, D. Golding and J. X. Kasperson (eds.), *Understanding Global Environmental Change: The Contributions of Risk Analysis and Management*, Worcester, MA: Clark University.

Lloyd-Jones, T. (2006), *Mind the Gap! Post-disaster Reconstruction and the Transition from Humanitarian Relief*, available at http://www.rics.org/site/download_feed.aspx?fileID=2263&fileExtension=PDF (accessed 14 August 2012).

Loker, W. (2009), 'A flood of Impressions: Riding out Mitch and its aftermath', in M. Ensor (ed.), *The Legacy of Hurricane Mitch: Lessons from Post-Disaster Reconstruction in Honduras*, Arizona: University of Arizona Press, pp. 67–99.

Lopez, H. (2002), 'Pro growth, Pro poor: Is there a trade off?', Pro Poor Growth program, PREM Poverty Group, World Bank (PRMPR), 11 January, available at http://siteresources.worldbank.org/INTPGI/Resources/15040_WBSWP3378.pdf (accessed 14 August 2012).

Lorch, D. (1995), 'Wave of rape adds new horror to Rwanda's trail of brutality', *New York Times*, 15 May 1995.

Lynch, M. (2007), *Weathering the Storm: A Crisis Management Guide for Tourism*, Leicester: Matador.

Lyotard, J.F. (1984), *The Postmodern Condition: A Report on Knowledge*, Mineapolis, MN: University of Minnesota Press.

MacDonald, L. (1994), 'Globalising civil society: Interpreting International NGOs in Central America', *Millenium*, **23** (2), 267–286.

MacDonald, L. (1997), *Supporting Civil Society: The Political Role of Non-Governmental Organisations in Central America*, London: Macmillan.

Macrae, J. (1998), 'The death of humanitarianism: An anatomy of the attack', *Disasters*, **22** (4), 309–317.

Marchand, M.H. and J. Parpart (eds.) (1995), *Feminism/ Postmodernism/ Development*, London: Routledge.

Martin, W.E. and I.M. Martin, B. Kent (2009), 'The role of risk perceptions in the risk mitigation process: The case of wildfire in high risk communities', *Journal of Environmental Management*, **91**, 489–498.

McGee, R. (2002), 'Participating in development', in U. Kothari, and M. Minogue (eds.), *Development Theory and Practice: Critical Perspectives*, Basingstoke: Palgrave, pp. 92–116.

McGray, H. (2007), 'Weathering the storm: Options for framing adaptation and development', World Resources Institute, available at http://pdf.wri.org/weathering_the_storm.pdf (accessed 14 August 2012).

McIlwaine, C. (1998a), 'Contesting civil society: Reflections from El Salvador', *Third World Quarterly*, **19** (4), 651–672.

McIlwaine, C. (1998b), 'Civil society and development geography', *Progress in Human Geography*, **22** (3), 415–424.

McIlwaine, C. (2002), 'Perspectives on poverty, vulnerability and exclusion', in C. McIlwaine and K. Willis (eds.), *Challenges and Change in Middle America: Perspectives on Development in Mexico, Central America and the Caribbean*, Harlow: Prentice Hall/Pearson, pp. 82–109.

Meltzer, H. and B. Gill, M. Petticrew, K. Hinds (1995), *OPCS Surveys of Psychiatric Morbidity in Great Britain: Report 1: the Prevalence of Psychiatric Morbidity among Adults Living in Private Households*, London: HMSO.

Merton, R. (1970), 'Foreword', in A.H. Barton (ed.), *Communities in Disaster*, Garden City, NY: Doubleday.

Mesch, D.J. (2010), 'Women give 2010', Women's Philanthropy Institute at the Center on Philanthropy at Indiana University, available at http://www.philanthropy.iupui.edu/womengive/docs/womengive2010 report.pdf (accessed 14 August 2012).

Messing, U. (1999), 'Introduction', in A.R. Morrison and M.L. Biehl, (eds.), *Too Close to Home: Domestic Violence in the Americas*, Washington, DC: Inter-American Development Bank/John Hopkins University Press, pp. xi–xiii.

Mies, M. (1982), *Lace Makers of Narsapur*, London: Zed Books.

Mileti, D. (1995), 'Factors related to flood warning response', US-Italy Research Workshop on the Hydrometeorology, Impacts and Management of Extreme Floods, Perugia Italy, November 1995, available at http://www.engr.colostate.edu/~jsalas/us-italy/papers/46mileti.pdf (accessed 14 August 2012).

Miller, D. and J. Rivera (2007), 'Landscapes of disaster and place orientation in the aftermath of hurricane Katrina', in D. Brunsma, D. Overfelt and J.S. Picou (eds.), *The Sociology of Katrina: Perspectives on a Modern Catastrophe*, Maryland: Rowman and Littlefield, pp. 141–154.

Mills, K. (2005), 'Neo-Humanitarianism: The role of international humanitarian norms and organisations in contemporary conflict', *Global Governance*, **11** (2), 161–183.

Mishra, P. (2009), 'Let's share the stage: Involving men in gender equality and disaster risk reduction', in E. Enarson and D. Chakrabarti (eds.), *Women, Gender and Disaster: Global Issues and Initiatives*, India: Sage, pp. 29–39.

Mitchell, T. and M. van Aalst (2008a), *Convergence of Disaster Risk Reduction and Climate Change Adaptation: A Review for DFID*, available at http://www.preventionweb.net/files/7853_Convergenceof DRRandCCA1.pdf (accessed 14 August 2012).

Mitchell, T and M. van Aalst (2008b), 'Disaster risk reduction and climate change adaptation: Closing the gap', *id21 highlights*, **71**, 1.

Moghadam, V. (1992), 'Development and women's emancipation: Is there a connection?', *Development and Change*, **3**, 215–255.

Mohanty, C.T. (1991), 'Under Western eyes: Feminist scholarship and colonial discourses', in C.T. Mohanty, A. Russo and L. Torres (eds.), *Third World Women and the Politics of Feminism*, Bloomington, IN: Indiana University Press, pp. 51–80.

Mohanty, C.T. (1997), 'Feminist encounters: Locating the politics of experience', in L. McDowell and J. Sharp (eds.), *Space, Gender, Knowledge: Feminist Readings*, London: Edward Arnold, pp. 82–97.

Mohanty, C.T. (2003), *Feminism without Borders: Decolonizing Theory, Practising Solidarity*, Durham and London: Duke University Press.

Molyneux, M. (1985), 'Mobilization without emancipation? Women's interests, the state, and revolution in Nicaragua', *Feminist Studies*, **11** (2), 227–254.

Molyneux, M. (2006), 'Mothers at the service of the new poverty agenda: PROGRESA/ Oportunidades, Mexico's Conditional Transfer Programme', *Journal of Social Policy and Administration*, Special Issue on Latin America, **40** (4), 425–449.

Molyneux, M. (2007), 'Two cheers for conditional cash transfers', *IDS Bulletin*, **38** (3), 69–75.

Molyneux, M. (2009), 'Conditional cash transfers: pathways to women's empowerment?', Research Paper, IDS Series on Social Policy in Developing Countries.

Molyneux, M. and A. Cornwall (eds.) (2008), *The Politics of Rights: Dilemmas for Feminist Praxis*, London: Routledge.

Molyneux, M. and S. Lazar (2003), *Doing The Rights Thing: Rights-Based Development And Latin American NGOs*, London: Intermediate Technology Development Group Publishing.

Morrison, A. and M. Ellsberg, S. Bott (2007), 'Addressing gender-based violence: A critical review of interventions', *The World Bank Observer*, **22** (1), 25–51.

Morrow, B. (1997), 'Stretching the bonds: The families of Andrew', in W.G. Peacock, B.H. Morrow and H. Gladwin (eds.), *Hurricane Andrew: Ethnicity, Gender and the Sociology of Disasters*, Miami: International Hurricane Center, pp. 141–170.

Morrow, B.H. and E. Enarson (1996), 'Hurricane Andrew through women's eyes: issues and recommendations', *International Journal of Mass Emergencies and Disasters*, **14** (1), 1–22.

Moser, C. (1989a), 'The impact of recession and adjustment at the micro level: Low-income women and their households in Guayaquil, Ecuador', in UNICEF (ed.), *Invisible Adjustment*, Vol. 2, New York: UNICEF, Americas and Caribbean Regional Office.

Moser, C. (1989b), 'Gender planning in the Third World: Meeting practical and strategic gender needs', *World Development*, **17** (11), 1799–1825.

Moser, C. (1992), 'Adjustment from below: Low-income women, time and the triple role in Guayaquil, Equador', in H. Afshar and C. Dennis (eds.), *Women and Adjustment Policies in the Third World*, London: Macmillan Academic and Professional Ltd, pp. 87–116.

Moser, C. (1993), *Gender and Development Planning*, London: Routledge.

Moser, C. (1996), *Confronting Crisis: Household Response to Poverty and Vulnerability*, TWURD, World Bank, Washington, DC: Mimeo.

Moser, C. (1998), 'The Asset Vulnerability Framework: Reassessing Urban Poverty Reduction Strategies', *World Development*, **26** (1), 1–19.

Moser, C. and C. McIlwaine (2001), 'Gender and social capital in contexts of political violence: community perceptions from Colombia and Guatemala', in C. Moser and F. Clark (eds.), *Victims, Actors or Perpetrators? Gender, Armed Conflict and Political Violence*, London: Zed Books, pp. 178–200.

Mukhopadhyay, M. (2004), 'Mainstreaming gender or "streaming" gender away: Feminists marooned in the development business', *IDS Bulletin*, **35** (4), 95–103.

Myers, D. (1994), 'Psychological recovery from disaster: Key concepts for delivery of mental health services', *NCP Clinical Quarterly*, **4** (2), Spring 1994.

Myrdal, G. (1957), *Economic Theory and Underdeveloped Regions*, London: Duckworth.

Nan, N. (2010), 'New Humanitarianism with old problems: The forgotten lessons of Rwanda', *The Journal of Humanitarian Assistance*, October 2010, available at http://sites.tufts.edu/jha/archives/780 (accessed 14 August 2012).

Nathan, F. (2008), 'Risk perception, risk management and vulnerability to landslides in the hill slopes in the city of La Paz, Bolivia. A preliminary statement', *Disasters,* **32** (3), 337–357.

Neumayer, E. and T. Plümper (2007), 'The gendered nature of natural disasters: The impact of catastrophic events on the gender gap in life expectancy, 1981–2002', *Annals of the Association of American Geographers*, **97** (3), 551–566.

Nguyen, G.T. (2012), 'Building coalitions and rebuilding Versailles: Vietnamese American women's environmental work after Hurricane Katrina', in E. David and E. Enarson (eds.), *The Women of Katrina: How Gender, Race and Class Matter in an American Disaster*, Nashville, TN: Vanderbilt University Press, pp. 198–209.

Norris, F.H. (2009), 'The impact of disasters and political violence on mental health in Latin America', *PTSD Research Quarterly*, **20** (4), 1–3.

Norris, F.H. and D.L. Weisshaar, M.L. Conrad, E.M. Diaz, A.D. Murphy, G.E. Ibañez (2001), 'A qualitative analysis of posttraumatic stress among Mexican victims of disaster', *Journal of Traumatic Stress*, **14**, 741–756.

Nussbaum, M.C. (1995), 'Human capabilities, female human beings', in M. Nussbaum and J. Glover (eds.), *Women, Culture and Development: A Study of Human Capabilities,* Oxford: Clarendon Press, pp. 61–105.

O'Brien, K. and L. Sygna, R. Leichenko, W.N. Adger, J. Barnett, T. Mitchell, L. Schipper, T. Tanner, C. Vogel, C. Mortreux (2008), 'Disaster Risk Reduction, Climate Change Adaptation and Human Security', Report for the Royal Norwegian Ministry of Foreign Affairs by the Global Environmental Change and Human Security (GECHS) Project, *GEHCS Report* 2008: 3, available at http://www.adpc. net/DDRCCA/GECHS-08/GECHS_Report_3-2008.pdf (accessed 14 August 2012).

Oliver-Smith, A. (1992), 'Disasters and development', *Environmental and Urban Issues,* **20** (1), 1–3.

Oliver-Smith, A. (1998), 'Global changes and the definition of disaster', in E.L. Quarantelli (ed.), *What is a Disaster? Perspectives on the Question,* London and New York: Routledge, pp. 177–194.

Oliver-Smith, A. (2002), 'Theorizing disasters: Nature, power and culture', in S. Hoffman and A. Oliver-Smith (eds.), *Catastrophe & Culture: The Anthropology of Disaster,* New Mexico: School of American Research Press, pp. 23–48.

Olsen, G.R. and N. Carstensen, K. Hoyen (2003), 'Humanitarian crises: What determines the level of emergency assistance? Media coverage, donor interests and the aid business', *Disasters,* **27** (2), 109–126.

Olson, M. (1971), *The Logic of Collective Action: Public Goods and the Theory of Groups,* New York: Schocken books.

Olson, M. (1982), *The Rise and Decline of Nations,* Cambridge, MA: MIT Press.

Olson, R.S. and V.T Gawronski (2003), 'Disasters as critical junctures? Managua, Nicaragua 1972 and Mexico City 1985', *International Journal of Mass Emergencies and Disasters,* **21** (1), 5–35.

ONS (2000), *Psychiatric Morbidity Among Adults Living in Private Households in Great Britain,* London: HMSO.

Organization of African Unity (2000), International Panel of Eminent Personalities Report, 'Rwanda: the preventable genocide', available at http://www.africa-union.org/official_documents/reports/report_ rowanda_genocide.pdf (accessed 14 August 2012).

Osofsky, H. and J. Osofsky, M. Kronenberg, A. Brennan, T. Cross Hansel (2009), 'Posttraumatic stress symptoms in children after hurricane Katrina: Predicting the need for mental health services', *American Journal of Orthopsychiatry,* **79** (2), 212–220.

Ostergaard, L. (ed.) (1992), *Gender and Development,* London: Routledge.

O'Toole, L.L. and J.R Schiffman (eds.) (1997), *Gender Violence: Inter-disciplinary Perspectives*, New York and London: New York University Press.

Overton, L. (2007), 'Flirting with disaster: Gendered impacts of women's access to land and housing in post-tsunami Sri Lanka', unpublished dissertation, Middlesex University, August 2007.

Owen, D (2008), 'Can a perception of blame influence donations to humanitarian crises?' unpublished dissertation, Middlesex University, August 2007.

Oxfam (2000), 'Growth with equity is good for the poor: Poverty reduction rather than growth: focusing on equity and types of growth rather than growth alone', June 2000, available at http://remi.bazillier.free.fr/oxfam_equity.pdf (accessed 14 August 2012).

Oxfam (2005), 'The Tsunami's Impact on women', Oxfam Briefing Note, Oxfam International, available at http://www.preventionweb.net/files/1502_bn050326tsunamiwomen.pdf (accessed 14 August 2012).

Oxfam (2006), 'The Tsunami two years on: Land rights in Aceh', Oxfam Briefing Note, 30 November 2006, available at http://www.oxfam.org/en/policy/bn_tsunami_2yrs_landrights_0612 (accessed 14 August 2012).

Oxfam (2009), 'Collaboration in crises: Lessons in community participation from the Oxfam International Tsunami research program', 26 December 2009, available at http://www.oxfam.org/en/policy/collaboration-crises (accessed 14 August 2012).

Oxfam (2010) 'Reconstruction in Haiti, "What do we know from previous disasters?"', Oxfam, Great Britain, available at http://www.preventionweb.net/english/professional/news/v.php?id=12475 (accessed 14 August 2012).

Oxfam (2011), 'From relief to recovery supporting good governance in post-earthquake Haiti', 142 Oxfam Briefing Paper, available at http://www.oxfam.de/sites/www.oxfam.de/files/20110106_fromrelieft recovery_379kb.pdf (accessed 14 August 2012).

PAHO (2003), *Violence Against Women: The Health Sector Responds*, Washington, DC: Pan American Health Organization.

Paine, R. (2002), 'Danger and the no-risk thesis', in S. Hoffman, and A. Oliver-Smith, A. (eds.), *Catastrophe & Culture: The Anthropology of Disaster*, New Mexico: School of American Research Press, pp. 67–90.

Parker, D.J. and S.J. Priest, S.M. Tapsell (2009), 'Understanding and enhancing the public's behavioural response to flood warning information', *Meteorological Applications*, **16**, 103–114.

Parpart, J. (1993), 'Who is the "other"?', *Development and Change*, **24**, 439–464.

Parpart, J. (1995), 'Post-modernism, gender and development', in J. Crush (ed.), *Power of Development*, New York: Routledge, pp. 253–265.

Parsons, T. (1960), *Structure and Process in Modern Societies*, New York: Free Press.

Pearson, R. (2000), 'Which men, why now? Reflections on men and development', *IDS Bulletin*, **31** (2), 42–48.

Petchesky, R.P. (2000), 'Reproductive and sexual rights: Charting the course of transnational women's NGOs', Geneva 2000, paper No. 8, United Nations Research Institute for Social Development, June 2000.

Petras, J. (1997), 'Imperialism and NGOs in Latin America', *Monthly Review*, **49** (7).

Pettit, J. and J. Wheeler (2005), 'Developing rights? Relating discourse to context and practice', *IDS Bulletin*, **36** (1), 1–8.

Phillips, B.D. (2009), 'Engendering Disaster Risk Reduction: A North American perspective', *Regional Development Dialogue*, **30** (1), 52–60.

Phillips, B.D. and M. Fordham (2009), 'Understanding social vulnerability', in B.D. Phillips, D. Thomas, A. Fothergill and L. Blinn-Pike (eds.), *Social Vulnerability to Disasters*, Boca Raton, FL: CRC Press, pp. 1–26.

Phillips, B.D. and B.H. Morrow (eds.) (2008), *Women and Disasters: From Theory to Practice*, PA: Xlibris (International Research Committee on Disasters).

Phillips, B.D and B.H. Morrow (2007), 'Social science research needs: A focus on vulnerable populations, forecasting and warnings', *Natural Hazards Review*, 61–68.

Phillips, B.D. and A. Fothergill, L. Blinn-Pike (eds.) (2010), *Social Vulnerability to Disasters*, Boca Raton, FL: CRC Press.

Phillips, B.D. and P. Jenkins , E. Enarson (2010), 'Violence and disaster vulnerability', in B. Phillips, D. Thomas, A. Fothergill and L. Blinn-Pike (eds.), *Social Vulnerability to Disasters*, Boca Raton, FL: CRC Press, pp. 279–306.

Pickup, F. and S. Williams, C. Sweetman (2001), *Ending Violence Against Women: A Challenge for Development and Humanitarian Work*, Oxford: Oxfam.

Piron, L. (2005), 'Rights-Based Approaches and bilateral aid agencies: More than metaphor?', *IDS Bulletin*, **36** (1), 19–30.

Porter, F. and C. Sweetman (2005), *Mainstreaming Gender in Development: A Critical Review. Has Gender Mainstreaming Made a Difference after 10 Years?*, Oxford: Oxfam.

Potter, R. and T. Binns, J.A. Elliott, D. Smith (2008), *Geographies of Development*, third edition, Harlow: Pearson Eduction.

Prendergast, J. (1995), *Tie Humanitarian Assistance to Substantive Reform*, Washington Report on Middle East Affairs, July/August 1995.

Prendergast, J. (1996), *Frontline Diplomacy: Humanitarian Aid and Conflict in Africa*, Boulder, CO: Lynne Reinner Publishers.

ProVention/Alnap (2005), *South Asia Earthquake 2005: Learning from Previous Recovery Operations*, London: Active Learning Network for Accountability and Performance (ALNAP), December 2005, available at http://www.alnap.org/pool/files/ALNAPLessonsEarthquakes.pdf (accessed 14 August 2012).

Prowse, M. (2003), 'Towards a clearer understanding of "vulnerability" in relation to chronic poverty', *CPRC Working Paper 24*, Chronic Poverty Research Centre, University of Manchester.

Prowse, M. and L. Scott (2008), 'Assets and adaptation: An emerging debate', *IDS Bulletin*, **39**, 42–52.

PTSD Research Quarterly (2009), special edition on 'The Impact of Disasters and Political Violence on Mental Health in Latin America', **20** (4).

Punamäki, R.L. and I.H. Komproe, S. Qouta, M. Elmasri, J.T. de Jong (2005), 'The role of peritraumatic dissociation and gender in the association between trauma and mental health in a Palestinian community sample', *American Journal of Psychiatry*, **162** (3), 545–551.

Puntos de Encuentro, available at www.puntos.org.ni/ (accessed 14 August 2012).

Putman, R.D. (1993), *Making Democracy Work: Civic Traditions in Modern Italy*, Princeton, NJ: Princeton University Press.

Quarantelli, E.L. (1985), 'An assessment of conflicting views on mental health: The consequences of traumatic events', in C. Figley (ed.), *Trauma and its Wake*, New York: Brunner-Mazel, pp. 173–218.

Quarantelli, E.L. (ed.) (1998), *What is a Disaster? Perspectives on the Question*, London and New York: Routledge.

Radcliffe, S. and S. Westwood (eds.) (1993), *Viva: Women and Popular Protest in Latin America*, London: Routledge.

RADIX, 'Radical Interpretations of Disaster', available at http://www.radixonline.org/ (accessed 14 August 2012).

Rahnema, M. and V. Bawtree (eds.) (1997), *The Post-development Reader*, London and New Jersey: Zed Books.

Rakodi, C. (2002), 'A livelihood approach – Conceptual issues and definitions', in C. Rakodi and T. Lloyd-Jones (eds.), *Urban Livelihoods: A People-centred Approach to Reducing Poverty*, London: Earthscan publications, pp. 3–22.

Rapley, J. (2007), *Understanding Development*, London: UCL Press.

Rathgeber, E. (1990), 'WID, WAD, GAD: Trends in research and practice', *Journal of Developing Areas*, **24**, 489–502.

Ravallion, M. (1997), 'Can high inequality developing countries escape absolute poverty?', *Economics Letters*, **56**, 51–57.

Ravallion, M. (2001), 'Growth, inequality and poverty: Looking beyond averages', *World Development*, **29** (11), 1803–1815.

Ravallion, M. (2002), 'Is global inequality rising?', transcript of an IMF Economic Forum, International Monetary Fund, Washington, DC, 8 October, 2002, available at http://www.imf.org/external/np/tr/2002/tr021008.htm (accessed 14 August 2012).

Rawlings, (2004), 'A new approach to social assistance: Latin America's experience with conditional cash transfer programs', *World Bank Social Safety Nets Primer Notes*, **15**, Washington, DC: World Bank.

Razavi, S. (ed.) (2003), *Agrarian Change, Gender and Land Rights*, Oxford: UNRISD/Blackwell.

Redman, P. (1996), '"Empowering men to disempower themselves": Heterosexual masculinities, HIV and the contradictions of anti-oppressive education', in M. Mac An Ghaill (ed.), *Understanding Masculinities: Social Relations and Cultural Arenas*, Buckingham: Open University Press, pp. 168–182.

Rieff, D. (1999), 'Moral imperatives and political realities: Response to "principles, politics, and humanitarian action"', *Ethics and International Affairs*, **13** (1) 35–42.

Rieff, D. (2002), *A Bed For the Night: Humanitarianism in Crisis*, London: Vintage.

Rieffer-Flanagan, B. (2009), 'Is neutral humanitarianism dead? Red Cross neutrality: walking the tightrope of neutral humanitarianism', *Human Rights Quarterly*, **31**, 888–915.

Ritchie, B. (2009), *Crisis and Disaster Management for Tourism*, Bristol: Channel View Publications.

Roberts, P. (1991), 'Anthropological perspectives on the household', *IDSBulletin*, **22** (1), 60–65.

Robertson, C.J, (2004), 'Flood risk communication – Why does the message fail to reach ethnic communities?', Masters research, unpublished.

Robinson, P. (2002), *The CNN Effect: The Myth of News, Foreign Policy and Intervention*, London: Routledge.

Rosenbaum, J. (2012), 'Listening for gender in Katrina's Jewish voices', in E. David and E. Enarson (eds.), *The Women of Katrina: How Gender, Race and Class Matter in an American Disaster*, Nashville, TN: Vanderbilt University Press, pp. 190–197.

Rosenhouse, S. (1989), 'Identifying the poor: Is "headship" a useful concept?' *World Bank Living Standards Measurement Study Working Paper*, No. 58. Washington, DC: The International Bank for Reconstruction and Development/World Bank.

Rosenthal, U. (1998), 'Future disasters, future defiitions', in E.L. Quarantelli, (ed.) (1998), *What is a Disaster? Perspectives on the Question*, London and New York: Routledge, pp. 147–160

Rosenthal, U. (1999), 'Challenges of crisis management in Europe', International Conference on The Future of European Crisis Management, The Hague, November 7–9, 1999.

Ross, L.J. (2012), 'A feminist perspective on Katrina', in E. David and E. Enarson (eds.), *The Women of Katrina: How Gender, Race and Class Matter in an American Disaster*, Nashville, TN: Vanderbilt University Press, pp. 15–24.

Rostow, W.W. (1960), *The Stages of Economic Growth: A Non-Communist Manifesto*, Cambridge: Cambridge University Press.

Rowlands, J. (1997), *Questioning Empowerment: Working with Women in Honduras*, Oxford: Oxfam.

Rubio, M. (1997), 'Perverse Social Capital – Some evidence from Colombia', *Journal of Economic Issues*, **XXXI** (3), 805–816.

Ruppert, U. (2002), 'Global women's politics: Towards the "globalising" of women's human rights', in M. Braig and S. Wölte (eds.), *Common Ground or Mutual Exclusion: Women's Movements and International Relations*, London and New York: Zed Books, pp. 147–159.

Saad, S.G. (2009), 'Environmental management and disaster mitigation: Middle Eastern gender perspective', in E. Enarson and D. Chakrabarti (eds.), *Women, Gender and Disaster: Global Issues and Initiatives*, India: Sage, pp. 89–98.

Sabates-Wheeler, R. and S. Devereux (2008), 'Transformative social protection: The currency of justice', in A. Barrientos and D. Hulme (eds.), *Social Protection for the Poor and the Poorest: Concept, Policies, Politics*, Basingstoke: Palgrave MacMillan, pp. 64–84.

Samuels, A. (2010), 'Remaking neighbourhoods in Banda Aceh: Post-tsunami reconstruction of everyday life', in M. Clarke and I. Fanany (eds.), *Post-disaster Reconstruction*, London: Earthscan pp. 210–223.

Sanz, K. and I. Kelman, A. Adebola, J. Chacon, R. Sanchez, Gender and Disaster Network Members (2009), 'From the inside out: Reflections on gendering Disaster Risk Reduction', *Regional Development Dialogue,* **30** (1), 14–21.

Saunders, K. (2002), 'Towards a deconstructive post-development criticism', in K. Saunders (ed.), *Feminist Post-development Thought*, London and New York: Zed Books, pp. 1–38.

Sayeed, A. (2009), 'Victims of earthquake and patriarchy: The 2005 Pakistan earthquake', in E. Enarson and D. Chakrabarti (eds.), *Women, Gender and Disaster: Global Issues and Initiatives*, India: Sage, pp. 142–151.

Schlager, E. and E. Ostrom (1992), 'Property-rights regimes and natural resources: A conceptual analysis', *Land Economics*, **68**, 249–262.

Scott, A.M. (1986), 'Women and industrialisation: Examining the "female marginalisation" thesis', *Journal of Development Studies*, **22** (4), 649–680.

Scott, C. and R. Hopkins (1999), 'The economics of non-governmental organisations', *The Development Economics Discussion Paper Series*, No. 15, STICERD, London School of Economics and Political Science.

Scott, J. (1996), *Only Paradoxes to Offer: French Feminists and the Rights of Man*, Cambridge, MA: Harvard University Press.

Sen, A. (1981), *Poverty and Famines: An Essay on Entitlements and Deprivation*, Oxford: Clarendon Press.

Sen, A. (1984), *Resource Values and Development*, Cambridge, MA: Harvard University Press.

Sen, A. (1987), 'Gender and co-operative conflicts', World Institute for Development Economics Research, *Working Paper*, No.18, Helsinki.

Sen, A. (1990a), 'Gender and co-operative conflicts', in I. Tinker (ed.), *Persistent Inequalities: Women and World Development*, Oxford: Oxford University Press.

Sen, A. (1990b), 'More than 100 million women are missing', *New York Review of Books*, **37** (20).

Sen, A. (1999), *Development as Freedom*, Oxford: Oxford University Press.

Sen, G. and C. Grown (1988), *Development, Crisis and Alternative Visions*, New York: Monthly Review Press.

Shanmugaratnam, N. (2005), '"Tsunami Victims." Perceptions of the proposed buffer zone and its implications in Eastern Sri Lanka', unpublished manuscript, available at http://www.sacw.net/free/SriLankaTsunami_Reflections.pdf (accessed 14 August 2012).

Sheehan, L. and K. Hewitt (1969), 'A pilot survey of global natural disasters of the past twenty years', *Working Paper*, No. 11. Boulder, CO: Institute of Behavioral Science, University of Colorado.

Showalter, E. (1985), *The Female Malady: Women, Madness and English Culture, 1830–1980*, New York: Penguin Books.

Sjoberg, L. (2000), 'Factors in risk perception', *Risk Analysis*, **20** (1), 1–11.

Skutsch, M. (2004), *Mainstreaming Gender into the Climate Change Regime (COP 10)*, Buenos Aires: Genanet.

Smith, K. (1992), *Environmental Hazards – Assessing Risk and Reducing Disaster*, second edition 1996, London and New York: Routledge.

Smith, K. and D.N. Petley (1991), *Environmental Hazards: Assessing Risk and Reducing Disaster,* fifth edition 2009, London and New York: Routledge.

Staudt, K. (2002), 'Dismantling the master's house with the master's tools: Gender work in and with powerful bureaucracies', in K. Saunders (ed.), *Feminist Post-development Thought: Rethinking Modernity, Postcolonialism and Representation,* London: Zed Books.

Stephens, S. (2002), 'Bounding uncertainty: The post-Chernobyl culture of radiation protection experts', in S. Hoffman and A. Oliver-Smith (eds.), *Catastrophe & Culture: The Anthropology of Disaster,* New Mexico: School of American Research Press, pp. 91–111.

Sterett, S. (2012), 'State policy and disaster assistance: Listening to women', in E. David and E. Enarson (eds.), *The Women of Katrina: How Gender, Race and Class Matter in an American Disaster,* Nashville, TN: Vanderbilt University Press, pp. 118–129.

Stevens, A. (2007), 'World Bank, IMF charged with short-changing women', *Women's e-news,* Tuesday 20 November, 2007, available at http://www.womensenews.org/story/the-world/071120/world-bank-imf-charged-short-changing-women (accessed 14 August 2012).

Stiglmayer, A. (1993), 'The rapes in Bosnia-Herzegovina', in A. Stiglmayer (ed.), *Mass Rape: The War Against Women in Bosnia-Herzegovina,* trans. Marion Faber, Lincoln, NE: University of Nebraska Press.

Stockton, N. (1998), 'In defence of Humanitarianism', *Disasters,* **22** (4), 352–360.

Stoddard, A. (2003), 'Humanitarian NGOs: challenges and trends', *HPG Briefing,* **12**, Humanitarian Policy Group, ODI, available at http://www.odi.org.uk/resources/docs/349.pdf (accessed 14 August 2012).

Stonich, S. (1999), 'Comments', *Current Anthropology,* **40** (1), 23–24.

Subrahmanian, R. (2004), 'Making sense of gender in shifting institutional contexts: Some reflections on gender mainstreaming', *IDS Bulletin,* **35** (4), 89–94.

Sugden, R. (1984), 'Reciprocity: The supply of public goods through voluntary contributions', *Economic Journal,* **94** (376), 772–787.

Summerfield, D. (1999), 'A critique of seven assumptions behind psychological trauma programs in war-affected areas', *Social Science and Medicine,* **48**, 1449–1462.

Tábora, R. (2000), 'Impacto diferencial de género del Huracán Mitch en Honduras', en CEM-H (ed.), *Encuentro Centroamericano de Las Mujeres en la Reconstrucción.* Tegucigalpa, Honduras: CEM-H.

Tanner T. (2007), 'Screening climate risks to Development Cooperation', *IDS In Focus Policy Briefing,* **2.5** (November).

Tearfund (2008), 'Linking climate change adaptation and disaster risk reduction', UK: Tearfund, available at http://www.preventionweb.net/files/3007_CCAandDRRweb.pdf (accessed 14 August 2012).

Telford, J. and J. Cosgrave (2006), *Joint Evaluation of the International Response to the Indian Ocean Tsunami: Synthesis Report*, London: Tsunami Evaluation Coalition.

Thomalla F. and T. Downing, E. Spanger-Springfiel, G. Han, J. Rockstrom (2006), 'Reducing hazard vulnerability: Towards a common approach between disaster risk reduction and climate adaptation', *Disasters*, **30** (1), 39–48.

Thomas, A. (2000), 'Meaning and views of development', in T. Allen and A. Thomas (eds.), *Poverty and Development into the 21st Century*, Oxford: Oxford University Press, pp. 23–48.

Ticktin, M. (2011), 'The gendered human of humanitarianism: Medicalising and politicising sexual violence', *Gender and History*, **23** (2), 250–265.

Tierney, K. (2000), 'Controversy and consensus in disaster mental health research', paper passed on a presentation at the UCLA Conference on Public Health and Disasters, Redondo Beach, CA, 11–14 April, 1999.

Tierney, K. (2012), 'Critical disjunctures: Disaster research, social inequality, gender and Hurricane Katrina', in E. David and E. Enarson (eds.), *The Women of Katrina: How Gender, Race and Class Matter in an American Disaster*, Nashville, TN: Vanderbilt University Press, pp. 245–258.

Tierney, K. and C. Bevc (2007), 'Disaster as war: Militarism and the social construction of disaster in New Orleans', in D. Brunsma, D. Overfelt and J.S. Picou (eds.), *The Sociology of Katrina: Perspectives on a Modern Catastrophe*, Maryland: Rowman and Littlefield, pp. 35–49.

Timmons-Roberts, J. and A. Hite (eds.) (2000), *From Modernisation to Globalisation: Perspectives on Development and Social Change*, Oxford: Blackwell Publishing.

Tong, R. (1989), *Feminist Thought: A Comprehensive Introduction*, London: Routledge.

Tourism Concern (2005), 'Post-tsunami reconstruction and tourism: a second disaster?', report by Tourism Concern, October 2005, available at http://www.naomiklein.org/files/resources/pdfs/tourism-concern-tsunami-report.pdf (accessed 14 August 2012).

Toye, J. (1987), *Dilemmas of Development*, Oxford: Blackwell.

True, J. and M. Mintrom (2001), 'Transnational networks and policy diffusion: The case of gender mainstreaming', *International Studies Quarterly*, **45**, 27–57.

Tsikata, D. (2004), 'The Rights Based Approach to development: Potential for change or more of the same?', *IDS Bulletin*, **35** (4), 130–133.

Turner, J.F.C. (1976), *Housing by People: Towards Autonomy in Building Environments. Ideas in Progress*, London: Marion Boyars Publishers.

Turshen M. (2001), 'The political economy of rape: An analysis of systematic rape and sexual abuse of women during armed conflict in Africa', in C. Moser and F. Clarke (eds.), *Victors, Perpetrators or Actors: Gender, Armed Conflict and Political Violence*, London: Zed Books, pp. 55–68.

Twigg, J. (2007), 'Characteristics of a disaster-resilient community: A Guidance Note', Version 1 (for field testing), August, DFID Disaster Risk Reduction Interagency Coordination Group.

United Nations (1992), United Nations Framework Convention on Climate Change, available at http://unfccc.int/resource/docs/convkp/conveng.pdf (accessed 14 August 2012).

UN Millennium Development Goals (2000), available at http://www.un.org/millenniumgoals/.

UN/ADPC (2010), 'Disaster proofing the Millennium Development Goals (MDGs)', UN Millennium Campaign and the Asian Disaster Preparedness Center, available at http://www.adpc.net/v2007/downloads/2010/oct/mdgproofing.pdf (accessed 14 August 2012).

UNDP (1994), *'Disasters and development'*, United Nations Disaster Management Training Programme, second edition, available at http://iaemeuropa.terapad.com/resources/8959/assets/documents/UN%20DMTP%20-%20Disaster%20Preparedness.pdf.

UNIFEM (2003) 'Not a minute more: ending violence against women', UNIFEM, Rome, available at http://www.unifem.org/materials/item_detail86d2.html.

UNIFEM (2005), 'UNIFEM responds to the tsunami tragedy. One year later: A report card', UNIFEM, Rome, available at http://www.unifem.org/campaigns/tsunami/documents/TsunamiReportCard_1yrAnniversary.pdf.

UNISDR (2009a), 'Terminology on DRR', available at http://www.unisdr.org/we/inform/terminology (accessed 14 August 2012).

UNISDR (2009b), 'Making disaster risk reduction gender-sensitive: Policy and practical guidelines', UNISDR, UNDP and IUCN, Geneva, June 2009, available at http://www.preventionweb.net/files/9922_MakingDisasterRiskReductionGenderSe.pdf (accessed 14 August 2012).

UNISDR (2011), 'Themes and issues in disaster risk reduction', available at http://www.unisdr.org/files/23647_themesandissuesindisasterriskreduct.pdf (accessed 14 August 2012).

US National Earthquake Information Center, available at http://www. usgs.gov/ (accessed 14 August 2012).

Ussher, J. (1992), *Women's Madness: Misogyny or Mental Illness*, Amherst, MA: University of Massachusetts Press.

Uwantege Hart, S. (2011), 'Women only: violence and gendered entitlements in post-quake food distribution in Port-au-Prince, Haiti', available at http://graduateinstitute.ch/webdav/site/genre/shared/Genre_docs/Actes_2010/Actes_2010_UwantegeHart.pdf (accessed 14 August 2012).

Vakil, A. (1997), 'Confronting the classification problem: Toward a taxonomy of NGOs', *World Development*, **25** (12), 2057–2070.

Vakis, R. (2006), 'Complementing natural disasters management: The role of social protection', *Social Protection Discussion Paper*, No. 0543, Washington, DC: World Bank.

Varley, A. (1994a), 'The exceptional and the everyday: Vulnerability analysis in the International Decade for Natural Disaster Reduction', in A. Varley (ed.), *Disasters, Development and Environment*, Chichester; New York: John Wiley, pp. 1–11.

Varley, A. (1994b), *Disasters, Development and Environment*, Chichester; New York: John Wiley.

Visvanathan, N. and L. Duggan, L. Nisonoff, N. Wiegersma (eds.) (1997), *The Women, Gender and Development Reader*, London: Zed Books.

Walby, S. (1990a), *Theorising Patriarchy*, London: Wiley-Blackwell.

Walby. S. (1990b), 'A critique of postmodernist accounts of gender', paper presented at Canadian Sociological Association Meetings, Vancouver, Canada (27–30 May).

Walby, S. (2005), 'Gender mainstreaming: Productive tensions in theory and practice', *Social Politics: International Studies in Gender, State and Society*, **12** (3), 321–343.

Walker, A. (2000), 'A gendered response to disasters: A case study of two national NGOs in the disaster continuum of Hurricane Mitch', unpublished dissertation, Middlesex University.

WBGDG (2003), 'Gender Equality and the Millennium Development Goals', World Bank Gender and Development Group, April 2003, available at http://siteresources.worldbank.org/INTGENDER/Publications/20169280/gendermdg.pdf (accessed 14 August 2012).

Weinstein, N.D. (1980), 'Unrealistic optimism about future events', *Journal of Personality and Social Psychology*, **39**, 806–820.

Weiss, T.G. (1999), 'Principles, politics, and humanitarian action', *Ethics and International Affairs*, **13**, 1–22.

White, G.B. (1945), 'Human adjustment to floods, A geographical approach to the flood problem in the United States', Research Paper, Issue 29, University of Chicago, Department of Geography.

Whitehead, A. (2000), 'Continuities and discontinuities in political constructions of the working man in rural Sub-Saharan Africa: The "lazy man" in African agriculture', *The European Journal of Development Research*, **12**, 23–52.

WHO (2001), *The World Health Report 2001 – Mental Health: New Understanding, New Hope*, Geneva: World Health Organization.

WHO (2002), 'Gender and human rights: Sexual health', World Health Organisation, available at http://www.who.int/reproductivehealth/topics/gender_rights/sexual_health/en/ (accessed 14 August 2012).

WHO (2005), *Mental Health Atlas*, Geneva: Department of Mental Health and Substance Abuse, World Health Organization.

WHO (2006) 'World Mental Health Day 2006: Building awareness – Reducing risks: Suicide and mental illness', available at http://www.who.int/mediacentre/news/releases/2006/pr53/en/index.html (accessed 14 August 2012).

WHO (2010), 'Mental health and development: Targeting people with mental health conditions as a vulnerable group', WHO Press, Geneva, available at http://www.who.int/mental_health/policy/development/en/index.html (accessed 14 August 2012).

WHO (nd) 'Gender and women's mental health', available at http://www.who.int/mental_health/prevention/genderwomen/en/ (accessed 14 August 2012).

WICEJ (eds.) (2004), *Seeking Accountability on Women's Human Rights: Women Debate the Millennium*, New York: Women's International Coalition for Economic Justice.

Williams, S. (2005), 'Getting back home: impact on property rights of the Indian Ocean Earthquake-Tsunami 2004', *New Issues in Refugee Research Working Paper*, No. 122, Switzerland: UNHCR.

Williams, S. and J. Seed, A. Mwau (1994), *The Oxfam Gender Training Manual*, Oxford: Oxfam UK and Ireland.

Willinger, B. and J. Knight (2012), 'Setting the stage for disaster: Women in New Orleans before and after Katrina', in E. David and E. Enarson (eds.), *The Women of Katrina: How Gender, Race and Class Matter in an American Disaster*, Nashville, TN: Vanderbilt University Press, pp. 55–75.

Willis, K. (2005), *Theories and Practices of Development*, London: Routledge.

Willits King, B. and P. Harvey (2005), *Managing the Risks of Corruption in Humanitarian Relief Operations*, London: Overseas Development Institute, Humanitarian Policy Group.

Wilson, J. and B. Phillips, D. Neal (1998), 'Domestic violence after disaster', in E. Enarson and B. Morrow (eds.), *The Gendered Terrain of Disasters*, Westport; CT; London: Praeger, pp. 115–122.

Wilson, P. and C. So-Kum Tang (2007), *Cross-Cultural Assessment of Psychological Trauma and PTSD*, New York: John Springer.

Wisner, B. and J.C. Gaillard, I. Kelman (2012), 'Framing disaster: theories and stories seeking to understand hazards, vulnerability and risk', in B. Wisner, J.C. Gaillard and I. Kelman (eds.), *Handbook of Hazards and Disaster Risk Reduction*, London: Routledge, pp. 18–33.

Wölte, S. (2002), 'Claiming rights and contesting spaces: Women's movements and international women's human rights discourse in Africa', in M. Braig and S. Wölte (eds.), *Common Ground or Mutual Exclusion: Women's Movements and International Relations*, London and New York: Zed Books, pp. 171–188.

Wood, A. and R. Apthorpe, J. Borton (eds.) (2001), *Evaluating Humanitarian Action*, London: Zed Books.

Woodford-Berger, P. (2004), 'Gender mainstreaming: What is it (about) and should we continue doing it?', *IDS Bulletin*, **35** (4), 65–72.

Woodward, S. (2001), 'Humanitarian war: A new consensus?', *Disasters*, Special Issue: Politics and humanitarian aid, **25** (4), 331–344.

World Bank (2001a), *Social Protection Strategy: From Safety Net to Springboard*, Washington, DC: World Bank.

World Bank (2001b), *Engendering Development Through Gender Equality in Rights, Resources, and Voice*, New York: Oxford University Press.

World Bank (2002), 'Poverty reduction strategy source book', Washington, DC: World Bank.

World Bank (2003), 'Mental health', in *At a Glance series*, World Bank Health-Nutrition-Population, October 2003, available at http://www.jhsph.edu/mental_health_initiatives/Events/2010_Symposium/Baingana_Word_Bank_Information_MH.pdf (accessed 14 August 2012).

World Bank (2004), *Mental Health and the Global Development Agenda: What Role for the World Bank?*, Proceedings of a November 2003 Seminar and an Overview of World Bank Interventions in Mental Health, Washington, DC: World Bank.

Young, K. (1993), *Planning Development with Women*, Basingstoke: Macmillan.

Zagefka, H. and H. Zagefka1, M. Noor, R. Brown, G. Randsley de Moura, T. Hopthrow (2010), 'Donating to disaster victims: Responses to natural and humanly caused events', *European Journal of Social Psychology*, **41** (3), 353–363.

Zotti, M.E. and V.T. Tong, L, Kieltyka, R. Brown-Bryant (2012), 'Factors influencing evacuation decisions among high risk pregnant and post-partum women', in E. David and E. Enarson (eds.), *The Women of Katrina: How Gender, Race and Class Matter in an American Disaster*, Nashville, TN: Vanderbilt University Press, pp. 90–104.

Index